Modern Technologies in Web Services Research

Liang-Jie Zhang
IMB T.J. Watson Research Center, USA

IGI PUBLISHING
Hershey • New York

Acquisition Editor:	Kristin Klinger
Senior Managing Editor:	Jennifer Neidig
Managing Editor:	Sara Reed
Assistant Managing Editor:	Sharon Berger
Development Editor:	Kristin Roth
Copy Editor:	Katie Smalley
Typesetter:	Jamie Snavely
Cover Design:	Lisa Tosheff
Printed at:	Yurchak Printing Inc.

Published in the United States of America by
  IGI Publishing (an imprint of IGI Global)
  701 E. Chocolate Avenue
  Hershey PA 17033
  Tel: 717-533-8845
  Fax: 717-533-8661
  E-mail: cust@idea-group.com
  Web site: http://www.idea-group.com

and in the United Kingdom by
  IGI Publishing (an imprint of IGI Global)
  3 Henrietta Street
  Covent Garden
  London WC2E 8LU
  Tel: 44 20 7240 0856
  Fax: 44 20 7379 0609
  Web site: http://www.eurospanonline.com

Library of Congress Cataloging-in-Publication Data

Modern technologies in Web services research / L.J. Zhang.
  p. cm.
Summary: "Web service technologies are constantly being recreated, continuously challenging Web service professionals and examiners. This book facilitates communication and networking among Web services and e-business researchers and engineers in a period where considerable changes are taking place in Web services technologies innovation"—Provided by publisher.
Includes bibliographical references and index.
ISBN 978-1-59904-280-0 (hardcover)—ISBN 978-1-5904-282-7 (ebook)
1. Web services. I. Zhang, Liang-Jie.
TK5105.88813.M64 2006
006.7'6—dc22
                                    2006033768

British Cataloguing in Publication Data
A Cataloguing in Publication record for this book is available from the British Library.

Modern Technologies in Web Services Research

Table of Contents

Preface

Nowadays, Web services are becoming a major research topic for computer scientists, engineers and business consulting professionals. Therefore, there appear a large number of topics and research about the Web services from various aspects. This book provides researchers, scholars, professionals, and educators with the most current research and architecture on Web services with organizations and individuals worldwide.

Chapter I, "Challenges and Opportunities for Web Services Research," by Liang-Jie Zhang, IBM T. J. Watson Research Center (USA), analyzes the trend of the increasing business requirements and points out the necessity of capturing and mapping it into a solution skeleton for Web services solution creators and researchers. This chapter presents some challenges incurred by the current Web services research topics from the modeling, interoperability, and mathematical foundations points of view, followed by some observations about the opportunities and possible directions for moving Web services forward via illustrative ideas such as business semantic computing as well as killer application driven Web services research approach.

Chapter II, "Authentication Techniques for UDDI Registries," by Elisa Bertino, Purdue University (USA); Barbara Carminati, and Elena Ferrari, University of Insurbia at Varese (Italy), shows that the key role in the Web Service architecture is played by UDDI registries, i.e., a structured repository of information that can be queried by clients to find the Web services that better fit they needs. This chapter proposes an approach based on Merkle hash trees, which provides a flexible authentication mechanism for UDDI registries, as well as its two relevant benefits.

Chapter III, "Web Services Enabled E-Market Access Control Model," by Harry Wang and Leon Zhao, University of Arizona (USA); and Hsing K. Cheng, University of Florida (USA), discusses the pressing need for a comprehensive access control model to support secure e-market operations. By integrating several access control models such as role-based access control, coalition-based access control, and relationship driven access control, this chapter proposes a comprehensive security control mechanism to support advanced access control in e-markets, which is referred as e-market access control (EMAC) model. It also illustrates how the EMAC model can support e-market access control via an automotive e-market example.

Chapter IV, "Dynamically Adaptable Web Services Based on the Simple Object Access Protocol," by Kevin Curran and Brendan Gallagher, University of Ulster (UK), introduces the simple object access protocol (SOAP) from its definition, its function and other aspects. This chapter describes a SOAP Web service, and demonstrates how SOAP's platform and language independence can be used to overcome common limitations such a bandwidth, memory capacity, as well as disparate programming environments.

Chapter V, "Advanced Data Compression Techniques for SOAP Web Services," by Christian Werner, Carsten Buschmann and Stefan Fischer, Institute of Telematics and University Lübeck (Germany), introduces a new experimental concept for SOAP compression based on differential encoding, which makes use of the commonly available WSDL description of a SOAP Web service. This chapter explores compression strategies and supplies a detailed survey and evaluation of state of the art binary encoding techniques for SOAP. Moreover, it discusses different strategies for compressing SOAP messages more efficiently than gzip does as well as some future work.

Chapter VI, "Mobile Agents Meet Web Services," by Cristian Mateos, Alejandro Zunino and Marcelo Campo, Universidad Nacional al Centro (Argentina), presents MoviLog, a novel programming language for enabling mobile agents to consume Web services. This chapter introduces Web services and the Semantic Web, the related work, and MoviLog. Furthermore, it explains the approach for integrating MoviLog and Web services, and describes an agent implemented with MoviLog.

Chapter VII, "RAWS & UWAS: Reflective and Adaptable Web Services Running on the Universal Web Application Server," by Javier Parra-Fuente and Marta Fernández-Alarcón, Computer Languages and Systems Department, Pontifical University of Salamanca, Madrid campus (Spain); and Salvador Sánchez-Alonso, Information Engineering Research Unit, University of Alcala (Spain), introduces the basic concepts of reflection which will be applied to Web services (the introspective characteristics and the analysis of the structural and behavioral reflection of the Web service), the architecture model of a reflective and adaptable Web service, and the automatic generation mechanism to obtain the reflective infrastructure needed for a Web service to be dynamically adaptable. This chapter presents the RAWS and the universal web application server (UWAS) architectures; in order to show how Web service can behave like a reflective and adaptable Web service by modifying the original code, it also introduces the dynamic generation process of a meta-Web service.

Chapter VIII, "Metadata Based Information Management Framework for Grids," by Wei Jie, Tianyi Zang, Terence Hung, Institute of High Performance Computing (Singapore); and Stephen Turner, and Wentong Cai, Nanyang Technological University (Singapore), presents an information management framework, a hierarchical structure which consists of VO layer, site layer and resource layer, for a grid virtual organization (VO). This information management framework is a three-layer structure supporting information generation, collection, updates and accessing. This chapter proposes different models of information data organization for information management in grids and simulation experiments conducted to evaluate the performance of these models.

Chapter IX, "Architectural Foundations of WSRF.NET," by Glenn Wasson and Marty Humphrey, University of Virginia (USA), discusses the architectural foundations of WSRF.NET, which is an implementation of the full set of specifications for WSRF and WS-notification on the Microsoft.NET framework. In this chapter, a concrete example of the design, implementation and deployment of a WSRF-compliant service and its accompanying WSRF-compliant client are used to guide the discussion. Meanwhile, it describes a use-case scenario for constructing and consuming a WSRF-compliant Web service in WSRF.NET.

Chapter X, "QoS-Aware Web Services Discovery with Federated Support for UDDI," by Chen Zhou, Liang-Tien Chia and Bu-Sung Lee, Nanyang Technological University (Singapore), presents a UX architecture that is QoS-aware and facilitates the federated discovery for Web services. With the need to provide QoS-awareness in UDDI and service discovery between enterprise domains, this chapter proposes a solution called UDDI eXtension (UX). Differing from the original UDDI system, the new system is aware of the basic service performance information with relatively small overhead from the feedback.

Chapter XI, "Proactively Composing Web Services as Tasks by Semantic Web Agents," by Vadim Ermolayev and Natalya Keberle, Zaporozhye National University, (Ukraine); Oleksandr Kononenko, Nokia Research Center (Finland); and Vagan Terziyan, University of Jyvaskyla (Finland), presents the framework for agent-enabled dynamic composition of Semantic Web services. This chapter focuses on one of the major open problems—dynamic composition of a desired complex service by a coalition of rational cooperative freelance software agents—and it offers a new understanding of a service as an intelligent agent capability implemented as a self-contained software component.

Chapter XII, "Web Services Identification: Methodology and CASE Tool," by Hemant Jain and Huimin Zhao, University of Wisconsin-Milwaukee (USA); and Nageswara R. Chinta, Tata Consultancy Services (India), proposes a formal approach to Web services identification, which is a critical step in designing and developing effective Web services. By discussing the Web services identification problem and reviewing approaches being used in identifying reusable assets and in designing business components, the authors then presents a formal approach to Web services identification. It also describes the implementation of the approach in a CASE tool and its application to identifying Web services for auto insurance claim system.

Since Web services are indispensable and becoming more and more significant in the modern world, how to use high-tech methods to make Web services be utilized by people more efficiently is the crucial problem. Now you don't need to worry about this. As an outstanding collection of the latest research associated with the Web services this book presents different kinds of research of the Web services to people of all circles.

Chapter I

Challenges and Opportunities for Web Services Research

Liang-Jie Zhang, IBM T.J. Watson Research Center, USA

Abstract

Web services are becoming a major research topic for computer scientists, engineers and business consulting professionals. In this preface, I would like to outline the challenges of the current Web services research topics from the modeling, interoperability, and mathematical foundations points of view. Then I will introduce some research opportunities and possible future directions for moving Web services forward via some illustrative ideas such as business semantic computing as well as killer application driven Web services research approaches. For the business semantic computing aspect I will present some example application domains such as federated Web services discovery, dynamic Web services composition and extended business collaboration.

Introduction

Web services refer to networked and modular applications, as well as a set of enabling technologies, such as simple object access protocol (SOAP), Web services definition language (WSDL), universal description, discovery and integration (UDDI) protocol, and emerging Web services flow specifications like business process execution language for Web services (BPEL4WS) and Web services chorography interface (WSCI). Since business requirements are becoming the major driving force for creating Web services research topics to support business process integration, collaboration, and management, the business context should be captured and transmitted into appropriate partners. Being Web services solution creators and researchers, we would like to start with capturing the business requirements, and then mapping them into a solution skeleton. Afterward, we can realize the skeleton by linking activities to a set of predefined Web services.

I would like to outline some challenges of the current Web services research topics from the modeling, interoperability, and mathematical foundations points of view followed by some observations about the opportunities and possible directions for moving Web services forward via illustrative ideas such as business semantic computing as well as killer application driven Web services research approach.

Challenges and Opportunities for
Web Services Research

The basic challenges are still focused on Web services modeling, interoperability and mathematical foundations for supporting federated Web services discovery, dynamic Web services composition, Web services monitoring and management, Web services security (Naedele, 2003) and privacy, and Web services semantic computing.

Web Services Modeling

We always ask ourselves, what kind of information should be used to describe a Web service? Currently, Web services definition language (WSDL) is used to describe the basic static information such as an abstract interface and bindings to particular message formats and protocols as well as location of the service.

Here I would like to present some ideas on what other information should be covered in a Web services model. I suggest that a multidimensional model should be created for Web services to cover three types of information about a Web service. That is, the static information about the descriptions of individual Web services, the dynamic information about the behaviors of individual Web services, and the relationships among the Web services and their corresponding service providers. The goal of this multidimensional model is to help in extracting or exchanging information from/within UDDI registries, and automatically analyzing, clustering and indexing Web services. The multidimensional Web services model is a fundamental concept that not only presents the semantic information of individual Web services, but also the relationships among Web services. In particular, the quality of services (QoS) (Mani, 2002;Menasce, 2002) can be part of the semantic information of individual Web services. A business information database can be built to carry correct category information and Web services reputation and recommendation ratings, so that service requestors can quickly find Web services from this reliable source. The Semantic Web community is working on the generic semantic representation for individual Web services (McIlraith, 2001, 2003). I think the comprehensive semantic information for domain specific applications will play a very important role in speeding up the adoption of Web services. Especially, if the semantic information is focused on e-business integration, collaboration, and management solutions (Zhang, 2000b) I call this kind of semantic information "business semantic computing" that will be described in detail later.

Web Services Interoperability

Web services interoperability addresses the integration guidelines for Web services that are deployed on multiple platforms or included in multiple applications. The Web services can also be implemented in multiple programming languages. Web Services Interoperability (WS-I) Organization is created to enable the interoperability among Web services. The goal of WS-I is to encourage Web services adoption based on introducing conventions and best practices. The Basic Profile 1.0 specification has been released as a key milestone for Web services interoperability. Using Basic Profile, WS-I defines individual profiles for specific purposes (e.g., WS-I Security Profile). The flow of the WS-I working group covers scenarios and sample applications, Web services basic profile, and testing tools and materials. The detailed guidelines will simplify the developer's job when they faces multiple development tools from multiple vendors.

A big effort is still needed for the Web services community to achieve the goal of the real interoperability among Web services. Theoretically, even if we have BPEL4WS and WSCI as two Web services flow representations, we can create a middle layer to hide the difference between those two specifications. This middle layer could become a WS-I profile for business process integration.

Facing the challenging issues on the modeling and interoperability in the Web services research community, we should perform deep investigations on these challenges and build mathematical foundations for the emerging Web services technologies and solutions. In my point of view, Web services itself is a system with inputs and outputs. The mathematical foundation of Web services modeling should focus on the system interaction behaviors based on the interface descriptions.

Business Semantic Computing

As we know, the pure Web services infrastructure can not fully understand the business context of an e-business solution. For example, basic Web services information is described in WSDL. The fact is that the current Web services specifications and UDDI specification are lacking in the definitions and descriptions of the relationships among Web services. Zhang's (2002a) proposed Web services relationship language (WSRL) captures the Web services relationships at different granularities (i.e., enterprise level, service level and operation level), which we think will be an important facilitator in selecting and composing the right set of services that meets the customer's requirements. Therefore, in order to bridge the gap between the generic Web services infrastructure and the business solution context, we have to build and collect business semantic information by defining business semantic computing enabling technologies, models and mechanisms.

Based on this concern, I have taken the Web services solution life cycle as a starting point to describe an emerging research direction called Web services collaboration, in Zhang (2003c), which is an example of a business semantic computing scenario in the Web services based enterprises collaboration domain. In the Web services collaboration, some core enabling technologies examples—including federated Web services discovery, dynamic Web services flow composition, Web services relationship, and business collaboration protocols—are briefly introduced in the context of Web services solution lifecycle. For example, finding an appropriate Web service is an important step before a Web service is invoked. Especially when there are hundreds or thousands of Web services published in multiple UDDI registries or Web services inspection language (WSIL) documents, the semantic information for assisting the Web services discovery engine is becoming very important. Some example semantic information includes the location of the UDDI registries or WSIL documents, priorities, the mapping between key words and UDDI categories, backup registries, aggregation means, the relationship between Web services, etc. Using this kind of semantic information, the federated Web services discovery engine should support the search across Web services registries in a uniform way that hides the complexities of individual programming models for Web services discovery, and the result aggregation for obtaining more accurate search results.

Based on this idea, Zhang et al. (2003a) have created a UDDI search markup language (USML) based federated Web services discovery model, namely, business explorer for Web services (BE4WS) and WSIL explorer, which are part of IBM Emerging Technologies Toolkit (ETTK). BE4WS was initially designed to support Web services lookup from multiple UDDI registries with result aggregation. WSIL Explorer was created to support transversal WSIL document exploration with result aggregation and categorization. WSIL explorer has been successfully integrated with BE4WS by using USML for supporting both Web services registries at the same time. However, the mathematical foundations for the search result caching, aggregation, and categorization can be further explored.

As we know, selection and composition of Web services in a drag-and-drop manner is time consuming. That is why dynamic composition of Web services flow has become a hot research topic. Let us take an example of dynamic Web services composition framework, namely, Web services outsourcing manager (WSOM), to explore the idea of model driven Web services composition based on business semantic annotations (Zhang, 2003b). The customer requirements are analyzed to generate an annotation document for business process outsourcing. The business requirement annotations include service flow rules, customer preferences, and business rules. The captured business requirements and preferences are used to guide service discovery and selection. The business process templates (represented in UML or BPEL4WS abstract) and the business process requirement annotations are used to optimize the composed process. That is, this service-oriented architecture allows effective searching for appropriate Web services and integrating them into one composite Web service to form a specific business process. The WSOM framework automates the generation of scripts (e.g., USML) for searching for Web services using BE4WS, for example. Then, it streamlines the process of selecting Web services from the narrowed down potential Web services from the Web services discovery engine (e.g., BE4WS) by using a "pluggable" optimization framework. Some example optimization algorithms, such as Genetic algorithm and integer programming, can be used in the pluggable optimization module in WSOM. Once the Web services are bound to a specific business process it can be translated into a flow language such as WSFL (Leymann, 2001), BPEL4WS and passed to a business process execution engine.

After the individual Web services or Web services flows are ready, the next challenging issue is how the enterprises use them. The organizational behaviors of an enterprise, its relationship with other enterprises, the project or task disseminations, and some low level specifications should be captured in the same business context in order for Web services to collaborate with other solution components within an enterprise or across multiple enterprises. As introduced in Sayah (2003), extended business collaboration is a framework that facilitates business process integration between enterprises by managing and monitoring the exchange of business information. In order to enable extended business collaboration, Sayah et al. (2003)

have been working on a resource definition framework (RDF) based business collaboration data model that includes the organizational behaviors, a flexible business protocol creation and an enabling platform. This enabling infrastructure allows one to create an extensible message structure for carrying non-structural information, as well as to dynamically configure B2B business protocols for on-demand business process execution. I believe that those are key challenging issues when connecting the business level and IT (information technology) level.

From this sample business computing scenario, we can extend the application domain from extended business collaboration to other areas. Moreover, the RDF based business collaboration data model can link to all different kinds of business semantic annotations described in Web services discovery and composition. These illustrate that business semantics can help build Web services solutions in an efficient and effective manner. Again, the most important part is to capture the business semantics from disaggregated data sets or examples.

Killer Application Driven Web Services Research

Creating killer business solutions using Web services is the best approach to move Web services research forward. The following successful solution examples trigger the Web services community to build more mission-critical Web services solutions.

In the latest years, the Grid computing community has started to leverage Web services to define grid services in the Open Grid Services architecture (OGSA) at Global Grid Forum (GGF). It facilitates achieving an environment of always on and reducing complexity in a distributed environment. The virtualization capability of grid computing enables the access and sharing resources over the Internet based on open protocols and interfaces defined in Web services. Grid computing has become a good deployment infrastructure for life science solutions, financial solutions, engineering design collaborations, etc. Grid service in OGSA carries state information and versioning information, which is not defined in regular Web services interface. Successful OGSA-based grid solutions will be driving the development of Web services specifications. Traditional Internet solutions are moving to a services-oriented infrastructure. As the Internet search solution provider, Google has created Web services interface to allow its search services to be embedded in developers' own computer programs (Google APIs) developed in different programming languages. The biggest Internet commerce site Amazon.com provides Web services interfaces so that Web services developers can invoke e-commerce transactions and catalog browsing in their own applications (Amazon.com—Web services) on multiple platforms.

From the killer application solution creation processes, we can enhance the existing Web services specifications, create more domain specific semantics, and define business collaboration protocols when addressing the challenging problems that we may have.

Conclusion

I have addressed the research challenges and opportunities in the areas of Web services modeling, Web services interoperability, and mathematical foundations for enabling federated Web services discovery, dynamic Web services composition and business semantic computing. We can envision that some interesting topics like WS-I Discovery Profile for supporting federated Web services discovery, WS-I collaboration profile for supporting the Web services collaboration across multiple enterprises, WS-I composition profile for supporting dynamic Web services flow composition, WS-I Relationship Profile for supporting Web services relationships at all the three levels described above, and other WS-I profiles will become real driving forces for Web services research if we can bring Web services to the killer application scenarios.

References

Amazon.com. (n.d.). *Web services*. Retrieved from www.amazon.com/gp/aws/land-ing.html

BPEL4WS. (n.d.). *Specification: Business process execution language for Web services, Version 1.1*. Retrieved May 5, 2003, from http://www-106.ibm.com/developerworks/webservices/library/ws-bpel/

IBM. (n.d.). *ETTK, emerging technologies toolkit*. Retrieved from alphaWorks, http://www.alphaworks.ibm.com

Global Grid Forum (GGF). (n.d.). Retrieved from www.ggf.org

Google. (n.d.). *Google APIs, develop your own applications using Google*. Retrieved from http://www.google.com/apis/

Zhang, L. J., et al. (Eds.). (2003).In *Proceedings of the 2003 International Conference on Web Services (ICWS)*. CSREA Press.

Leymann, F. (2001). *Web services flow language (WSFL), Version 1.0*. IBM. Retrieved from http://www-4.ibm.com/software/solutions/webservices/pdf/WSFL.pdf

Mani, A., & Nagarajan, A. (2002). Understanding quality of service for Web services. *IBM DeveloperWorks*. Retrieved from http://www-106.ibm.com/developer-works/webservices/library/ws-quality.html

McIlraith, S. A., & Martin, D. L. (2003). Bringing semantics to Web services. *IEEE Intelligent System*, 90-93.

McIlraith, S. A., Son, T. C., & Zeng, H. (2001). Semantic Web services. *IEEE Intelligent Systems*, *16*(2), 46-53.

Menasce, D. A. (2002). QoS issues in Web services. *IEEE Internet Computing*, *6*(6), 72-75.

Naedele, M. (2003). Standards for XML and Web services security. *IEEE Computer*, *36*(4), 96-98.

Sayah, J., & Zhang, L.-J. (2003, September 30). *On-demand business collaboration enablement with Web services* (IBM Research Report, No. RC22926, W0309-191). IBM T. J. Watson Research Center.

Staab, S., van der Aalst, W., Benjamins, V. R., Sheth, A., Miller, J. A., Bussler, C., et. al. (2003). Web services: Been there, done that? *IEEE Intelligent Systems*, *18*(1), 72 -85.

WSCI. (n.d.). *Web service choreography interface (WSCI), Version 1.0* (W3C Note). Retrieved August 8, 2002, from http://www.w3.org/TR/wsci/

WS-I. (n.d.). *Web Services Interoperability Organization*. Retrieved from http://www.ws-i.org

Web services outsourcing manager (WSOM). (2002). *IBM alphaWorks*. Retrieved from www.alphaworks.ibm.com/tech/wsom

Zhang, L.-J., Chang, H., & Chao, T. (2002a). Web services relationships binding for dynamic e-business integration. In *Proceedings of the International Conference on Internet Computing (IC '02)*, Las Vegas, NV (pp. 561-567).

Zhang, L.-J., Chang, H., Chao, T., Chung, J. -Y., Tian, Z., et. al. (2002b). Web services hub framework for e-Sourcing. *IEEE Conference on System, Man, and Cybernetics (SMC '02)*, *6*, 163-168.

Zhang, L.-J., Chao, T., Chang, H., & Chung J. -Y. (2003a). XML-based advanced UDDI search mechanism for B2B integration. *Electronic Commerce Research Journal*, *3*, 25-42.

Zhang, L.-J., Li, B., Chao, T., & Chang, H. (2003b). On demand web services-based business process composition. In *Proceedings of 2003 IEEE Conference on System, Man, and Cybernetics(SMC '03)*.

Zhang, L.-J., & Jeckle, M (2003c). The next big thing: Web services collaboration. In *Proceedings of the 2003 International Conference on Web Services—Europe (ICWSEurope '03)* (LNCS 2853, pp. 1-10). Springer.

Chapter II

Authentication Techniques for UDDI Registries

Elisa Bertino, Purdue University, USA

Barbara Carminati, University of Insubria at Varese, Italy

Elena Ferrari, University of Insubria at Varese, Italy

Abstract

A Web service is a software system designed to support interoperable application-to-application interactions over the Internet. Web services are based on a set of XML standards, such as Web services description language (WSDL), simple object access protocol (SOAP) and universal description, discovery and integration (UDDI). A key role in the Web service architecture is played by UDDI registries, i.e., a structured repository of information that can be queried by clients to find the Web services that better fit their needs. Even if, at the beginning, UDDI has been mainly conceived as a public registry without specific facilities for security, today security issues are becoming more and more crucial, due to the fact that data published in UDDI registries may be highly strategic and sensitive. In this chapter, we focus on authenticity issues, by proposing a method based on Merkle hash trees, which does not require the party managing the UDDI to be trusted wrt authenticity. In the chapter, besides giving all the details of the proposed solution, we show its benefit wrt standard digital signature techniques.

Introduction

A Web service is a software system designed to support interoperable application-to-application interactions over the Internet. Web services are based on a set of XML standards, such as Web services description language (WSDL) (Christensen, Curbera, Meredith, & Weerawarana, 2001), simple object access protocol (SOAP) (Mitra, 2003), and universal description, discovery and integration (UDDI) (Clement, Hately, von Riegen, & Rogers, 2002). A key role in the Web service architecture is played by UDDI registries. UDDI is an XML-based registry with the primary goal of making widely available information on Web services. It thus provides a structured and standard description of the Web service functionalities as well as searching facilities to help in finding the provider(s) that better fit client requirements. In the beginning, UDDI was mainly conceived as a public registry without specific facilities for security. Today, security issues are becoming more and more crucial, due to the fact that data published in UDDI registries may be highly strategic and sensitive. In this respect, a key issue regards authenticity: For a client querying a UDDI registry it should be possible to first verify that the received answer is actually originated at the claimed source, and, then, that the party managing the UDDI registry has not maliciously modified some of answer portions before returning them to the client. To deal with this issue the current version of UDDI specifications allows one to optionally sign some of the elements in a registry, according to the W3C XML signature syntax (Eastlake, Reagle, & Solo, 2001).

UDDI can be implemented according to either a third party or two party architecture. A third party architecture consists of a *service provider*, that is, the owner of the services, the *service requestors*, that is, the parties who request the services, and a *discovery agency*, that is, the UDDI registry, which is responsible for managing (a portion of) the service provider information and for answering service requestors queries. By contrast, in a two party architecture, there is no distinction between the service provider and the discovery agency. Authenticity issues are particularly crucial when UDDI registries are managed according to a third party architecture. For this reason, in the chapter we focus on authenticity issues for third party implementations of UDDI. In this architecture the main problem is how the owner of the services can ensure the authenticity of its data, even if the data are managed by a third party (i.e., the discovery agency). The most intuitive solution is that of requiring the discovery agency to be trusted with respect to authenticity. However, the main drawback of this solution is that large Web-based systems cannot be easily verified to be trusted and can be easily penetrated. For this reason, in this chapter, we propose an alternative approach, previously developed by us for generic XML data distributed, according to a third party architecture (Bertino, Carminati, Ferrari, Thuraisingham, & Gupta, 2004). The main benefit of the proposed solution is that it does not require the discovery agency to be trusted wrt authenticity.

It is important to remark that in the scenario we consider it is not possible to directly apply standard digital signature techniques to ensure authenticity. Indeed, since a client may retrieve only selected portions of a document, depending on its needs, it will not be able to validate the signature generated on the whole document. For this reason, we apply an alternative solution that requires the owner to send the discovery agency, in addition to the information it is entitled to manage, a summary signature, generated using a technique based on Merkle hash trees (Merkle, 1989). The idea is that when a client submits a query to a discovery agency requiring any portion of the managed data, the discovery agency sends it, alongside the query result, the signatures of the documents on which the query is performed. In this way, the client can locally re-compute the same bottom-up hash value signed by the owner, and by comparing the two values it can verify whether the discovery agency has altered the content of the query answer and can thus verify its authenticity. The problem with this approach is that since the client may be only returned selected portions of a document, they may not be able to re-compute the summary signature, which is based on the whole document. For this reason, the discovery agency sends the client a set of additional hash values, referring to the missing portions that make the client able to locally perform the computation of the summary signature.

In the current chapter, we show how this approach can be applied to UDDI and we discuss its benefits. Additionally, we describe the prototype implementation we have developed for supporting the proposed approach. The remainder of this chapter is organized as follows. The "Background" section briefly overviews the authentication mechanisms devised so far for third party architectures and summarizes the basic concepts of UDDI registries. The section "XML Merkle Tree Authentication" presents in detail the Merkle tree-based authentication method conceived for XML documents. In the "Applying the Merkle Signature to UDDI Registries" section, we show how this authentication mechanism can be exploited in the UDDI environment. In "Merkle Signatures vs. XML Signatures in UDDI Registries," we compare our approach with the traditional digital signature techniques. Then, in "Prototype of an Enhanced UDDI Registry," we give some details about the prototype implementation. Finally, "Conclusion" ends the chapter.

Background

In this section we provide the reader with some background that can be useful while reading the chapter. In particular, we start by reviewing the mechanisms introduced so far to face up the authenticity issues in third party architectures. We then summarize the basic concepts of UDDI registries.

Authentication Mechanisms for Third Party Architectures

Mechanisms exploiting traditional digital signatures are not suitable for third party architectures. This is mainly due to the fact that users must be able to validate the owner's signature even if they received a selected portion of the signed data. A naive solution to overcome this problem, by still exploiting traditional signature schemes, is to impose the owner to separately sign each possible portion of data. This set of digital signatures can be outsourced together with the data, and properly returned to users by the third party. However, this solution implies an enormous overhead, both in owner computation and in query answer size. For this reason, in the recent years several alternative strategies have been presented. We can group these strategies on the basis of the underlying adopted techniques. In particular, there are two main exploited techniques, that is, Merkle tree authentication (Merkle, 1989) and signature aggregation (Boneh, Gentry, Lynn, & Shacham, 2003). In what follows we present them by introducing some of the related proposals.

Merkle Tree Authentication

Merkle (1989) proposed a method to sign multiple messages by producing a unique digital signature. The method exploits a binary hash tree generated by means of the following bottom-up recursive construction: At the beginning, for each different message m, a different leaf containing the hash value of m is inserted in the tree; then, for each internal node, the value associated with it is equal to $H(h\_l || h\_r)$, where $h\_l || h\_r$ denotes the concatenation of the hash values corresponding to the left and right children nodes, and $H()$ is an hash function. The root node of the resulting binary hash tree can be considered as the digest of all messages, and thus it can be digitally signed by using a standard signature technique and distributed. The main benefit of this method is that a user is able to validate the signature by having a subset of messages, providing him/her with a set of additional hash values. Indeed, a user, by having hash values of the missing messages, is able to locally build up the binary hash tree and thus to validate the signature.

Merkle hash trees have been used in several computer areas for certified query processing. For instance, they have been exploited by Naor and Nissim (Naor & Nissim, 1998) to create and maintain efficient authenticated data structures holding information about certificate validity. More precisely (Naor & Nissim, 1998), proposed as data structure a sorted hash tree, which is built in such a way that tree leaves correspond to revoked certificates. Thus, verifying that a certificate is revoked or not is equivalent to verify the existence of certain leaves in the tree. Similar schemes have also been used for micro-payments (Charanjit & Yung, 1996), where Merkle hash trees are used to minimize the number of public key signatures that are required in issuing or authenticating a sequence of certificates.

Merkle hash trees have also been exploited for data outsourcing. For instance, (Devanbu, Gertz, Martel, & Stubblebine, 2000) Devanbu et al. adapt Merkle hash trees to the relational data model to prove the completeness and authenticity of query answers. In particular, in Devanbu et al. approach for each relation R a different Merkle hash tree is generated, in such a way that leaf nodes represent hash values of tuples.

Merkle hash trees have been investigated also for third party distribution of XML data (Bertino et al., 2004;Devanbu et al., 2001). Here the challenge is how the XML hierarchical data model can be exploited in construction of Merkle trees. A brief introduction to Merkle tree application to XML documents is given in the "XML Merkle Tree Authentication" section, where we refer interested readers to (Bertino et al., 2004) for a deeper presentation of it.

Signature Aggregation Schemes

Another technique recently exploited to ensure authenticity in third party architectures is based on signature aggregation. In general, signature aggregation schemes allow one to aggregate into a unique digital signature n distinct signatures generated by n distinct data owners (Boneh et al., 2003). The validation of this unique digital signature implies the validation of each component signature. Aggregate signature schemes have also been investigated to aggregate into a unique signature n generated by the same owner. This last kind of aggregation scheme can be adopted to ensure authenticity in third party scenarios. Indeed, according to this solution, data owners could generate a distinct signature for each distinct message and then aggregate them into a unique digital signature. By having only the aggregate signature and by simply validating it, a user is able to authenticate selected messages received by the third party. Such kind of solution has been proposed by Mykletun, Narasimha and Tsudik (2004) for relational data, where two different aggregate signature schemes, namely condensed-RSA and Boneh et al. (2003), have been compared.

UDDI Registries

The main goal of a UDDI registry (Clement et al., 2002) is to supply potential clients with the description of businesses and the services they publish, together with technical information about the services, making thus the requestor able to directly require the service that better fits its needs. The UDDI registry organizes all these descriptions into a single entry.

Figure 1. UDDI main data structutres

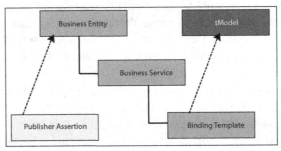

Figure 2. The BusinessEntity element

```
<?xml version="1.0" encoding="UTF-8"?>
 <businessEntity businessKey="9ECDC890-23EC-11D8-B78C-89A8511765B5" operator="jUDDI.org"
authorizedName="Carminati">
  <discoveryURLs>
   <discoveryURL useType="BusinessEntity"> http://www.dicom.uninsubria.it/ </discoveryURL>
   <discoveryURL
useType="businessEntity">http://localhost:8080/juddi/discovery?businessKey=9ECDC890-23EC-11D8-
B78C-89A8511765B5</discoveryURL>
  </discoveryURLs>
  <name xml:lang="it">DICOM</name>
  <description xml:lang="it">Dipartimento d'Informatica e Comunicazione</description>
  <contacts>
   <contact>
    <personName>Barbara Carminati</personName>
    <email>barbara.carminati@uninsubria.it</email>
    <address>
     <addressLine>Via Mazzini, 5</addressLine>
     <addressLine>21100 Varese </addressLine>
    </address>
   </contact>
  </contacts>
  <businessServices>
   <businessService serviceKey="9F063DB0-23EC-11D8-B78C-ECBB5F8B0CFC" businessKey="9ECDC890-23EC-
11D8-B78C-89A8511765B5">
    <name>Service 1</name>
    <description>Example service</description>
    <bindingTemplates>
     <bindingTemplate bindingKey="9F063DB0-23EC-11D8-B78C-F7A09CE94F7B" serviceKey="9F063DB0-23EC-
11D8-B78C-ECBB5F8B0CFC">
      <description>Binding Example 1</description>
      <accessPoint URLType="www.example.it/service.asmx"></accessPoint>
      <tModelInstanceDetails />
     </bindingTemplate>
    </bindingTemplates>
   </businessService>
  </businessServices>
  <identifierBag />
  <categoryBag />
 </businessEntity>
```

More precisely, each entry is composed of five main data structures (see Figure 1), namely, the BusinessEntity, the BusinessService, the BindingTemplate, the publisherAssertion and the tModel, which are briefly described in what follows.

The BusinessEntity provides general information about the business or the organization providing the Web services (e.g., the name of the organization, the contact person). Additionally, a UDDI entry contains one BusinessService data structure for each service provided by the business or organization and described by the BusinessEntity. This data structure contains a technical description (i.e., the BindingTemplate data structure) of the service, and information about the type of the service (i.e., the tModel data structure). By contrast, the PublisherAssertion data structure models the relationships existing among different BusinessEntity elements. For example, by this data structure it is possible to represent the relationships among the UDDI entries corresponding to subsidiaries of the same corporations.

Figure 2 reports an example of the XML representation of a UDDI entry. In particular, this entry represents the DICOM organization (i.e., the name element contained in the BusinessEntity element), which has specified only one contact person, that is, Barbara Carminati (i.e., the personName element contained in the BusinessEntity element). According to Figure 2, the DICOM organization provides only one service, called Service1 (i.e., the name element contained in the BusinessService element), whose binding template is accessible at URL www.example.it/service.asmx (i.e., the accessPoint element contained in the bindingTemplate   element).

UDDI registries provide clients searching facilities for provider(s) that better fits the client requirements. More precisely, according to the UDDI specification, UDDI registries support two different types of inquiry: The drill-down pattern inquiries (i.e., get_xxx API functions), which return a whole core data structure (e.g., BusinessTemplate, BusinessEntity, operationalInfo, BusinessService, and tModel), and the browse pattern inquiries (i.e., find_xxx API functions), which return overview information about the registered data.

XML Merkle Tree Authentication

The approach we propose in Bertino et al. (2004) for applying the Merkle tree authentication mechanism to XML documents is based on the use of the so-called *Merkle signatures*. This signature allows one to apply a unique digital signature on an XML document by ensuring at the same time the authenticity of both the whole document, as well as of any portion of it (i.e., one or more of its elements/attributes). The peculiarity of the Merkle signature is the algorithm used to compute the digest value of the XML document to being signed. This algorithm, which exploits the Merkle tree authentication mechanism (see "Authentication Mechanisms for Third Party Architectures" section), associates a different hash value, called Merkle hash value, with each node (i.e., elements/attributes) in the graph representing an XML document. Before presenting the function computing these Merkle hash values, we need to introduce the notation we adopt throughout the chapter. Given an element *e*, we use the dot notation *e.content* and *e.tagname* to denote the data content and the tagname of e, respectively. Moreover, given an attribute a, the notation $a.val$ and $a.name$ is used to denote the value and the name of attribute a, respectively.

Definition 1. *Merkle hash function*(). Let d be an XML document, and v a node of d (i.e., an element, or an attribute). The Merkle hash value associated with a node v of d, denoted as $MhX_d(v)$, is computed by the following function:

$$MhX_d(v)=\begin{cases} h(h(v.val)\|h(v.name)) & \text{if } v \text{ is an attribute} \\ \\ h(h(v.content)\|h(v.tagname)\|MhX_d(child(1,v))\|\ldots \end{cases}$$

$\|MhX_d(child(Nc_v,v)))$ if v is an element where '$\|$' denotes the concatenation operator, and function $child(i,v)$ returns the i-th child of node v, with Nc_v denoting the number of children of node v.

According to Definition 1, the Merkle hash value associated with an attribute is the result of an hash function applied to the concatenation of the hashed attribute value and the hashed attribute name. By contrast, the Merkle hash value of an element is obtained by applying the same hash function over the concatenation of the hashed element content, the hashed element tagname, and the Merkle hash values associated with its children nodes, both attributes and elements.

As an example, consider the XML document d in Figure 2, containing the BusinessEntity element defined according to the UDDI specification. The Merkle hash value of the contacts element (MhX_d(contacts)) is the result of the hash function computed over the concatenation of the element content, if any, the element tagname, and the Merkle hash values associated with its children nodes (i.e., contact elements).

The important point of the proposed approach is that if the correct Merkle hash value of a node v is known by a client, an untrustworthy third party or an intruder cannot forge the value of the children of node v, as well as its content and tagname. Thus, by knowing only the Merkle hash value of the root element of an XML document, the client is able to verify the authenticity and integrity of the whole XML document. To ensure the integrity of the Merkle hash value of the document root element we impose that the owner of the data signs this value, and we refer to this signature as the Merkle signature of the document.

The main benefit of the proposed technique wrt traditional digital signature technique is when a third party architecture is adopted like the UDDI, that is, when there exists a third party that may prune some nodes from a document as a result of the query evaluation. In this case, the traditional approach of digital signatures is no longer applicable, since its correctness is based on the assumption that the signing and verification processes are performed on exactly the same bits. By contrast, if the Merkle signature is applied, the client is still able to validate the signature, provided that it receives from the third party a set of additional hash values, referring to the missing document portions. This makes the client able to locally perform the computation of the summary signature and comparing it with the received one. We refer to this additional information as the *Merkle hash path*, defined in what follows.

Merkle Hash Paths

Intuitively, the Merkle hash paths can be defined as the hash values of those nodes pruned during query evaluation, and needed by the client for computing the Merkle signature. In general, given two nodes v,w in an XML document d, such that v belongs to the path connecting w to the root, the Merkle hash path between w and v, denoted as $MhPath(w,v)$, is the set of hash values necessary to compute the Merkle hash value of v having the Merkle hash value of w. The formal definition is given in what follows.

Definition 2. *Merkle Hash Path – MhPath().* Let d be an XML document, and let v,w be two nodes in d such that $v \in Path(w)$, where $Path(w)$ denotes the set of nodes connecting w to the root of the corresponding document. $MhPath(w,v)$ is a list consisting of the following hash values:

- $\{h(f.content), h(f.tagname)|\ \forall\ f \in Path(w,v) \setminus \{w\}\}$
- $\{MhX_d(e)|\ \forall\ e \in sib(f),$ where $f \in Path(w,v) \setminus \{v\}\}$

where $sib()$ is a function that, given a node f, returns f's siblings.

Thus, the Merkle hash path between w and v consists of the hash values of the tagname and content of all the nodes belonging to the path connecting w to v (apart from w), plus the Merkle hash values of all the siblings of the nodes belonging to the path connecting w to v (apart from v).

To better clarify how the proposed approach works, consider Figure 3, which depicts three different examples of Merkle hash paths. In the graph representation adopted in this chapter we do not distinguish elements from attributes by treating them as generic nodes. In the figure, the triangle denotes the view returned to the client, whereas black circles represent the nodes whose Merkle hash values is returned together with the view, that is, the Merkle hash paths. Consider the first example reported in

Figure 3. Examples of Merkle hash paths

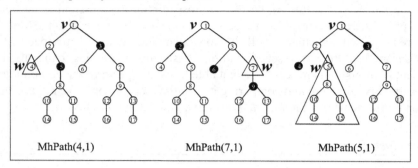

MhPath(4,1)   MhPath(7,1)   MhPath(5,1)

Figure 3. The Merkle hash path between nodes 4 and 1 consists of the Merkle hash values of nodes 5 and 3, plus the hash values of the tagname and content of nodes 2 and 1. Indeed, by using node *w*, the Merkle hash value of node 5, and the hash value of the tagname and content of node *2*, it is possible to compute the Merkle hash value of node 2. Then, by using the Merkle hash values of nodes 2 and 3, and the hash values of the tagname and content of node 1, it is possible to compute the Merkle hash value of node 1. In the second example in Figure 3, the view consists of a non-leaf node. In such a case *MhPath*(7,1) contains also the Merkle hash values of the child of node 7, that is, node 9. Thus, by using the Merkle hash value of node 9 and the hashed content of node 7, it is possible to compute the Merkle hash value of node 7. Then, by using this value, the Merkle hash value of node 6 and the hash values of the tagname and content of node 3, it is possible to generate the Merkle hash value of node 3. Finally, by using the Merkle hash values of nodes 3 and 2, and the hash values of the tagname and content of node 1, it is possible to generate the Merkle hash value of node 1. By contrast, in the third example the view consists of the whole sub-tree rooted at node 5. In such a case, *MhPath*(5,1) does not contain the hash values of the children of node 5. Indeed, since the whole sub-tree rooted at 5 is available, it is possible to compute the Merkle hash value of node 5 without the need of further information. Then, similarly to the previous examples, by using the Merkle hash values of nodes 5 and 4, and the hash values of the tagname and content of node 2 (these last values supplied by *MhPath*(5,1)), it is possible to compute the Merkle hash value of node 2. Finally, by having the Merkle hash values of nodes 2 and 3, and the hash values of the tagname and content of node 1, it is possible to compute the Merkle hash value of node 1. We can note that if the query result consists of an entire sub-tree, the only necessary Merkle hash values necessary are those associated with the siblings of the node belonging to the path connecting the subtree root to the document root.

Applying the Merkle Signature to UDDI Registries

In this section, we show how we can apply the authentication mechanism, illustrated in the previous section, to UDDI registries. As depicted in Figure 4, the proposed solution implies that the service provider first generates the Merkle signature of the BusinessEntity element, and then publishes it, together with the related data structures, in the UDDI registry. Then, when a client inquiries the UDDI, the Merkle signature as well as the set of necessary hash values (i.e., the Merkle hash paths, computed by the UDDI) are returned by the UDDI to the requesting client together with the inquiry result.

Adopting this solution requires to determine how the Merkle signature and the Merkle hash paths have to be enclosed in the BusinessEntity element, and inquiry result, respectively. To deal with this issue, we make use of the dsig:Signature element introduced in the latest UDDI specification (Clement, Hately, von Riegen, & Rogers, 2002). Indeed, to make the service provider able to sign the UDDI entry the latest UDDI specification supports an optional dsig:Signature element that can be inserted into the following elements: BusinessEntity, BusinessService, bindingTemplate, publisherAssertion, and tModel. Thus, according to the XML Signature syntax (Eastlake, Reagle, & Solo, 2001), a service provider can sign the whole element to which the signature element refers to, as well as it can exclude selected portions from the signature, by applying a transformation.

Therefore, in order to apply the Merkle signature to the UDDI environment, and at the same time to be compliant with the UDDI specification, we represent both

Figure 4. The Merkle signature in UDDI environment

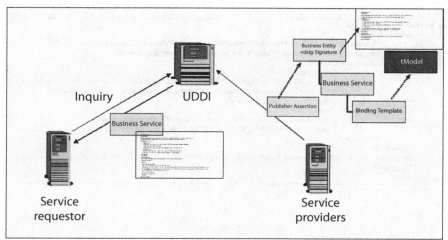

the Merkle signature and the Merkle hash paths according to the XML signature syntax (i.e., by using the dsig:Signature element). In the following sections, we give more details on the proposed representation.

Merkle Signature Representation

In Figure 5 we show how the dsig:Signature element can be used to wrap the Merkle signature. Note that the URI attribute of the Reference element is empty and thus it identifies the XML document where the Signature element is contained, that is, the BusinessEntity element. In addition to the required enveloped signature and scheme centric canonicalization transformations, the dsig:Signature element specifies also a Merkle transformation, through a Transform element whose Algorithm attribute is equal to "Merkle." This last transformation indicates to the client and UDDI registries that the service provider has computed the Merkle signature on the BusinessEntity element.

It is important to note that the syntax of the Transforms element implies an order according to which the various transformations should be applied. In particular, this order is given by the order in which the corresponding Transform elements appear in their parent element. Thus, to generate the digital signature contained into the dsig:Signature element, presented in Figure 5, it is first necessary to apply the enveloped signature transformation and the scheme centric canonicalization. Then, the Merkle hash function is computed on the obtained result. Finally, the obtained digest value is digitally signed according to the XML Signature Recommendation.

Figure 5. An example of signature element storing the Merkle signature

```
<dsig:Signature>
<           SignedInfo>
                    <CanonicalizationMethod Algorithm="http://www.w3.org/TR/2001/REC-xnl-c14n-20010315"/>
                    <SignatureMethod Algorithm="http://www.w3.org/2000/09/xmldsig#dsa-sha1"/>
                    <Reference URI="">
<                        Transforms>
                                <Transform Algorithm="http://www.w3.org/2000/09/xmldsig#enveloped-signature"/>
                                <Transform Algorithm="urn:uddi-org:schemaCentricC14N:2002-07-10"/>
<                        Transform Algorithm="Merkle"/>
<                        /Transforms>
<                        DigestMethod Algorithm="http://www.w3.org/2000/09/xmldsig#sha1"/>
<                        DigestValue>1fR07/Z/XFW375JG22bNGmFblMY=</DigestValue>
                    </Reference>
<           /SignedInfo>
<           SignatureValue> W0uO9b47TqmlpunAwmF4ubn1mdsb4HYR17c+3ULmLL2BxslwSsl6kQ
            </SignatureValue>
</ dsig:Signature>
```

Merkle Hash Path Representation

According to the strategies depicted in Figure 4, once client inquiries a UDDI registry, the UDDI registry computes the corresponding Merkle hash path and returns it to the client together with the inquiry result. As we will see in the next section, the latest UDDI specification states that for some kind of inquiries (i.e., the get_xxx inquiries), the UDDI registry has to include in the inquiry answer also the dsig: Signature element corresponding to the data structure returned as inquiry result. For this reason, we represent also the Merkle hash paths into the dsig:Signature element, supplying thus the client with the additional information needed for verifying the authenticity and integrity of the inquiry results.

To enclose this information into the dsig:Signature element, we exploit the dsig:SignatureProperties element, in which additional information useful for the validation process can be stored.

In Figure 6 we present an example of dsig:Signature element containing the dsig:SignatureProperties element, which is inserted as direct child of an Object element. It is important to note that, according to the XML Signature generation process, the only portion of the dsig:Signature element which is digitally signed is the SignedInfo element.

Thus, by inserting the Object element outside the SignedInfo element the UDDI registry does not invalidate the signature. This allows the UDDI to complement the dsig:Signature element representing the Merkle signature of the BusinessEntity element with the dsig:SignatureProperties element containing the appropriate Merkle hash paths, and then to insert it into the inquiry answer. More precisely, during the Merkle signature validation, the client must be able to recompute the Merkle hash value of the BusinessEntity element, to compare it with the Merkle signature. In order to do that, the client must know the Merkle hash value of each subelement of the BusinessEntity element not included into the inquiry answer (i.e., the Merkle hash path). To make the validation simpler, the Merkle hash paths are organized into an empty BusinessEntity element (see Figure 6), whose children contain a particular attribute, called hash, storing the Merkle hash value of the corresponding element. This BusinessEntity element is inserted into the dsig:SignatureProperties element.

Merkle Signatures vs. XML Signatures in UDDI Registries

In this section, we explain the differences and the benefits that could be attained by adopting in UDDI registries the Merkle signature approach instead of the tra-

Figure 6. An XML signature element complemented with Merkle hash paths

```
<dsig:Signature>
       <SignedInfo>
              <CanonicalizationMethod Algorithm="http://www.w3.org/TR/2001/REC-xnl-c14n-20010315"/>
              <SignatureMethod Algorithm="http://www.w3.org/2000/09/xmldsig#dsa-sha1"/>
              <Reference URI="">
                     <Transforms>
                            <Transform Algorithm="http://www.w3.org/2000/09/xmldsig#enveloped-signature"/>
                            <Transform Algorithm="urn:uddi-org:schemaCentricC14N:2002-07-10"/>
                     <Transform Algorithm="Merkle"/>
                     </Transforms>
                     <DigestMethod Algorithm="http://www.w3.org/2000/09/xmldsig#sha1"/>
                     <DigestValue>1fR07/Z/XFW375JG22bNGmFblMY=</DigestValue>
              </Reference>
       </SignedInfo>
       <SignatureValue>
       W0uO9b47TqmlpunAwmF4ubn1mdsb4HYR17c+3ULmLL2BxslwSsl6kQ
       </SignatureValue>
       <Object>
              <SignatureProperties>
                     <SignatureProperty Target="MerkleHashPath">
                            <businessEntity autorizhedName="valore"  operator="juddi.org" hash="sldghoghor....">
                            <discoveryURLs hash="fdsgbdsl...." />
                            <identifierBag hash="57438tgfkv...." />
                                    <categoryBag hash="57438tgfkv...." />
                            <businessServices>
                                    <businessService>
                                           <description hash="gherogh..." />
                                           <bindingTemplates hash="hgkvdlsfv...." />
                                           <categoryBag  hash="hdsbghfdlb..." />
                                    </businessService>
                                    <businessService>
                                           <description hash="gherogh..." />
                                           <bindingTemplates  hash="hgkvdlsfv...." />
                                           <categoryBag  hash="hdsbghfdlb..." />
                                    </businessService>
                            </businessServices>
                            </businessEntity>
                     </SignatureProperty>
              </SignatureProperties>
       </Object>
</dsig:Signature>
```

ditional digital signature techniques. Before we do that it is interesting to note that similarly to Merkle signature also the XML signature syntax allows one to generate a different hash value for each different node of the XML document, and then to generate a unique signatures of all these values. This feature is obtained by means of the Manifest element, which creates a list of Reference elements, one for each hashed node. However, this solution does not care about the structure of the XML document, ensuring thus only the authenticity of the data content and not of the relationships among nodes.

In the following, we separately consider the possible inquiries that a client can submit to a UDDI registry, that is, the find_xxx and get_xxx inquiries.

get_xxx Inquiries

According to the UDDI latest specification, the service provider can complement all the data structures that could be returned by a get_xxx API call with a dsig:Signature element. However, to ensure the authenticity and integrity of all the data structures the service provider must compute five different XML signatures (one for each different element). Whereas, by using the Merkle signature approach the service provider generates only one signature, that is, the Merkle signature of the BusinessEntity element. Thus, a first benefit of our approach is that by generating only a unique signature it is possible to ensure the integrity of all the data structures. When a client submits a get_xxx inquiry, the UDDI returns the whole requested data structure, where the inserted dsig:Signature element contains the Merkle signature generated by the service provider, together with the Merkle hash path between the root of the returned data structure and the BusinessEntity element.

As an example, consider the get_bindingDetail inquiry. The UDDI specification states that the answer to the get_bindingDetail inquiry must be the BindingTemplates element, containing a list of BindingTemplate elements together with the corresponding dsig:Signature elements. In such a case, a UDDI registry exploiting the Merkle signature approach should substitute each dsig:Signature element contained into the bindingTemplate elements with the signature generated by the service provider, that is, the dsig:Signature element published together with the BusinessEntity. Moreover, according to the representation proposed in the previous sections, the UDDI registry should insert into the dsig:Signature element the dsig:SignatureProperties subelement, which stores the Merkle hash path between the bindingTemplate element and the BusinessEntity element.

find_xxx Inquiries

We now analyze the other types of inquiry, that is, the find_xxx inquiries. We recall that these inquiries return overview information about the registered data. Consider, for instance, the inquiry API find_business that returns a structure containing information about each matching business, including summaries of its business services. This information is a subset of those contained in the BusinessEntity element and the BusinessService elements. For this kind of inquiries, the UDDI specification states that if a client wants to verify the authenticity and integrity of the information contained in the data structures returned by a find_xxx API call, he/she must retrieve the corresponding dsig:Signature elements by using the get_xxx API calls. This means that if a client wishes to verify the answer of a find_business inquiry, it must retrieve the whole BusinessEntity element, together with the corresponding dsig:Signature element, as well as each BusinessService element, together with its dsig:Signature element.

By contrast, if we consider the same API call performed by using the Merkle signature approach, to make the client able to verify the authenticity of the inquiry result it is not necessary to return the client the whole BusinessEntity element and the BusinessService elements, together with their signatures. By contrast, only the Merkle hash values of the missing portions are required, that is, those not returned by the inquiry. These Merkle hash values can be easily stored by the UDDI into the dsig: Signature element (i.e., dsig:SignatureProperties subelement) of the BusinessEntity.

As discussed previously, the main problem in applying the Merkle signature to the find_xxx inquiries is that the expected answers, defined by the UDDI specification, do not include the dsig:Signature element. For this reason, we need to modify the data structure returned by the UDDI by inserting one ore more dsig:Signature elements. In particular, to state where the dsig:Signature element should be inserted, we need to recall that the find_xxx API calls return overview information taken from different nodes of the BusinessEntity element, and wrapped into a fixed element. For instance, the find_business API returns a BusinessList structure, which supplies information about each matching businesses, together with summary information about its services. All this information is wrapped into the BusinessInfo element, which contains the name and the description of the service provider, and a different serviceInfo element for each published service.

We can say thus that the find_xxx API returns a list of results, each of them wrapped by a precise element (i.e., BusinessInfo for find_business API), which will be called, hereafter, *container* element. The proposed solution is thus to insert the dsig:Signature element, complemented with the appropriate Merkle hash paths, into each *container* element.

Figure 7 reports an algorithm for generating the answer for a find_xxx inquiry. The algorithm receives as input the answer returned according to the UDDI specification (i.e., the xxxList). Then, in step 1, the algorithm interactively considers each *container* element contained into the xxxList, and for each of them it creates the appropriate dsig:Signature element. This implies, as a first step, the generation of the Merkle hash values associated with the BusinessEntity element to which the information contained into the container element belong to. Note, that according to Definition 2, it is not necessary to create all the Merkle hash values; by contrast, the only hash values needed are those corresponding to the nodes pruned during the inquiry evaluation. Then, the obtained hash values are inserted into the dsig:SignatureProperty element, according to the strategies illustrated previously. Then, in step 1d, the resulting dsig: SignatureProperty element is inserted into the dsig:Signature element generated by the service provider and published together with the BusinessEntity element. Finally, the resulting dsig:Signature element is inserted into the xxxList as direct child of the corresponding container element.

As an example, let us suppose that a client submits a find_business inquiry on the BusinessEntity presented in Figure 2. The answer generated by UDDI according to Algortihm 1 is shown in Figure 8. Given this answer the client is able to verify the

Figure 7. Computation of find_xxx *inquiry answers exploiting the Merkele signatures*

Algorithm 1

Input

      xxxList the answer of a find_xxx API call

Output

    T   he xxxList complemented by the disg:Signature element

1. For each container n into the xxxList:
   a. Let MhX be the set of Merkle Hash values associated with the businessEntity to which n belongs to
   b. Create the dsig:SignatureProperties element using the Merkle hash values in MhX
   c. Let *Sign* be the dsig:Signature element of the businessEntity to which n belongs to
   d. Insert the dsig:SignatureProperties element into *Sign*
   e. Insert the obtained *Sign* element as direct child of the n
   EndFor
2. Return xxxList

Merkle signature generated by the service provider. In order to do that the client exploits the Merkle hash values stored into the dsig:SignatureProperty element, which correspond to those nodes of the BusinessEntity not included in the find_business answer. In order to compute the Merkle hash value of the BusinessEntity element, and thus to verify the Merkle signature, the client needs to have all the Merkle hash values of all children of the BusinessEntity element. The find_business inquiry returns to client only the name and description element (see Figure 8). For this reason the dsig:SignatureProperty element contains the Merkle hash values of all the remaining children nodes, that is the discoveryURLs, the contacts, identifierBag and categoryBag element. Another Merkle hash value needed for the validation of the Merkle signature is the one corresponding to the BusinessService element. The find_business inquiry returns only the name of the services (i.e., the name element contained into the BusinessService element), whereas the description, the bindingTemplate and the categoryBag element are omitted. According to Definition 1, to compute the Merkle hash value of the BusinessService element, the client must have the Merkle hash values of all its children. These values are contained into the dsig:SignatureProperty element.

Prototype of an Enhanced UDDI Registry

In this section, we describe the prototype we have developed for implementing a UDDI registry exploiting the Merkle signature technique. The prototype consists

Figure 8. An example of find_xxx *answer generated according the algorithm in Figure 7*

```
<?xml version="1.0" encoding="UTF-8"?>
<soapenv:Envelope xmlns:soapenv="http://schemas.xmlsoap.org/soap/envelope/"  xmlns:xsd="http://www.w3.org/2001/XMLSchema"
xmlns:xsi="http://www.w3.org/2001/XMLSchema-instance">
<soapenv:Body>
   <businessList generic="2.0" operator="jUDDI.org" xmlns="urn:uddiorg:api_v2">
      <businessInfos>
         <businessInfo businessKey="9ECDC890-23EC-11D8-B78C-89A8511765B5">
            <name xml:lang="it">DICOM</name>
            <description xml:lang="it">Dipartimento d'Informatica e Comunicazione</description>
            <serviceInfos>
                  <serviceInfo serviceKey="E27F6560-2579-11D8-A560-A95B48063A06">
                        <name>Service 1</name>
                  </serviceInfo>
            </serviceInfos>
            <Signature>
                  <SignedInfo>
                        <Reference URI="">
                              <Transforms>
                                    <Transform Algorithm="http://www.w3.org/2000/09/xmldsig#enveloped-signature"/>
                                    <Transform Algorithm="urn:uddi-org:schemaCentricC14N:2002-07-10"/>
                                       <Transform Algorithm="Merkle"/>
                              </Transforms>
                              <DigestMethod Algorithm="http://www.w3.org/2000/01/xmldsig/sha1"/>
                              <DigestValue>CysG5cZQelvxENwHwxBXLMBYGgo=</DigestValue>
                        </Reference>
                        <CanonicalizationMethod Algorithm="http://www.w3.org/1999/07/WD-xml-c14n-19990729"/>
                        <SignatureMethod Algorithm="http://www.w3.org/2000/01/xmldsig/rsa"/>
                  </SignedInfo>
                  <SignatureValue>n2XH0Jk6g7jVgGnZxp+7PyBEJhCrVXNx2bdjgzN4zOu1Q52jOfFh3VHMMi6nZsRHHZb5TgqFl
QFgG/Z3JGZJ9P1AWLUVn+kuX1ClZPxKdZ12oe4w/pa/qqXex/K8szgmrBUDIzXNfGEgQIUF+Nbh2WpHK/tVumLNfF+hIg+
jD+StWLTalqlV4jfJbdaeEO7EQyiS3AJ+FByvd7qtArlJvzAwAQ8WLIO6uprG+
/soHewJLNNgHywPjpSh9FMKraFSyhyjVcrXXgX4Aauv5M3YM6k7ZOEDfD0WVQTMk8ukbU31rQ9dlPOgJvp/aRQPtBb4D
CqD4tM0701s1a6Pxmf+8p7IvvfKWWHy3nWNXTLZtGIYssN/BN3clLuiXijW3sIaBU=
                  </SignatureValue>
                  <KeyInfo>
                        <KeyValue>
                              <RSAKeyValue>
                                    <Modulus>ALkV0Yv6NSWMQ/GxX7VElnUCmBiBB2kA92iRuXzjr+TesJ6mJWsu
NrQTdaLXNUeLaCfTyibXCHEo8GKhGr3+6UlxkNfPbApqRMG2Z6f
                                    </Modulus>
                                    <Exponent>AQAB</Exponent>
                              </RSAKeyValue>
                        </KeyValue>
                  </KeyInfo>
                  <Object>
                        <SignatureProperty Target="MerkleHashPath">
                              <businessEntity authorizedName="Barbara" operator="jUDDI.org">
                                    <discoveryURLs hash="sB/kzmjVacE9iBuLdyxC5S2Ha9E="/>
                                    <contacts hash="bMwPAQ5nAZZhhKcAMswsxDAfPeY="/>
                                    <identifierBag hash="PFIc19Gspd46sXkdP4f2+i8yajk="/>
                                    <categoryBag hash="ako/7rv5NZdxp5qjDGQ/W0++acY="/>
                                    <BusinessServices>
                                          <BusinessService>
                                                <description hash="az8oQfVMxw1C7Dtf5logCtlZNtQ="/>
                                                <bindingTemplates hash="cQw/q+Z4iL50QOA/7hj0jnXhkmg="/>
                                                <categoryBag hash="ako/7rv5NZdxp5qjDGQ/W0++acY="/>
                                          </BusinessService>
                                    </BusinessServices>
                              </businessEntity>
                        </SignatureProperty>
                  </Object>
            </Signature>
         </businessInfo>
      </businessInfos>
   </businessList>
</soapenv:Body>
</soapenv:Envelope>
```

of two different components: the UDDI registry, called *enhanced-UDDI registry* and a UDDI client, playing the role of both service provider publishing data to a UDDI, and service requestor inquiring the enhanced UDDI registry.

As reported in Figure 9, the enhanced-UDDI registry is built on top of jUDDI, which is a Java open source implementation of a UDDI registry. In particular, in the prototype jUDDI exploits a MySQL database as UDDI entries repository. Moreover, since the latest jUDDI implementation has been developed according to UDDI version 2 that, unlike the latest specification, does not provide support for the dsig:Signature element, we have integrated the prototype also with the IAIK Java cryptography extension (JCE) toolkit. This last component makes the prototype able to exploit hash functions, symmetric and asymmetric encryption, and thus to validate the Merkle signature. Thus, in the current version of our enhanced-UDDI registry the standard API functions are implemented by means of jUDDI, whereas the functionalities devoted to the Merkle signature management are implemented by two distinct java classes, directly invoked by jUDDI. These functionalities are the generation of the Merkle hash paths, and the generation of inquiry answers. More precisely, the last task implies the insertion of the computed Merkle hash path into the dsig:Signature element and the insertion of the obtained element into the inquiry answer.

The UDDI client plays the role of both service provider and requestor. To support both these tasks, the UDDI client exploits UDDI4j, a Java class library providing APIs for interacting with a UDDI registry. UDDI4j supports the UDDI version 2. For this reason, the UDDI client makes also use of additional Java classes, implementing the functionalities devoted to Merkle signatures management, that is, the Merkle signature generation and the Merkle signature validation. Such classes are directly invoked by the UDDI4j implementation (see Figure 9), and exploit IAIK JCE for signature generation and validation. An example of BusinessEntity generated

Figure 9. The enhanced IDDI registry

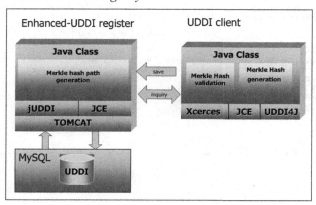

Figure 10. The BusinessEntity *element generated by UDDI client*

```
<?xml version="1.0" encoding="UTF-8"?>
<save_business xmlns="urn:uddi-org:api_v2" generic="2.0">
 <authInfo xmlns="">authToken:9EF0E0F0-23EC-11D8-B78C-8DDAF5C9614A</authInfo>
 <businessEntity xmlns="" businessKey="9ECDC890-23EC-11D8-B78C-89A8511765B5"
operator="jUDDI.org" authorizedName="Barbara">
  <discoveryURLs>
   <discoveryURL useType="BusinessENtity"> http://www.dicom.uninsubria.it/ </discoveryURL>
   <discoveryURL
useType="businessEntity">http://localhost:8080/juddi/discovery?businessKey=9ECDC890-23EC-11D8-
B78C-89A8511765B5</discoveryURL>
  </discoveryURLs>
  <name xml:lang="it">DICOM</name>
  <description xml:lang="it">Dipartimento d'Informatica e Comunicazione</description>
  <contacts>
   <contact>
    <personName>Barbara Carminati</personName>
    <email>barbara.carminati@uninsubria.it</email>
    <address>
     <addressLine>Via Mazzini, 5</addressLine>
     <addressLine>21100 Varese</addressLine>
    </address>
   </contact>
  </contacts>
  <businessServices>
   <businessService serviceKey="9ECF4F30-23EC-11D8-B78C-D4B4D63A03DD" businessKey="9ECDC890-
23EC-11D8-B78C-89A8511765B5">
    <name>Service 1</name>
    <description>Example service</description>
    <bindingTemplates>
     <bindingTemplate bindingKey="9ED25C70-23EC-11D8-B78C-E6B2648DFC70" serviceKey="9ECF4F30-
23EC-11D8-B78C-D4B4D63A03DD">
      <description>Binding Example 1</description>
      <accessPoint URLType="www.example.it/service.asmx"></accessPoint>
      <tModelInstanceDetails />
     </bindingTemplate>
    </bindingTemplates>
   </businessService>
  </businessServices>
  <identifierBag />
  <categoryBag />
  <Signature>
   <SignedInfo>
    <CanonicalizationMethod Algorithm="http://www.w3.org/1999/07/WD-xml-c14n-19990729"/>
    <SignatureMethod Algorithm="http://www.w3.org/2000/01/xmldsig/rsa"/>
    <Reference URI="">
     <Transforms>
      <Transform Algorithm="http://www.w3.org/2000/09/xmldsig#enveloped-signature" />
       <Transform Algorithm="urn:uddi-org:schemaCentricC14N:2002-07-10" />
       <Transform Algorithm="Merkle" />
     </Transforms>
     <DigestMethod Algorithm="http://www.w3.org/2000/01/xmldsig/sha1" />
     <DigestValue>PyAeAtNeYcRQq2gI6Fq7NXOgEnI=</DigestValue>
    </Reference>
   </SignedInfo>
   <SignatureValue>pJQn61Vo7ZjzBQNh944I1aMMJPO/ofR16CdHmTNpEYEoI8f3U0dI2OIjR9u+JiBA2MaN7TlwxnKR
ks/mdnWCL85SABOADHwqD1+zoF/VLnaFeGfCJfbWfOTiTNOxjxZFkYISPbfrM6hLFG/qhMb1RRmMp9v+jJKNh00ktpx9Vn
g=</SignatureValue>
   <KeyInfo>
    <KeyValue>
     <RSAKeyValue>
      <Modulus>ALkV0Yv6NSWMQ/GxX7VElnUCmBiBB2kA92iRuXzjr+TesJ6mJWsuEjWgU2CkezriMRsu1MbRGeXb
E0RSXluH4VPcE4IYECEb5pheQCeAleFHdS+BHAXmFIx0sNrQTdaLXNUeLaCfTyibXCHEo8GKhGr3
+6UlxkNfPbApqRMG2Z6f </Modulus>
      <Exponent>AQAB</Exponent>
     </RSAKeyValue>
    </KeyValue>
   </KeyInfo>
  </Signature>
 </businessEntity>
</save_business>
```

by the UDDI client, and published to the enhanced-UDDI registry is reported in Figure 10.

Conclusion

In this chapter we have presented an approach based on Merkle hash trees, which provides a flexible authentication mechanism for UDDI registries.

The proposed approach has two relevant benefits. The first is the possibility for the service provider to ensure the authenticity and integrity of the whole data structures by signing a unique small amount of data, with the obvious improvement of the performance. The second benefit regards browse pattern inquiries (i.e., find_xxx API), which return overview information taken from one or more data structures. According to the UDDI specification, in such a case if a client wishes to verify the authenticity and integrity of the answer, it must request the whole data structures from which the information are taken. Besides being not efficient, this solution is not always applicable. Indeed, the information contained in the data structures may be highly strategic and sensitive, and thus may not be made available to all the clients. In such a case, if the client does not have the proper authorization it is not able to verify the authenticity and integrity of the received answer. By contrast, the proposed solution supports the browse pattern inquiries by ensuring at the same time the confidentiality of the data, in that, by using Merkle hash paths it is not necessary to send clients the whole data structures.

We plan to extend this work along several directions. One extension regards the support for additional security properties, such as for instance confidentiality and completeness, using strategies similar to those presented in Bertino, et al. (2004) and an extensive testing and performance evaluation of our prototype.

References

Bertino, E., Carminati, B., Ferrari, F., Thuraisingham, B., & Gupta A. (2004). Selective and authentic third-party distribution of XML documents. *IEEE Transactions on Knowledge and Data Engineering(TKDE)*, *16*(10), 1263-1278.

Boneh, D., Gentry, C., Lynn, B., & Shacham, H. (2003). Aggregate and verifiably encrypted signatures from bilinear maps. In *Proceedings of Advances in Cryptology, International Association for Cryptologic Research*. Berlin, Germany: Springer-Verlag.

Charanjit, S., & Yung, M. (1996). Paytree: Amortized signature for flexible micropayments. In *Proceedings of the 2nd USENIX Workshop on Electronic Commerce.*

Christensen, E., Curbera, F., Meredith, G., & Weerawarana, S. (2001). *Web services description language (WSDL), Version 1.2* (World Wide Web Consortium recommendation). Retrieved from http://www.w3.org/TR/wsdl12/

Clement, L., Hately, A., Von Riegen, C., & Rogers, T. (2002). *Universal description, discovery and integration (UDDI), Version 3.0* (UDDI Spec Technical Committee specification). Retrieved from http://uddi.org/pubs/uddi-v3.00-published-20020719.htm

Devanbu, P., Gertz, M., Martel, C., & Stubblebine, S. G. (2000). Authentic third-party data publication. In *Proceedings of the 14th Annual IFIP WG 11.3 Working Conference on Database Security*, Schoorl, The Netherlands.

Devanbu, P., Gertz, M., Kwong, A., Martel, C., Nuckolls, G., & Stubblebine, S.G. (2001). Flexible authentication of XML documents. In *Proceedings of the 8th ACM Conference on Computer and Communications Security*. ACM Press.

Eastlake, D., Reagle, J., & Solo, D. (2001). *XML signature syntax and processing 2001* (World Wide Web Consortium Recommendation). Retrieved from http://www.w3.org/TR/2001/CR-xmldsig-core-20010419/

Merkle, R. C. (1989). A certified digital signature. In *Proceedings of Advances in Cryptology-Crypto '89.*

Mitra, N. (2003). *Simple object access protocol (SOAP), Version 1.1* (World Wide Web Consortium recommendation). Retrieved from http://www.w3.org/TR/SOAP/

Mykletun, E., Narasimha, M., & Tsudik, G. (2004), Authentication and integrity in outsourced databases. In *Proceedings of Network and Distributed System Security (NDSS 2004).*

Naor, M., & Nissim, K. (1998). Certificate revocation and certificate update. In *Proceedings of the 7th USENIX Security Symposium.*

Chapter III

Web Services Enabled E-Market Access Control Model

Harry Wang, University of Delaware, USA

Hsing K. Cheng, University of Florida, USA

Leon Zhao, University of Arizona, USA

Abstract

With the dramatic expansion of global e-markets, companies collaborate more and more in order to streamline their supply chains. Small companies often form coalitions to reach the critical mass required to bid on large volume or wide ranges of products. Meanwhile, they also compete with one another for market shares. Because of the complex relationships among companies, controlling the access to shared information found in e-markets is a challenging task. Currently, there is a lack of comprehensive access control approaches that can be used to maintain data security in e-markets. We propose to integrate several known access control mechanisms such as role-based access control, coalition-based access control, and relationship driven access control into an e-market access control model (EMAC). In this chapter, we present a Web services-based architecture for EMAC and the associated concepts and algorithms. We also illustrate, via an automotive e-market example, how the EMAC model can support e-market access control.

Introduction

Aimed to make business contact and transactions easier and more cost effective, e-markets have emerged in several industries. For instance, Covisint, an e-market owned by a group of the biggest auto manufacturers, is anticipated to handle $240 billion per year, which is greater than the GDP of Sweden (Feldman, 2000). Many companies have begun the evolution from traditional business practices to e-business to strengthen customer service, streamline supply chains, and reach existing and new partners.

E-markets open up new possibilities of trade by providing various tools and services. E-catalogs and sourcing directories help both suppliers and buyers increase market visibility, shorten processing time and easily locate business partners (Baron, Shaw, & Bailey, Jr., 2000). E-auctions make prices more dynamic and responsive to economic conditions (Feldman, 2000). Scrutiny of the participating companies by e-markets increases the trust between trading partners and makes the establishment of new business relationship easier. Process collaboration tools help companies integrate their processes, which simplifies the work and avoids duplications (eMarket Services, 2002).

As e-markets develop and offer more advanced services, many serious challenges have been presented. Among those challenges, security has been highlighted as a critical issue that must be dealt with. Businesses generally perform controls over the internal use of their business processes. In the e-market environment, this controlled access must be extended to outside the company boundaries (Medjahed, Benatallah, Bouguettaya, Ngu, & Elmagarmid, 2003). Depending on the business situation, participating companies may want e-markets to hide their identities, current trading positions, sensitive catalog items, history, or ongoing activities with other players (Feldman, 2000). This gives rise to the need for advanced access control mechanisms.

Although there have been many research efforts in access control in recent years (Joshi, Aref, Ghafoor, & Spafford, 2001), there is a lack of comprehensive methods that can be used directly in the context of e-market access control. We propose to integrate several existing access control models to meet the needs of data security in the presence of complex relationships among companies that participate in an e-market, which we refer to as *e-market access control model* (EMAC). Among the known access control models, we mainly draw ideas from the models of role-based access control (Sandhu, Coyne, Feinstein, & Youman, 1996), task-based access control (Thomas & Sandhu, 1997), coalition-based access control (Cohen, Thomas, Winsborough, & Shands, 2002), and relationship-driven access control (Zhao et al., 2002). We argue that the complex relationships among companies that participate in an e-market require the enforcement of security authorization constraints that are more complex than those found in each of the access control models aforementioned. Therefore, these focused access control models must be integrated into a new access control model that is comprehensive enough to satisfy the needs of e-markets.

In e-markets, the need to interoperate multiple types of systems has risen due to the increased level of connectivity and data complexity (Medjahed et al., 2003). In this chapter, we use Web services to enable a distributed architecture for the implementation of our EMAC model, as Web services have been embraced by the software industry as the universal standard for open interoperability (Kreger, 2003). We encapsulate advanced security mechanisms inside Web services and provide standard interfaces for different security systems to communicate with one another. In particular, we extend some emerging standards such as security assertion markup language (SAML) and XML access control markup language (XACML) with features in the EMAC model.

We first review the relevant literature on access control models. Then, we develop the e-market access control (EMAC) model and related concepts including four types of relationships, specification language, and EMAC authorization algorithm. We also present EMAC architecture that consists of three layers, namely, inter-organizational workflow layer, advanced security management layer, and e-market resources layer. Finally, we summarize our contributions and discuss future research directions.

Literature Review

Ferraiolo et al. (2001) proposed the role-based access control (RBAC) model to simplify management of authorization while providing an opportunity for greater flexibility in specifying and enforcing enterprise-specific protection policies. In RBAC model, roles represent business functions in a given organization, such as CEO, purchasing manager, buyer, etc. Authorizations are then granted to roles, rather than users. The authorizations granted to a role are strictly related to the data objects and resources that are needed for executing the functions associated with that role (Bertino, Bonatti, & Ferrari, 2001). Even though RBAC has reached a good maturity level, there are still significant application requirements that have not been addressed by various versions of RBAC. Therefore, many extensions to

RBAC models have been proposed, such as task-based access control (TBAC) and coalition-based access control (CBAC).

TBAC uses tasks as an important parameter for access control and authorization (Thomas, 1997; Thomas & Sandhu, 1997). It is an active security model that is well suited for information processing activities where users access data and applications in order to perform certain tasks. TBAC approaches security management from an application perspective rather than from a system-centric subject-object view. In the subject-object paradigm, access decision function checks whether a subject has the required permissions for the operation, but it does not take into account the context of the access. In addition, TBAC paradigm also considers the temporal constraints where access is permitted based on a just-in-time fashion for the activities or tasks in consideration.

Cohen et al. (2002) argued that businesses, governments, and other organizations form coalitions to enhance their success. Commercial coalitions include supply chain arrangements, subcontracting relationships, and joint marketing campaigns. Such coalitions may be dynamic, because changes in business environments or trust relationships often result in new missions and modifications to coalition member-ship. To effectively participate in modern coalitions, member organizations must be able to share specific data and functionality with other coalition partners, while ensuring that their resources are safe from inappropriate access.

Kang, Park, and Froscher (2001) suggested that as more businesses engage in glo-balization and inter-organizational collaborative computing grows in importance, the access control requirements for inter-organizational workflow must be met by new access control solutions in a multi-organizational environment. Their proposal emphasized the separation of inter-organizational workflow security from organi-zation level security enforcement. Further, they described workflow-based access control requirements such as dynamic constraints, fine-grained and context-based access control, and the need to insulate inter-organizational workflows from orga-nization level changes.

In B2B e-commerce environments, particularly e-markets, companies form alliances to improve operational efficiency and gain competitive advantages, and meanwhile these companies compete with one another for market shares. The dynamic and complex relationships among companies impose more access control requirements for the shared resources in e-markets, as addressed by the relationship-driven access control (RDAC) model (Zhao et al., 2002). RDAC states that the access decision of certain shared resources is based on the relationship between access requester company and the owner company of the shared resources. For instance, company X can set an access control policy on its shared e-catalog that any company can see the quantity of the product but only buyer companies can see the price. Here, "buyer companies" is no longer a static role as defined in the role-based access control model. Instead, it represents the dynamic and bi-directional relationship between companies. Therefore, a role-based access control model is not sufficient for access control of shared e-market data. For the same reason, the extended RBAC models like TBAC and CBAC are not sufficient either.

The complexity of various trading functions and dynamic company relationships require e-markets to enforce authorization constraints that are more complex than those found in each of the access control models aforementioned. Therefore, we propose an EMAC model by integrating all these specialized access control models to satisfy the needs of e-markets. In this chapter, we provide guidelines for designing an access control infrastructure in e-markets and propose a Web services enabled architecture and associated techniques based on emerging Web services security standards. To the best of our knowledge, EMAC model is the first comprehensive access control model specially designed for e-markets.

E-Market Access Control Model (EMAC)

Relationship Hierarchy in E-Markets

Company relationships are important for managing security in an e-market because a company determines information sharing policies based on its relationships with other companies. Figure 1 shows a relationship hierarchy in an automotive e-market, containing four types of relationships.

The first type of relationship is between roles and their companies. Roles have been used as the basic way of authorizing users to access certain information. In the literature, a role is a semantic abstraction of specific job competency within a company (Sandhu, Coyne, Feinstein, & Youman, 1996). Role hierarchy is often used to refer to a set of roles found in a company. This relationship is straightforward within a single organizational security domain, while in e-markets this relationship is more complex. In e-markets, users from one security domain need to frequently access protected resources of another security domain, where roles in one security domain have to be correctly recognized and mapped to another security domain.

The second type of relationship is between two companies. As shown, complex relationships among companies exist. For example, Company 1 is a supplier of Company 2, because Company 1 sells product P1 to Company 2. At the same time, Company 1 is also a buyer of product P2 from Company 2. Company 1 and Company 3 are identified as competitors on P1, because both of them sell the same product P1 to a third party, which is Company 2 in this case. In sum, companies can have multiple relationships among one another.

Figure 1. Relationship hierarchy in an automotive e-market

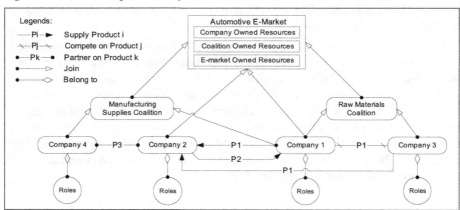

The third type of relationship is based on companies' membership in coalitions. In e-markets, small companies often form strategic coalitions to reach the critical mass required to bid on large volume or wide ranges of products. These coalitions are frequently formed and dissolved as company objectives and relationships change. Companies can choose not to join coalitions or to join any number of coalitions. For example, Company 1 participates in both a manufacturing supplies coalition and a raw materials coalition while Company 2 is not a member of any coalitions as shown in Figure 1.

The fourth type of relationship is based on companies' membership in e-markets. E-markets are often closed to companies that are not members. Sometimes only registration is required to become a member, while in other cases companies have to be invited by an existing member or go through a qualification process to get into e-markets (eMarket Services, 2002). Each coalition member company has to register independently to join the e-market regardless whether the coalition is a member of the e-market or not.

Figure 1 also illustrates that shared resources in e-market are classified into three categories: Market owned resources, coalition owned resources, and company owned resources. Market-owned resources include all trading services and facilities, which are open to all market participating companies. Coalition owned resources are shared among coalition member companies, but the access is often subject to certain access control rules. For instance, a coalition could have various classes of membership with different privileges. Company owned resources can be accessed by its own employees and the employees of other companies according to certain authorization constraints. Coalition owned resources and company owned

Figure 2. E-market access control reference model

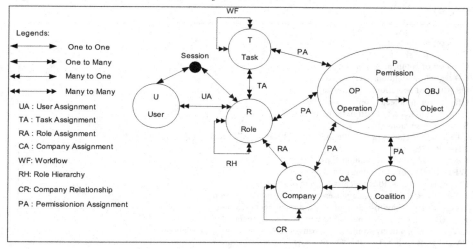

resources can be stored either by e-markets, by coalition and companies, or both. Take e-catalog as an example. Companies can upload their e-catalogs to e-markets or they can host their e-catalogs and only provide links for e-markets to redirect e-catalog access requests.

Specification of EMAC Model

Figure 2 shows a reference model for EMAC that integrates the concepts from RBAC, TBAC and CBAC. We extend the role-based constraints language presented in Ahn and Sandhu (2000) by incorporating more access control aspects from other models, resulting in the e-market access control language (EACL). This language is formal and rigorous since any expression written in EACL can be translated to an equivalent expression in a restricted form of first-order logic (Ahn & Sandhu, 2000; Bertino, Catania, Ferrari, & Perlasca, 2003).

The basic elements and functions on which EACL is based are defined in Table 1. For specifications related to RBAC, we refer readers to (Ahn & Sandhu, 2000) and focus the discussion on our extensions in the next subsection. EACL has three new entity sets named tasks (T), companies (C), and coalitions (CO), which are key elements in e-market access control scenarios.

Table 1. Basic elements and functions for e-market access control language (EACL)

U = a set of users, $\{u_1,\ldots,u_i\}$.
R = a set of roles, $\{r_1,\ldots,r_j\}$.
T = a set of tasks, $\{t_1,\ldots t_k\}$.
C = a set of companies, $\{c_1,\ldots,c_l\}$.
CO = a set of coalitions, $\{co_1,\ldots,co_m\}$.
OP = a set of operations, $\{op_1,\ldots,op_n\}$.
OBJ = a set of objects, $\{obj_1,\ldots,obj_p\}$.
$P = OP \times OBJ$, a set of permissions, $\{p_1,\ldots,p_q\}$.
S = a set of sessions, $\{s_1,\ldots,s_o\}$.
CT = types of classification, {"role," "task," "company," "relationship," "coalition"}.
$RH \subseteq R \times R$, role hierarchy.
$CR \subseteq C \times C$, company relationships.
$WF \subseteq T \times T$, workflows constituted by a set of tasks.
$CLS \subseteq R \cup T \cup C \cup CR \cup CO$, classification of an object.
$UA \subseteq U \times R$, a many-to-many user-to-role assignment relation.
$TA \subseteq R \times T$, a many-to-many role-to-task assignment relation.
$RA \subseteq R \times C$, a many-to-one role-to-company assignment relation.
$CA \subseteq C \times CO$, a many-to-many company-to-coalition assignment relation.
$PA \subseteq P \times R \cup P \times T \cup P \times C \cup P \times CO$, a many-to-many permission assignment relation, which can be permission-to-role, permission-to-task, permission-to-company or permission-to-coalition.
sessionuser: $S \rightarrow U$, a function mapping each session s_o to a single user.
user: $R \rightarrow U$, a function mapping each role r_j to a set of users.
role: $U \cup P \cup S \rightarrow R$, a function mapping the set U, P, and S to a set of roles.
task: $U \rightarrow T$, a function that returns the current task of the user.
company: $U \rightarrow C$, a function mapping each user u_i to a set of companies.
session: $U \rightarrow S$, a function mapping each user u_i to a set of sessions.
permission: $R \cup T \cup C \cup CO \rightarrow P$, a function mapping the set R, T, C and CO to a set of permissions.
operation: $R \times OBJ \rightarrow OP$, a function mapping each role r_j and object obj_p to a set of operations.
relationship: $C \times C \rightarrow CR$, a function mapping two companies c_i, c_i' to a set of company relationships.
affiliation: $C \rightarrow CO$, a function mapping company c_i to a set of coalitions.
owner: $OBJ \rightarrow C \cup CO$, a function returns the owner(s) of a object obj_p.
classification: $OBJ \times CT \rightarrow CLS$, a function mapping each object obj_p and classification type to a set of classifications.

Authorization Constraints

Given the complex relationships in e-markets and various ways of sharing resources, advanced authorization constraints that are more sophisticated than those in existing access control models must be enforced. Being an important aspect of access control, authorization constraints have been extensively studied. As one of the basic security constraints, separation of duty (SOD) is known and practiced long before the existence of computers. The goal of SOD is to reduce the possibility for fraud or significant errors by partitioning tasks and the associated privileges so that cooperation of multiple users is required to complete sensitive tasks (Ahn & Sandhu, 2000). Ferralolo et al., (2001) defined static separation of duty (SSOD) and dynamic separation of duty (DSOD) in the context of role-based access control model. Bertino, Ferrari, and Atluri (1999) investigated the enforcement of SOD in workflow management systems. In particular, they systematically addressed the problem of assigning roles and users to tasks in a workflow. Because role-based access control and task-based access control are main components of EMAC model, all these authorization constraints still hold. In this section, we specify four more authorization constraints from the perspective of shared resources and provide corresponding EACL expressions:

- **Role authorization constraints:** Conventionally, a role authorization constraint specifies that a user must play certain roles in order to access specific resources and related applications. For instance, company X may only allow other companies' buyers to access its shared e-catalog to improve the confidentiality. The EACL expression for role authorization is $|$ role(U) $\cap$ classification (OBJ, "role") $| \geqq 1$.

- **Task authorization constraints:** Task authorization constraints have been discussed in the literature such as task-based authorization (Thomas & Sandhu, 1997), separation of duties, binding of duties, restricted task execution, and cooperation and inhibition (Casati, Castano & Fugini, 2001). Essentially, this constraint specifies that a user must be participants of certain task to get the access. For example, sometimes the price and quantities of specific products are only visible during the auction (task); when the auction finishes, the access of these information will be revoked. The EACL expression is $|$ task(U) $\cap$ classification (OBJ, "task") $| = 1$.

- **Company authorization constraints:** A company authorization constraint expresses an authorization that depends on company relationships. Authorization to company-owned information can be specified based on the user company's relationship with the information owner (Zhao, et al., 2002). In order to reduce computational overhead, authorization can be specified on a higher level of data granularity such as product category instead of product type. This constraint is specified by EACL as: $\{|$ C(U) $\cap$ classification (OBJ, "company") $| = 1\} \cap \{|$ relationship(company(U), owner(OBJ)) $\cap$ classification (OBJ, "relationship") $| = 1\}$.

- **Coalition authorization constraints:** A coalition authorization constraint indicates additional privileges for coalition members. An example of coalition authorization is that specific discount information is only accessible to certain classes of member companies of the coalition. In EACL, this is expressed as $|$ affiliation(company(U)) $\cap$ classification (OBJ, "coalition") $| \geqq 1$.

By applying combinations of these four types of authorization constraints, we can support more advanced levels of access control in e-markets. The question is that what happens when those constraints conflict with one another. In this case, we use a "Deny-overrides" (OASIS, 2003) rule to resolve the conflicts. If any one of

Figure 3. Authorization process in EMAC

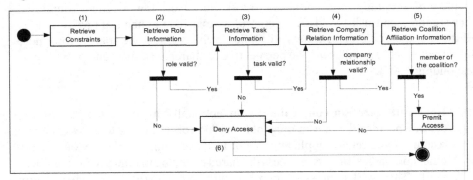

Table 2. Algorithm for EMAC authorization process

INPUT: user u_i and object obj_p
OUTPUT: permission P
Begin

If *classification(obj_p, "role")* <> N/A Then
　　If *classification(obj_p, "role")* <> *role* (u_i) Then return FALSE and Exit
　　　　Endif
Endif

If *classification(obj_p, "task")* <> N/A Then
　　If *classification(obj_p, "task")* <> *task(u_i)* Then return FALSE and Exit
　　　　Endif
Endif

If *classification(obj_p, "company")* <> N/A Then
　　If *classification(obj_p, "company")* <> company(u_i) Then return FALSE and Exit
　　　　Endif
Endif

If *classification(obj_p, "relationship")* <> N/A Then
　　If *classification(obj_p, "relationship")* <> relationship(company$((u_i)$, owner(OBJ))
　　Then return FALSE and Exit
　　　　Endif
Endif

If *classification(obj_p, "coalition")* <> N/A Then
　　If *classification(obj_p, "coalition")* <> affiliation(company(u_i))) Then return FALSE and Exit
　　　　Endif
Endif

Return P
End

the four constraints is not satisfied, then, regardless of the evaluation results of the other constraints, the access request is denied. When an access request is received, the EMAC model uses the authorization process shown in Figure 3 to evaluate the access control policies and make the final authorization decision.

This authorization process is sequential while the exact sequence of Step 2 to Step 5 depends on the authorization decision maker's policy. Table 2 shows the algorithm for the implementation of EMAC authorization process.

An Illustrative Example

Next, we use an example to illustrate how the EMAC model works. Figure 4 describes an e-market trading process.

Table 3 shows a database schema needed to implement the EMAC access control mechanism. The underlined attributes denote primary keys while foreign keys are in italic.

We can use the following query to get an object's classification constraints information (For ease of presentation, we select names instead of IDs.):

Figure 4. An e-market trading process

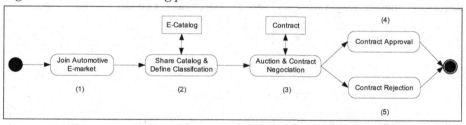

Table 3. A sample relational schema

User(<u>U_ID</u>, U_Name, Position, Login, Password, *C_ID*)
Role(<u>R_ID</u>, R_Name,R_Desc)
Task(<u>T_ID</u>,T_Name, T_Desc, Start, Expiration, End, *W_ID*)
Workflow(<u>W_ID</u>, W_Name, W_Desc, Start, End)
Company(<u>C_ID</u>, C_Name, Location, Phone, *Coal_ID*)
Coalition(<u>Coal_ID</u>, Coal_Name, Coal_Desc)
Object(<u>O_ID</u>, O_Name, O_Desc, *Con_ID*)
ObjectConstraints (<u>O_ID</u>, <u>Con_ID</u>, Desc)
Constraints(<u>Con_ID</u>, *R_ID, T_ID, C_ID*, C_Type, *Coal_ID*, Permission, Start, End)
UserRole(<u>U_ID</u>, <u>R_ID</u>, Desc, Status)
UserTask(<u>U_ID</u>, <u>T_ID</u>, Start, End)

SELECT o.O_Name, r.R_name, T.T_name, C.C_Name, con.C_Type, coal.Coal_Name, coal.
Permission

FROM Object o, Role r, Task t, Company c, Coalition coal, ObjectConstraints oc, Constraints
con

WHERE con.R_ID = R.R_ID and con.T_ID = T.T_ID and con.C_ID = C.C_ID and con.Coal_ID
= coal.Coal_ID and oc.O_ID = o.O_ID and oc.ConID = con.Con_ID;

We use the companies in Figure 1 in this example. Suppose at the beginning of the trading process there is no relationship between Company 1 and 2, and all other relationships are as shown in Figure 1. Raw material manufacturer Company 1 wants to sell aluminum (P1), and in order to improve its business visibility and reach more buyers, it joins the automotive e-market. Table 4 shows the structure of Company 1's e-catalog with the information on aluminum.

Before sharing their e-catalogs, the e-market requires participating companies to classify all the attributes in e-catalog according to EMAC authorization constraints. Table 5 shows the access control policies for each attribute of the e-catalog in Table 4 defined by Company 1. For instance, the policy of the price is defined as follows: The price is only visible to the buyers (role) of companies that have buying rela-

Table 4. An e-catalog item

Description	Manufacturer	Quant.(ton)	Price/ ton	Discount/ ton	Currency	Quality	Status
Aluminum	Company 1	2000	500	50	USD	High	Available

Table 5. Access control policies defined by Company 1

Attribute	Permission	Role	Task	Company	Relationship	Coalition
Description	Read	N/A	N/A	N/A	N/A	N/A
Manufacter	Read	N/A	N/A	N/A	Non-competitor	N/A
Quant.	Read	N/A	N/A	N/A	Non-competitor	N/A
Price	Read	Buyer	Auction	N/A	Non-competitor	N/A
Discount	Read	Buyer	N/A	N/A	Non-competitor	Manufacturing Supplies Coalition
Currency	Read	N/A	N/A	N/A	N/A	N/A
Qlty.	Read	N/A	N/A	N/A	Non-competitor	N/A
Status	Read	N/A	N/A	N/A	N/A	N/A

tionship with Company 1 during the auction (task). Except for attributes "Description," "Currency," and "Status," all other attributes have the company relationship constraint as "non-competitor." As a result, an employee from Company 3 can only see the information shown in Table 6 because of the competing relationship between Company 3 and Company 1, which amounts to essentially little information.

Non-buyer employees from all e-market participating companies that are not Company 1's competitors can get more information as shown in Table 7. Price and discount are still not available because of the role constraint on these two attributes.

Now, a buyer from Company 2 named John, and another buyer from Company 4 named Tom are searching in the e-market in order to buy aluminum (P1). Because Company 4 is a member of manufacturing supplies coalition, Tom can see the discount information besides the information in Table 6. After some initial contacts, both Company 2 and 4 are invited to attend the e-auction held by Company 1. Now both John and Tom are involved in auction (Task 3) and the price of the product is available because the constraints of role, task and relationship are satisfied. When the auction is over, the price is no longer accessible. After the contract negotiation, Company 2 is selected to be the buyer of Company 1 on product aluminum (P1). In order to keep the buying company updated with product price, Company 1 revises the access control policy of price attribute after establishing the relationship with company 2. The new policy is presented in Table 8. Now all the buyers from Company 2 can see the price.

Table 6. A data view to the employee of Company 3

Description	Manufacturer	Quant. (ton)	Price/ ton	Discount/ ton	Currency	Quality	Status
Aluminum	###	###	###	###	USD	###	Available

Table 7. A data view of non-buyer employees from non-competitor companies

Description	Manufacturer	Quant. (ton)	Price/ ton	Discount/ ton	Currency	Quality	Status
Aluminum	Company 1	2000	###	###	USD	High	Available

Table 8. New policy on price by Company 1

Attribute	Permission	Role	Task	Company	Relationship	Coalition
Price	Read	Buyer	N/A	N/A	Buying	N/A

This example illustrates the power of the EMAC model. First, role authorization constraints can be easily implemented. Second, when the user moves from one task to another, task authorization constraints take effect. Third, when the company relationship changes by creating a new contract, relationship authorization constraints are activated. Fourth, when a company joins a new coalition, the coalition authorization constraints are triggered. As such, we showed that the EMAC model can accommodate various conventional access control models in a unified manner.

Web Services Enabled EMAC Architecture

Figure 5 shows a generic access control system architecture (OASIS, 2003), which consists of four system entities for policy administration, storage, enforcement, and decision respectively. Policy administration point (PAP) manages all the access control policies and policy information point (PIP) maintains security related information for subjects, resources and environment. An access requester sends a request for access to the policy enforcement point (PEP), and PEP creates an access decision request to policy decision point (PDP). By evaluating access control policies with attributes of subjects, resources and environment, PDP renders authorization decisions. Finally, PEP executes access control: Permit or deny. Each subject is a security autonomy and its intra-organizational access control architecture is similar. But, when these autonomies collaborate with one another in an e-market, the architecture becomes more complex and more requirements are added.

First of all, cross-company process automation is a fundamental function provided by e-market. Within an individual company, workflow management system (WFMS) is usually implemented to streamline the business processes. It defines, creates and manages the execution of workflows, interacts with workflow participants, and invokes the use of IT tools and applications. According to EMAC model, information on roles and tasks is required to enforce task based constraints, which can be acquired from organization's internal WFMS. However, in an e-market, different

Figure 5. A generic access control system architecture

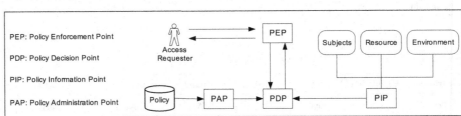

companies may have different WFMSs, which makes achieving interoperability among different WFMS a critical and challenging issue to enforce task-based constraints in e-markets. Second, companies have different access control policies and security systems. These access control policies need to be exchanged and understood by trading partners' security systems for e-market transactions. Therefore, how to make disparate security systems communicate with one another imposes another challenge for the e-market access control architecture.

Relationships between companies are important for data security in e-markets. But, how the relationship information is maintained and where it should be stored are interesting questions. In general, it is not appropriate for the e-market to serve as a centralized relationship information repository, although this method is easy to manage and implement. Because business relationship information is crucial and often top secret, companies are reluctant to let third parties, like e-markets, manage this information. The new e-market access control architecture must support security information exchanges between heterogeneous security systems in order to be successful.

Built on existing and emerging standards such as HTTP, extensible markup language (XML), simple object access protocol (SOAP), Web services description language (WSDL) and universal description, discovery and integration (UDDI), Web services allow business functions to be loosely integrated between companies more rapidly and less expensively than ever before. They also provide a unifying programming model so that application integration inside and outside the company can be done with a common approach, leveraging a common infrastructure. The integration and application of Web services can be done in an incremental manner by using existing languages and platforms and adopting existing legacy applications (Kreger, 2001). These characteristics make Web services the ideal enabling technology for our e-market access control architecture.

As shown in Figure 6, we propose a three-layer architecture for the implementation of EMAC model. Layer 1 is an inter-organizational workflow composed of tasks wrapped as Web services that interface with the private workflows of e-market companies. In this layer, business process information is exchanged among business partners with different process modeling and execution environments as described in (Lee, Yang, & Chung, 2002; Leymann, Roller, & Schmidt, 2002). The business process execution language for Web services (BPEL4WS) jointly proposed by BEA, IBM and Microsoft can be used as the inter-organizational workflow definition language (BEA, IBM, & Microsoft, 2002). In this way, each e-market participant can define its own business process using their internal process modeling language, while BPEL4WS is used by the e-market for process coordination, synchronization and exchange.

The second layer of the architecture is the EMAC access control engine implemented as a Web service. This engine communicates with the company security systems,

Figure 6. Three-layer EMAC architecture

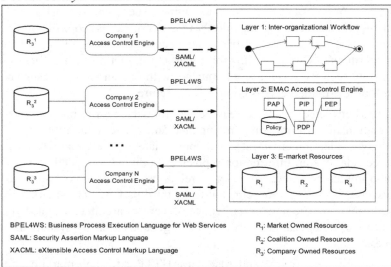

BPEL4WS: Business Process Execution Language for Web Services
SAML: Security Assertion Markup Language
XACML: eXtensible Access Control Markup Language

R_1: Market Owned Resources
R_2: Coalition Owned Resources
R_3: Company Owned Resources

which are also wrapped as Web services. This layer is responsible for coordinating with the inter-organizational workflow in Layer 1 to retrieve role and task related information and issue authorization request and decisions. In particular, security assertion makeup language (SAML) is used to communicate the authorization information among different companies (OASIS, 2002). SAML is a technology resulting from the increased trend toward sharing security information among different organizations. Although Web services technology facilitates inter-organizational computing and integration, there has been no standard on how to share security information across different security domains (Nagappan, Skoczylas, & Sriganesh, 2003). In SAML, the security information exchanged is in the form of an assertion about subjects.

There are three types of core assertions defined by SAML, namely, authentication assertion, attribute assertion, and authorization assertion. In the example presented in the previous section, when John from Company 2 wants to see the price of Company 1's aluminum, based on the constraints on price attribute, Company 1's PDP needs an assertion from Company 2 to show whether John's role is buyer. This attribute assertion request and corresponding response are expressed in SAML as shown in Listing 1.

In the same manner Company 1's PDP sends another task assertion request to the e-market asking for task information that John is currently involved. Based on the business process defined in BPEL4WS, the e-market returns a task name. Finally, after checking the relationship between Company 2 and Company 1, the PDP issues

Listing 1. SAML assertion request and response

```
Role assertion request from Company 1:
     <samlp:Request>
                    <samlp:AttributeQuery>

        <saml:Subject>

        <saml:NameIdentifier SecurityDomain ="Company 2" Name="John"/>

        </saml:Subject>

        <saml:AttributeDesignator AttributeName="role" AttributeNamespace="Company
     2"/>
                    </samlp:AttributeQuery>
     </samlp:Request>
Role assertion response from Company 2:
     <samlp:Response ...>
        <saml:Assertion ...>

        <saml:Conditions .../>

        <saml:AttributeStatement>

        <saml:Subject>

        <saml:NameIdentifier SecurityDomain ="Company 2" Name="John"/>

        </saml:Subject>

        <saml:Attribute AttributeName="role" AttributeNamespace="Company 2"/>

        <saml:AttributeValue>buyer</saml:AttributeValue>

        </saml:AttributeStatement>
        </saml:Assertion ...>
     </samlp:Response>
```

an authorization decision to PEP. Applications working with SAML can define their own specific assertions. However, this extensibility comes at the cost of interoperability. In this situation, e-markets can provide a standard specification of SAML assertions that all participants must follow.

As we can see in this example, the security policies of each e-market participant have many elements and points of enforcement. They can be enforced by different departments within the company, external business partners, or the e-market. To enable security policy exchange and distributed enforcement, security policies must be expressed in a unified format. The extensible access control markup language (XACML) is a technology that represents access control policies in a standard XML

Listing 2. An EMAC security policy in XACML

```
<?xml version=1.0" encoding="UTF-8"?>
<Policy xmlns="urn:oasis:names:tc:xacml:1.0:policy"
xmlns:xsi="http://www.w3.org/2001/XMLSchema-instance"
xsi:schemaLocation="urn:oasis:names:tc:xacml:1.0:policy
http://www.oasis-open.org/tc/xacml/1.0/cs-xacml-schema-policy-01.xsd"
PolicyId="identifier:example:Company1SamplePolicy"
RuleCombiningAlgId="identifier:rule-combining-algorithm:deny-overrides">
<Description>
        Company 1 Access Control Policy
</Description>
<Target>
        <Subjects><AnySubject/></Subjects>
        <Resources><AnyResource/></Resources>
        <Actions><AnyAction/></Actions>
</Target>
<Rule RuleId= "urn:oasis:names:tc:xacml:1.0:example:SimpleRule1" Effect="Permit">
        <Description>
                price is only visible to the buyers of companies that have buying
                relationship with Company 1 during the auction.
        </Description>
        <Subjects>
                <Subject>
                        <SubjectMatch MatchId="
                        urn:oasis:names:tc:xacml:1.0:function:Role-match">
                        <SubjectAttributeDesignator
                        AttributeId="urn:oasis:names:tc:xacml:1.0:subject:user-role"
                        DataType="urn:oasis:names:tc:xacml:1.0:data-type:Role"/>
                        <AttributeValue
                        DataType="urn:oasis:names:tc:xacml:1.0:
                        datatype:Role">buyer
                        </AttributeValue>
                        </SubjectMatch>

                        <SubjectMatch MatchId="
                        urn:oasis:names:tc:xacml:1.0:function:task-match">
                        <SubjectAttributeDesignator
                        AttributeId="urn:oasis:names:tc:xacml:1.0:subject:user-task"
                        DataType="urn:oasis:names:tc:xacml:1.0:data-type:Task"/>
                        <AttributeValue
```

Listing 2. continued

```
                              DataType="urn:oasis:names:tc:xacml:1.0:
                              datatype:Task">auction
                              </AttributeValue>
                              </SubjectMatch>

                              <SubjectMatch MatchId="
                              urn:oasis:names:tc:xacml:1.0:function:relationship-match">
                              <SubjectAttributeDesignator
                              AttributeId="urn:oasis:names:tc:xacml:1.0:subject:company-
relationship"
                              DataType="urn:oasis:names:tc:xacml:1.0:data-type:Relation-
ship"/>
                              <AttributeValue
                              DataType="urn:oasis:names:tc:xacml:1.0:
                              datatype:Relationship">buying
                              </AttributeValue>
                              </SubjectMatch>
                      </Subject>
              </Subjects>
              <Resources>
                      <Attribute AttributeId="urn:oasis:names:tc:xacml:1.0:resource:ufspath"
                              DataType="http://www.w3.org/2001/XMLSchema#anyURI">
                      <AttributeValue>Company1/ProductCatalog/attribtes/price</Attribute-
Value>
                      </Attribute>
              </Resources>
              <Actions>
                      <Attribute AttributeId="urn:oasis:names:tc:xacml:1.0:action:action-id"
                              DataType="http://www.w3.org/2001/XMLSchema#string">
                      <AttributeValue>read</AttributeValue>
                      </Attribute>
              </Actions>
      </Target>
</Rule>
...
</xacml:Policy>
```

format (OASIS, 2003). Using XACML, all authorization constraints in EMAC models can be specified in a standard way. For example, the access control policy for attribute price is that the price is only visible to the buyers of companies that have buying relationship with Company 1 during the auction, which can be expressed in the extended XACML as shown in Listing 2.

Layer 3 consists of e-market resources including market owned resources, coalition owned resources, and company owned resources. Market owned resources are centrally controlled by e-markets, while the management of the other two types of resources is handled by their owners: coalitions and companies, respectively. There are various ways of linking the coalition and company owned resources to the e-market. For instance, the relevant contents of a company database can be either uploaded physically to the e-market database or linked logically (Geppert, Kradolfer, & Tombros, 1998). As a result, the access control to the company owned resources may vary depending on whether or not the data are uploaded to the e-market.

The three-layer e-market access control architecture enables a loosely-coupled and distributed platform for implementing various access control mechanisms required by e-market information sharing. In addition, it also provides the flexibility and scalability that are critical for the dynamic e-market environment.

Conclusion

With market globalization and advance in Internet technology, various e-markets have emerged to help companies improve their product visibility and reach more customers. Security of e-markets has been identified as one of the most important concerns of participating companies. To be successful, e-markets must be able to provide advanced security mechanisms to protect companies' data.

A variety of access control models have been developed in response to system and security administration requirements. In particular, role-based access control (RBAC), task-based access control (TBAC), and team-based access control (TMAC) use "role," "task," and "team" respectively to model contextual information associated with organizational roles, task responsibilities and collaborative activities (Cohen, Thomas, Winsborough, & Shands, 2002; Sandhu, Coyne, Feinstein, & Youman, 1996; Thomas & Sandhu, 1997). Coalition-based access control (CBAC) model discusses the relationship between organizations through the memberships in a coalition, and the relationship-driven access control model takes into account the relationships among companies and proposes an object classification scheme (Zhao et al., 2002). However, each access control model aforementioned by itself cannot satisfy all access control requirements of secure e-market data sharing. Therefore, there is pressing need for a comprehensive access control model to support secure e-market operations.

In this chapter, we studied the resource sharing problem in e-markets by analyzing the relationships among companies and identifying four types of authorization constraints. By integrating several access control models, we proposed a comprehensive security control mechanism to support advanced access control in e-markets, which we refer as *e-market access control* (EMAC) model. An access control specification language is also proposed based on first order logic to model different authorization constraints. An example is presented to demonstrate the rich expressive power of EMAC in terms of modeling and enforcing various access control requirements. Another thrust of this study is the adoption of Web services as the enabling technology for EMAC implementation, leading to a loosely-coupled and distributed EMAC architecture.

References

Ahn, G., & Sandhu, R. (2000). Role-based authorization constraints specification. *ACM Transactions on Information and System Security*, 3(4), 207-226.

Baron, J. P., Shaw, M. J., & Bailey, A. D. (2000). Web-based e-catalog systems in B2B procurement. *Communications of the ACM*, 43(5), 93-100.

BEA System, IBM Corporation, & Microsoft Corporation, Inc. (2002). *Business process execution language for Web services, Version 1.0*. Retrieved from http://www.bim.com/developerworks/library/ws-bpel

Bertino, E., Bonatti, P. A., & Ferrari, E. (2001) TRBAC: A temporal role-based access control model. *ACM Transactions on Information and System Security*, 4(3), 191-223.

Bertino, E., Catania, B., Ferrari, E., & Perlasca, P. (2003). A logical framework for reasoning about access control models. *ACM Transactions on Information and System Security*, 6(1), 71-127.

Bertino, E., Ferrari, E., & Atluri, V. (1999). The specifiction and enformcement of authorization constraints in workflow management systems. *ACM Transactions on Information and System Security*, 2(1), 65-104.

Casati, F., Castano, S. & Fugini, M. (2001). Managing workflow authorization constraints through active database technology. *Information Systems Frontiers*, 3(3), 319-338.

Cohen, E., Thomas, R. K., Winsborough, W., & Shands, D. (2002) Models for coalition-based access control (CBAC). In *Proceedings of the 7th ACM Symposium on Access Control Models and Technologies*, Monterey, CA.

eMarket Services. (2002). *Introduction to eMarkets*. Retrieved from http://www.emarketservices.com

Feldman, S. (2000). Electronic marketplaces. *IEEE Internet Computing*, 93-95.

Ferralolo, D. F., Sandhu, R., Gavrila, S., Kuhn, D. R., & Chandramouli, R. (2001). Proposed NIST standard for role-based access control. *ACM Transactions on Information and System Security*, 4(3), 224-274.

Geppert, A., Kradolfer, M., & Tombros, D. (1998). *Federating heterogeneous workflow systems* (Tech. Rep. No. 05). Department of Computer Science, University of Zurich.

Joshi, J. B. D., Aref, W. G., Ghafoor, A. & Spafford, E. H. (2001). Security models for web-based applications. *Communications of the ACM*, 44(2), 38-44.

Kang, H. M., Park, J. S., & Froscher, J. N. (2001). Access control mechanisms for inter-organizational workflow. In *Proceedings of the 6th ACM Symposium on Access Control Models and Technologies* (pp. 66-74).

Kreger, H. (2003). Fulfilling the Web services promise. *Communications of the ACM*, 6(46), 29-34.

Kreger, H. (2001). *Web services conceptual architecture.* IBM Software Group. Retrieved from http://www-3.ibm.com/software/solutions/webservices/pdf/WSCA.pdf

Lee, J., Yang, J., & Chung, J. (2002). *Winslow: A business process management system with Web services.* Technical paper. IBM T. J. Watson Research Center.

Leymann, F., Roller, D., & Schmidt, M. T. (2002). Web services and business process management. *IBM Systems Journal, Special Issue on New Developments in Web Services and E-Commerce*, 41(2), 198-211.

Medjahed, B., Benatallah, B., Bouguettaya, A., Ngu, A. H. H., & Elmagarmid, A. K. (2003). Business-to-business interactions: Issues and enabling technologies. *The VLDB Journal*, 12, 59-85.

Nagappan, R., Skoczylas, R., & Sriganesh, R. P. (2003). *Developing Java Web services.* John Wiley & Sons.

OASIS. (2003). *eXtensible access control markup language (XACML), Version 1.0.* Retrieved from http://www.oasis-open.org/committees/xacml/repository/

OASIS. (2002). *Assertions and protocol for the OASIS security assertion markup language (SAML).* Retrieved from http://www.oasis-open.org/committees/security/docs/

Sandhu, R. S., Coyne, E. J., Feinstein, H. L., & Youman, C. E. (1996). Role-based access control models. *IEEE Computer*, 29(2), 38 -47.

Thomas, R. K. (1997, November 6-7). Team-based access control (TMAC): A primitive for applying role-based access controls in collaborative environments. In *Proceedings of the 2nd ACM Workshop on Role-Based Access Control* (pp. 13-19).

Thomas, R. K., & Sandhu, R. S. (1997, August 11-13). Task-based authorization controls (TBAC): A family of models for active and enterprise-oriented authorization management. In *Proceedings of the IFIP WG11.3 Workshop on Database Security*, Lake Tahoe, CA.

Zhao, J. L., Wang, H. J., Huang, S. S., & Chen, G. (2002). Relationship driven access control in a supply web. In *Proceedings of the 12th Workshop on Information Technology and Systems (WITS '02)*, Barcelona, Spain.

Chapter IV

Dynamically Adaptable Web Services Based on the Simple Object Access Protocol

Kevin Curran, University of Ulster, UK

Brendan Gallagher, University of Ulster, UK

Abstract

Dynamic protocol stacks enable a developer to select a particular protocol profile at bind time where each protocol profile is built from a rich library of protocol modules including UDP, packet loss detection, data encryption, TCP, Multicast among others. Communicating objects can be represented as object graphs that together realise the required behaviour built upon the IP service offered by the host computer. All protocols down to device driver level can be implemented at the user level, providing the maximum potential for configurability. The simple object access protocol (SOAP) is a lightweight remote procedure calling (RPC) protocol for the exchange of structured data in a decentralized environment. SOAP enables programs to run and interoperate with other SOAP applications (called Web services) in a distributed environment. The SOAP protocol is based on extensible markup language (XML) and hypertext transmission protocol (HTTP), which, it is claimed, makes it a language and platform neutral vehicle for RPC over the Internet and through firewalls. This chapter describes a SOAP Web service deployed which enables clients to download protocol stack components as simple MIME attachments.

Introduction

Mobile devices, such as PDAs and smart phones, can access the Internet and they must also use networking protocols similar to those used by the average desktop computer. These networking protocols, called a protocol stack, are layered such as file transfer protocol (FTP), hypertext transmission protocol (HTTP) and transmission control protocol (TCP). However, the protocols underlying the Internet were not designed for the latest cellular type networks with their low bandwidth, high error losses and roaming users. Thus, many 'fixes' have arisen to solve the problem of efficient data delivery to mobile resource constrained devices (Saber, 2003). Mobility requires adaptability, meaning that systems must be location-aware and situation-aware, taking advantage of this information in order to dynamically reconfigure in a distributed fashion (Katz, 1994; Solon, 2003; Matthur, 2003). However, situations, in which a user moves an end-device and uses information services, can be challenging. In these situations the placement of different co-operating parts is a research challenge. The heterogeneity is not only static but also dynamic as software capabilities, resource availability and resource requirements may change over time. The support system of a nomadic user must distribute, in an appropriate way, the current session among the end-user system, network elements and application servers. In addition, when the execution environment changes in an essential and persistent way, it may be beneficial to reconfigure the co-operating parts.

A protocol stack consists of a linear list of protocol objects, which between them can support a range of quality of service such as reliable delivery, virtual synchrony, or encrypted communication. Our framework, Webber, provides the inter-layer services necessary for supporting new communication protocols. Webber consists of a set of Java classes for representing uniform resource locators, protocol stacks, the framework API and posting objects. Dynamically composable protocol stacks overcome the limitations imposed by generic protocol stacks allowing optimisation for particular traffic. Some uses that dynamic protocols may be used for include using the best-fit protocol for a particular network and application behaviour, so that performance can always be optimal; upgrading network protocols at run-time without having to restart applications and increasing security at run-time.

The use of an object-oriented implementation language allows us to extensively use object-level design patterns. This makes any framework more generic and extensible, and creates a highly stylistic way for writing actual protocol implementations. With a suitable object oriented design tool, the outline for the classes needed to implement a new protocol can be created quickly. The actual implementation code for the protocol actions typically takes a little longer, depending on the complexity of the protocol. Performance will always be an issue with communications protocols. Even though processing power is constantly increasing, the new applications need ever-increasing bandwidth and reasonable transfer delay. The new protocols require large transfer capacity, short and fixed delay, and lots of cryptography, among other things. There are two facets to performance. First, the processing power available should be used as efficiently as possible. The importance of this will gradually decrease as processing power increases. Second, and more importantly, there should not be any design limitations, which set a theoretical limit to the performance of the protocols, no matter how much processing power we have. We want to allow as much parallelism as possible and build the protocol implementations such that they can be efficiently divided between multiple processors. Java, with its built-in threads and synchronization, allows parallelism to be utilised with relative ease.

Central to providing an adaptable QoS is the ability to maintain multiple protocol stacks. A protocol stack consists of a linear list of protocol objects and represents a quality of service such as reliable delivery or encrypted communication. We have developed a framework called Webber, which provides the services necessary for supporting new communication protocols and qualities of service. Webber consists of a set of Java classes for representing uniform resource locators, protocol stacks, the framework API and SOAP.

The Simple Object Access Protocol (SOAP)

SOAP is a lightweight XML-based protocol for exchange of structured data in a decentralized, distributed environment (Curbera, 2005). SOAP is a standard way of regulating data transmission between computers. The XML-based protocol is language and platform neutral, which means that information, can be shared and messages passed among disparate parties, across different platforms, languages and programming environments. SOAP is not a competitive technology to component systems and object-request broker architectures such as the CORBA and DCOM, but instead complements these technologies. CORBA, DCOM, and enterprise JavaBeans (EJB) enable resource sharing within a single organization while SOAP technology aims to bridge the sharing of resources among different organizations possibly located behind firewalls. SOAP applications exploit HTTP or SMTP to communicate with Web services to retrieve dynamic content. For example, real-time stock quote information of a stock portfolio can be graphed on the display of a cell phone or can be analysed within a spreadsheet program running on a desktop computer. This allows real-time 'what-if' scenarios and enables the development of agents that access real-time information. Other examples are the visualization of factory processes on PDAs, people sharing laboratory results using cell phones, or in the case of this project, the downloading of a new protocol stack from a remote server.

SOAP is a language and platform-neutral RPC protocol that adopts XML as the parameter encoding format. SOAP applications typically adopt HTTP as a firewall-friendly transport protocol. SOAP Web services are programs providing data and services to other applications over the Internet or intranet. A Web service can be as simple as a shell or Perl script that uses the common gateway interface (CGI) of a Web server such as Apache Tomcat. A Web service can also be a server-side ASP, JSP, or PHP script, or an executable CGI application implemented in any programming language for which an XML parser is available. Firewalls can be configured to selectively allow SOAP messages to pass through, because the intent of a message can be determined from the header part of the SOAP message. Web services description language (WSDL) is an XML format for describing network services as a set of endpoints operating on messages containing either document-oriented or procedure-oriented information. The operations and messages are described abstractly, and then bound to a concrete network protocol and message format to define an endpoint (Snell, 2001). WSDL is used to create a file that identifies the services provided by the server and the set of operations within each service that the server supports. For each of the operations, the WSDL file also describes the format that the client must follow in requesting an operation.

Basic Concepts of SOAP

The SOAP authors decided to specify SOAP only as a low-layer protocol for structured data exchange. The authors clearly stated that they did not want to define an entire distributed object system specification [Modi01]. Tarak Modi writes that the reason for SOAP being lightweight, "can be found upon examining the goals of SOAP. Besides extensibility, a major design goal of SOAP is simplicity. SOAP is designed to exchange structured and typed information. The data exchanged takes the form of an XML document. The SOAP specification mandates an XML vocabulary that is used for representing remote method parameters, return values, and (remote) exceptions. It is also a protocol specification for invoking methods over the Internet between geographically remote systems. This section briefly introduces the architecture of the SOAP protocol. The SOAP protocol consists of four parts:

1.   An **envelope** that defines a framework for describing what is in an XML-encoded SOAP message and how to process it
2.   A set of **encoding rules** that define a data serialization mechanism that can be used to express instances of application-defined data types in XML
3.   A convention for representing **remote procedure calls** and **responses**
4.   A **binding** convention for exchanging messages between systems using an underlying protocol; bindings describe how to use SOAP in combination with HTTP (Casner, 1999)

XML is a simple and extensible mark-up language. Because XML is just text, any application can understand it as long as the application understands the character encoding in use. By default, XML assumes that all characters belong to ISO/IEC 10646, known as the universal character set (UCS). The XML specification [XML02] mandates that all XML processors must accept character data encoded using the UCS transformation formats UTF-8 or UTF-16. Therefore, any XML data stream encoded in UTF-8 or UTF-16 can be understood regardless of platform or programming language. This makes XML a good choice for describing method invocations in a platform and language-neutral fashion. The basic SOAP payload structure consists of three parts:

1.   **SOAP envelope:** This is the root XML element in the XML document tree representing a message.
2.   **SOAP header:** This is a generic mechanism that adds characteristics to the SOAP message. SOAP defines several attributes that can be used to indicate who must process the message, and whether this process is optional or mandatory.

     SOAP body: This is the container for the mandatory information being sent to the message endpoint.

SOAP applications exploit a wire protocol (typically HTTP) to communicate with Web services to retrieve dynamic content. SOAP Web services are units of application logic providing data and services to other applications over the Internet or intranet. Web services can be a shell or Perl script. It can also be a server-side ASP, JSP, or PHP script, or an executable CGI application implemented in the programming language for which an XML parser is available. The SOAP protocol, and its industry-wide support, promises to make services available to users anywhere. In a SOAP RPC, the Web services are treated like methods or components are treated in traditional programming.

Security Considerations

Firewalls can easily distinguish SOAP packets based on their content type, and can filter based on the interface and method name exposed via HTTP headers. These headers include the Web service URI and the method name being invoked on that Web service. This information is culled from the payload before sending the HTTP request, and is required to match the payload. Since most firewalls block all but a few ports, such as the standard HTTP port 80, all of today's distributed object protocols (e.g., DCOM and IIOP) suffer because they rely on dynamically assigned ports for remote method invocations. To make matters worse, the clients of distributed applications that lie behind another corporate firewall and suffer the same problems. If clients don't configure their firewall to open the same port, they won't be able to use the distributed application. Making clients reconfigure their firewalls is just not practical.

Since SOAP relies on HTTP as the transport mechanism, and most firewalls allow HTTP to pass through, there is no problem invoking SOAP endpoints from either side of a firewall. SOAP makes it possible for system administrators to configure firewalls to selectively block out SOAP requests using SOAP-specific HTTP headers. Because SOAP is layered on top of HTTP, it may utilize any standard HTTP security feature or any endpoint application-specific security feature. The standard authentication mechanisms that are HTTP-friendly can be used with SOAP. These protocols can authenticate the server (and optionally the client), and can provide a confidential channel over which SOAP payload can travel. This demonstrates SOAP using what is already in place instead of reinventing the wheel and is another example of SOAP realizing its stated goal of lightweight simplicity.

Webber

Webber is a middleware framework, which supports reconfigurable dissemination oriented communication (see Figure 1). The abstraction is analogous to that of the various broadcast media in everyday use such as newspaper, radio and TV corresponding to text, audio and video components contained in multimedia applications. People like the various qualities of each and may listen to the radio while reading a newspaper. Likewise, Webber fragments the various media elements of a multimedia application and 'broadcasts' them over separate channels to be subscribed to at the receiver's own choice. We do not force the full range of media on any subscriber, a source simply transmits onto a specific channel, and receivers, which have subscribed to that channel, receive media streams (e.g., audio, text, and video) without explicit interactions with the source.

Figure 1. Webber in comparison to the OSI model

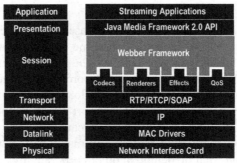

Webber separates the media into text, audio and video and distributes these to multicast groups. We also create multiple groups within each category (e.g., high, medium and low audio quality) thereby allowing receivers to subscribe to groups such as high audio with medium video and text or simply low audio. This is where our work is unique. No work that we know of has being done in this area where the various components of multimedia are separated and transported across the network according to their characteristics. We address the network congestion and heterogeneity problem by taking into account the differing nature and requirements of multimedia elements such as text, audio and video thereby creating tailored protocol stacks which distribute the information to different multicast groups allowing the receivers to decide which multicast group(s) to subscribe to according to processing power and network bandwidth availability.

Webber also uses transcoders to provide optimal service to heterogeneous clients. A transcoder is an application that can be placed at the far end of a low bandwidth connection, to down-grade a high bit rate stream, so that is can fit through the connection. Transcoders for video and audio can reduce the frame-rate and image quality, and audio transcoders can reencode the audio signal using a higher compression bandwidth scheme. A feature of audio transcoding is that it adds minimal delay to the signal when relaying it, as it can be done on a per packet basis. Apart from changing the bandwidth requirements of a stream, a transcoder can also introduce or remove forward error correction to counter packet loss. In scenarios such as Webbers typical multicast broadcasts, transcoders are positioned at the problematic cellular network link's base station, to reencode the stream to use lower bandwidth. The resulting stream is then remulticast to a new address. If all receivers beyond that link tune into the new customised stream, then there will be no bandwidth wasted, as the original stream no longer has to traverse the problematic link.

The primary goal of Webber is to provide an SOAP based infrastructure for building multimedia-computing platforms that support interactive mobile multimedia applications dealing with synchronised time-based media in a heterogeneous distributed mobile environment. Systems exist which support interactive applications, which deal with synchronised time-based media. Most existing systems however, operate in a stand-alone environment. Thus, the major focus of Webber is to support such applications in a heterogeneous distributed environment.

The development of distributed multimedia applications is supported by an increasing number of services. While such services pave the way towards sophisticated multimedia support even in distributed systems, using them still makes the task of developers quite tedious. This is because several inconsistent services have to be interfaced in order to reflect different aspects. Webber offers a means to alleviate this problem, by offering an encompassing web services framework in which all services would be offered under a unifying paradigm. Often, we would like to choose from a variety of mechanisms when the application is running. Consider for example the case of a mobile device moving from a LAN into a cellular network. As a result, the available bandwidth and the error rate change significantly. Ideally, the middleware (or proxy) should adopt bandwidth-conserving mechanisms, such as compressing the requests (i.e., trading off CPU for bandwidth). By using reflective techniques [Parr-Curran00] it is possible to create a middleware layer that can adapt itself to environmental changes. Applications can then always use optimised protocols and policies themselves. Instead the adaptation work is performed by the supporting middleware.

Dynamic Stacks

The protocol stack uses microprotocols in its implementation. A microprotocol (also called a layer) enforces a part of the quality of service properties guaranteed by the protocol stack as a whole. Creating a layer for each property and stacking them on top of each other achieve the properties desired by the user of a stack. Each layer has the same interface (by sub classing a common super-class), which allows stacking any layer on top of any other. However, random stacking of layers will probably not make sense semantically in most cases. All layers are instances of Java classes and are maintained by a ProtocolStack object which itself is connected to an instance of Stack. Adjacent layers are connected by two queues, one for storing messages to be sent down the stack, and the other one for messages traveling up the stack, which guarantees FIFO delivery of messages between layers. A message sent by ProtocolStack is simply passed to the protocol stack, which in turn forwards it to the top-most layer. Each layer performs some computation and then passes the message on to the layer below it. The bottom-most layer typically puts the message on the network. In the reverse direction, the bottom-most layer of a different protocol stack will receive the message from the network and pass it on to the layer above it. This layer will perform some computation (possibly strip a header from the message) and pass it on to the layer above it. The message travels up the stack until the ProtocolStack object, which puts it in a queue for client applications to receive, receives it. The message will be removed when Stack.Receive is called. Messages are simple Java classes and contain a destination- and source address and a byte buffer. Headers of arbitrary data can be added to a message and removed again later by the corresponding layer of a different stack, allowing layers to add protocol specific data, such as a checksum or a key for encryption. A message travelling down the stack would typically accumulate a number of headers (possibly one per layer); the corresponding layers would then remove them again from a message traveling up the stack. The value of layers is that they are self-contained small pieces of functionality, independent from other layers, although, since they are only a small part of the whole stack, they of course depend on other layers to be present, as they require their functionality. Since layers are relatively small, they can be verified for correctness more easily than large chunks of (interdependent) code. Also, the concept of layering forces better structuring; as code for a certain type of functionality is localised in one place, layers can be easily replaced/upgraded with new versions.

A protocol layer typically either modifies a message (e.g., by adding a header), or it may delay its delivery, for example to preserve ordering in a FIFO layer in case the message arrived out of sequence. When it is a protocol layer instead of the Stack object that sends a message, it will in most cases not need to travel up all the way to the Stack object in the receiving stack, but it should probably be caught by the corresponding layer and be processed there. To this purpose, each message has a layer type tag, describing the layer from which it originated. A layer generating a message stamps it with its type (all types in a stack have to be unique). Each layer checks whether a message's layer type matches its own. If this is the case, the message will be processed by the layer (and then possibly discarded), otherwise it will just be passed on to the next layer. The interface of a protocol layer contains methods to process messages from layers above or below (Down or Up) which will be called when a message passes through that layer. There are also methods to start and stop a

Figure 2. Dynamic creation of protocol stack for speech to text

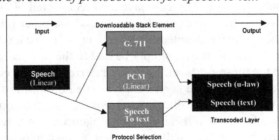

layer and to initialise it with data, these are invoked when setting up a new protocol stack or when shutting down an old one (e.g., when a member leaves).

Dynamically composable protocol stacks (as in Figure 2) overcome the limitations imposed by generic protocol stacks. A dynamically composable protocol stack allows optimisation for particular traffic. Here protocol layers such as real-time G.711 or PCM conversion capabilities could be deployed to address the 'impedance matching' across heterogeneous receivers. Protocol layers are created by the protocol stack (using a protocol profiler) according to a properties argument defined when creating an instance of Stack. The Webber framework allows protocol stacks to be composed dynamically at run-time, creating a flexible architecture suited to client application needs. The diagram in Figure 3 depicts three protocol stacks.

For instance, there might be a text stack is a stack that addresses applications that need to communicate reliably through private channels. We could also insert a CRYPT layer which would be in charge of encrypting and decrypting postings on the fly. Other layers could be responsible for taking care of retransmitting lost postings and of flow control. A video protocol stack is necessary for video applications that require that postings be communicated as efficiently as possible. Large postings that do not fit the UDP datagram could be fragmented and reassembled by the another dynamically insertable protocol layer. Distinct media formats deserve distinct transportation treatment. Webber filters the data depending on the source data stream, for example audio (microphone), video (camcorder) or text (file transfer), and composes one of a library of protocol stacks suitable for transmission of the media. The result is that separate streams from the same application are multicast to the same IP group address, and filters recompose the streams into an integrated

Figure 3. Flexible protocol object graphs

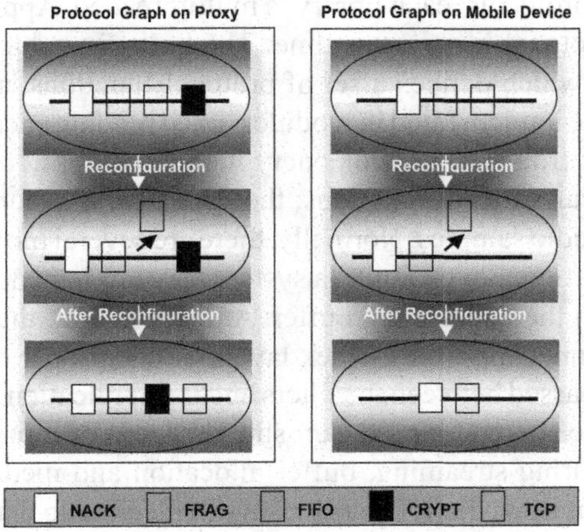

application. Protocol stacks can be compiled as late as run-time depending on the need for readaptability. There is a noticeable cost for stack reconfiguration but it is a reasonable overhead if it can be amortised over multiple subsequent data exchanges. Standard recognised objects are audio, video or text objects. These can be expanded to include more objects and specialised media types within these groups.

Webber provides a reconfigurable plug-and-play network protocol architecture intended for adaptive applications. The architecture revolves around the notion of a protocol stack. Such a stack is constructed from modules, which can be stacked and restacked in a variety of ways to meet the communication demands of its applications. Webber's protocols implement, among others, basic sliding window protocols, fragmentation and reassembly, flow-control, encryption and message ordering. Run-time protocol stacks are created according to the QoS string specified in the constructor. To transmit a posting over the network, the void push (WebberURL url, Posting p) operation is used. The URL denotes the channel on which the posting object will be transmitted by IP multicast or unicast, depending on whether the URL denotes a multicast address or not. Push is in one direction from the sender to the listeners, and non-blocking. An application can subscribe multiple receiver objects to the same channel, and also subscribe the same receiver object to multiple channels.

Protocol Stack Web Services

The protocol profiler is used to configure a protocol that satisfies the optimal protocol configuration as defined in the profiler for each media. A set of protocol class libraries contains the code that implements the communication protocols. For instance, typical protocol functions such as retransmission, flow control, check summing, and so forth, are located in the library. Given the timeout and retransmission mechanisms of reliable transport protocols, each library is multithreaded. Applications may link to more than one protocol library at a time. The basis for protocol configuration is a protocol graph, which defines a set of protocol functions and their relations. Protocol functions are implemented in modules. Each module encapsulates a typical task such as error control, flow control, encryption or decryption. Modules are not limited to the classical protocol functions; they are also used for displaying video frames and playing audio samples. Normally, there are several modules available for a single protocol function. For example, a system may implement a FIFO or a LIFO queuing algorithm in the end-system buffer. At a high level, the protocol profiler is responsible for connecting filters (stack layers) in the proper order. Control and status messages are passed between the filters and the application. Components that form a stream are the source filter, stream sink and zero or more transform filters between the two. During streaming, buffer allocation and media negotiation are performed at set-up by each filter. Upon arrival of video/audio data, the RTP source filter detects the new source endpoint, retrieves the data and passes the data on to an RTP receive payload handler. This handler reassembles the data packets into video/audio frames in accordance with the payload specification and forwards this data to the codec. The codec decodes the data and passes it to the video/audio sink filter for playback. All these actions use a single thread running on a RTP source filter without necessitating any interaction on the part of the application.

The payload handler components were designed from a class hierarchy for extensibility. We defined a generic handler in a base class, with all the basic fragmentation and reassembly functionality, which presents the external interface functions in the form of virtual functions. This allows us to derive payload classes from the generic base class and override virtual functions for any handling, which needs to be different for a specific payload class. New payload handlers can be added easily by deriving a new payload class and defining any different functionality. A protocol is configured by selecting modules for each protocol function such that the optimal protocol configuration for that situation is in force. The result of the protocol configuration is a module graph, which can be executed by the runtime environment after it is initiated. The properties of a media class are reflected in its protocol graphs. The protocol profiler, which is interposed between the data store and the protocol agent, orchestrates all data transformations to best adapt the multicast communication for the environment at hand. The protocol profiler is responsible for initiating the protocol conversion stage which bridges together diverse protocol families running in different sub-sessions across the network. Our premise is that the different regions of a diverse network environment might be best served by an equally diverse range of reliability mechanisms and each such region should be optimised by locally deploying the most suitable protocol (e.g., hop-wise ARQ might be appropriate to effectively accommodate the high loss-rates of a series of radio links, while SRM works well in a high-bandwidth LAN). To this end, the Webber framework allows us to seamlessly integrate a diverse set of protocols running across a disjoint set of network clouds. Webber supports two different variants of protocol conversion: Transport-level conversion and application-level conversion. In transport-level conversion, the protocol adapter acts as a bridge between two different transport protocols, such as an unreliable multicast protocol like UDP and some other protocol, say TCP.

In contrast to transport-layer conversion, application-layer conversion modifies the actual application objects to mitigate fundamental semantic discontinuities across diverse applications. In this case, the entire application-level data is transformed from one format to another. Examples of such adaptation include the following:

1.   Two desktop applications designed to implement a shared whiteboard without a common standard, will use completely different protocols and data formats for communication within the session. However, a transcoding proxy can

bridge the gap between these two applications. Such a proxy must maintain two data stores, one for each application format, and the protocol adapter must intelligently map objects and operations in one data store to the other.

2.   A second scenario is a proxy for communicating with computationally impoverished clients. Such a client (e.g., PDA) may be too limited to handle the full complexities of the application data. Hence the proxy must convert the entire data store to a much simpler representation before relaying it to the client.

3.   Another example is where data is been shipped over high capacity networks (e.g., backbone intercampus connections, where rates can exceed 500k). We can use the H.263 standard which is ideally suited to low bandwidth IP networks, however, research has shown that H.263 is not ideal for higher bit rates and dirty channels. In the case of a full motion video sequence of 20-30 frames/sec, the error resilient H.263 standard, upon detecting a channel error would reduce this to 10-15 frames/sec. Superior protocols exist for coping with this type of channel (Stefanov, 2000). Also, in large bandwidth/delay product networks where congestion control is only end-to-end packet acknowledgements, the state of the channel can change dramatically during one roundtip, and it may be not be possible to discover the reason simply from the acknowledgements. Therefore the dynamics of the packet loss process are different from lower bandwidth networks.

XML Deployment Descriptors

Apache SOAP utilizes XML documents called "deployment descriptors" to provide information to the SOAP server about the services that should be made available to clients.[1] Each separate Web service needs a separate deployment descriptor to expose their methods on the SOAP server to clients. The Web service being demonstrated here is illustrated in Figure 4.

The above deployment descriptor relates to the protocol stack retrieval Web service where the first line of the deployment descriptor, urn:mimetest identifies the URN of the Web services MimeTest.class. The element, methods="getStackElement"

Figure 4. Deployment descriptor 1: Protocol stack retrieval

```
<isd:service  xmlns:isd="http://xml.apache.org/xml-soap/deployment"  id="urn:
mimetest">
<isd:provider type="java" scope="Request" methods=" getStackElement ">
<isd:java class="samples.mime.MimeTest" static="false" />
</isd:provider>
</isd:service>
```

refer to the method which is to be exposed or deployed for use by SOAP clients. The element, class="samples.mime.MimeTest" is the fully qualified class name (i.e., packagename.classname) that contain the Web service methods being exposed. On the <isd:java> tag, there is an optional attribute called static, which may be set to either "true" or "false," depending upon whether or not the methods which are being exposed are static or not. getStackElement is not static so this attribute is set to "false." The <isd: provider> element also takes a scope attribute that indicates the lifetime of the instantiation of the implementing class. In this case of a deployment descriptor, "Request" indicates that the object will be removed after this request has completed.

RPC Client

A Webber Java client accepts the RPC parameters, builds the remote procedure call, sets the RPC parameters, invokes the remote procedure call and prints information about the attachment. The client application, called MimeTestClient, accepts three basic parameters which are the URL of the server where the Web service resides, the name of the Web service method to be called, and finally the full path to the stack element to be retrieved. In this case the element is a java source file representing a layer of the protocol stack.

```
public class MimeTestClient {
```

The second line shows that the client application is set up to accept RPC arguments of type String.

```
public static void main(String[] args) throws Exception {
```

The third line initialises the encodingStyleURI to the type of SOAP encoding to be used for the parameters.

```
String encodingStyleURI = Constants.NS_URI_SOAP_ENC;
```

The fourth line sets up the first argument as the URL of the SOAP server.

```
URL url = new URL(args[0]);
```

Building the remote procedure call In the first line of this code segment a new Call instance is created.

```
Call call = new Call();
```

The new call object is then used to setSOAPMappingRegistry. Java objects need to be serialized and encoded before they can be exchanged between the client and the server. The receiving Web service on the SOAP server needs to do the opposite by deserializing and decoding the SOAP message. The SOAPMappingRegistry provides the methods needed for serialization and deserialization (Modi, 2001).

```
call.setSOAPMappingRegistry(smr);
```

This line identifies the Web service that has been exposed or deployed on the SOAP server by the Web service developer. The SOAP server will need to check this urn against the urn listed in the deployment descriptor in order to ascertain whether or not it is one of the Web services deployed on the SOAP server. If both urn values do not match a fault is returned to the client.

```
call.setTargetObjectURI("urn:mimetest");
```

This line sets the method name to whatever the second RPC argument happens to be. The method specified in the second argument is the method invoked as part of the remote method invocation.

```
call.setMethodName(args[1]);
```

Here, the encoding style is set to the SOAP encoding style initialised earlier.
```
call.setEncodingStyleURI(encodingStyleURI);
```

When setting the RPC parameters, a Vector called params is created in order to hold the parameters.

```
Vector params = new Vector();
```

Below, each parameter is then added to the params vector. In order for the Web service on the SOAP server to be able to deal with an RPC parameter, it needs to know it's name (file-names), its data type (String[].class), its value(s), and an encoding style URI, which is null here.

```
params.addElement(new Parameter("filenms", String[].class, s, null));
```

Invoking the Remote Procedure Call and Checking the Response

Invoking the RPC involves using the call object's invoke method to remotely execute the Web service method residing at the SOAP server (also called the endpoint). The call object has already obtained the RPC parameters from the params vector using call.setParams(params). call.invoke invokes the call specifying the SOAP server endpoint URL as its first argument. The second argument is the value to be placed into the SOAP message header (this can be left empty is so desired). The resp object is set to the return value of the call.invoke method. If an exception occurs, it is caught and a fault code and exception message are returned. Assuming a SOAPException has not occurred, the resp object can check for faults and then extract the invocation result using the getReturnValue() method .

Printing Information about the Attachment and Creating the Image File

This section of code is used when the MIME attachment with the image file is sent back from the SOAP server. The printObject method call takes the msg.receive()object as its only argument. The function of msg.receive() is to receive the XML document created earlier. The printObject method takes the XML document received by msg.receive() and prints the information relating to the attachment carried within the message. The printObject method prints the datahandler name, its content type and its file name. The ByteArrayDataSource object (bds) is then used to physically construct the file using the DataSource getInputStream, DataHandler getContentType, and ByteArrayDataSource writeTo methods. The dh.getName() method returns a null value and as a result the file created will always be called 'null.out'. This generic output ensures scalability and means that the application is never tied to any particular file format thus allowing the client to specify any file format without touching the code.

On the client side, every remote procedure call uses the serializer from Apache SOAP's org.apache.soap.util.xml package to convert the java object(s) in the remote method parameters to produce a SOAP request message and then, upon a successful remote procedure call, the deserializer from the same package to convert the response message back into the Java object(s). On the server side, the deserializer can be used to convert a SOAP request message into the Java object(s), then execute the request method, and return the object(s) in the SOAP response by using the serializer to convert the object(s) into a SOAP response message.

Evaluation

Webber is ideal for circumstances where a protocol needs to be configured to match the characteristics of a specific network environment. One example could be a multimedia application, which requires congestion control but not ordered delivery, a service that TCP or UDP cannot provide. A scenario that we examine here is TCP over wireless networks. TCP performs well in wired networks with its low latency and low failure rate but overreacts in wireless networks where packet loss can occur for many reasons other than congestion (Wong, 2001). The principal problem is the congestion control algorithm. Nearly all TCP implementations nowadays assume that timeouts are caused by congestion, not by lost packets therefore when a timer expires; TCP retransmits the packet, but also invokes congestion control measures by reducing the TCP window size and throughput. The industry standards for versions of TCP such as Reno retransmit data on reception of 3 duplicate acknowledgements or the expiration of a retransmission timeout. This timeout however can be set very coarse, in the order of 350-500ms. Local area networks (LANs) and organisations fortunate enough to be connected directly (e.g., universities) to the backbone of the Internet quite often experience round-trips approximately 20-100ms, therefore due to the low latency of the network, faster retransmissions can be beneficial (Cheshire, 2000).

The goal here was to reconfigure the TCP retransmission timer over Wireless networks to react speedier to errors rather than assume congestion and 'back-off' incorrectly. To achieve this, we ran a series of comparisons between a Webber TCP Reno clone and a Webber TCP with a timeout value set to 150ms for Webber TCP and a time-out value of 400ms for TCP Reno (see Table 1). This testing involved running a Java RPC client and specifying the following parameters: SOAP endpoint server, Web service method and file(s) to be downloaded from SOAP server. The stack retrieval Web service using the VBScript was tested by running the client and passing requested stack elements as parameters.

The packet losses were simulated by a LOSSY protocol stack element. The LOSSY component simulated reordering and loss of messages (0% loss to 50% loss). We performed a series of 1000 runs of epoch sizes varying from 100-900 over our three-test bed networks. We used a Windows 98 Pentium Pro 500mhz PC Client, with 128 MB Ram connected via a 2 MB wireless LAN to a Windows 2000 Pentium III 800mhz Server with 128 MB RAM.

Table 1. Variable retransmission timer parameter

Variable Parameter	Time (ms)
retransmission_interval: the retransmission time-out	150-300

Figure 5. Latency comparisons of TCP versus optimised TCP over wireless LAN

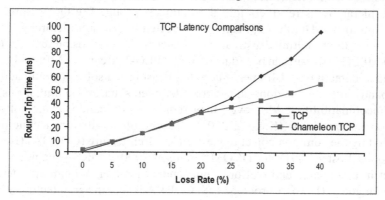

Figure 5 illustrates that our optimised TCP outperforms a standard TCP stack when faced with losses above a 20% threshold. This is achieved through the use of a retransmission timer, which is set to respond faster to lost messages.

Determining whether the application is streaming over a wired or on a wireless network can be determined at run-time by Webber. The assumption on the average packet loss rate for these networks is hidden in the protocol library for generic protocol stacks. Webber however provides the hooks for reconfiguring the environmental parameters involved. Webber does not require a total reloading of the stack into memory during run-time should a reconfiguration of the timer be requested. The timer interval is simply changed, buffers emptied and transmission continues as before with the new timer interval settings.

Related Work

The approaches taken by middleware solutions, such as WAP (2002) or MASE (Meggers, 1998) is to encapsulate the weaker process by creating simple APIs or reduced operating system calls. Proxies can also be used to hide the effects of error-prone and low-bandwidth wireless links (Huang, 2002; Yoshimura, 2002) applies the proxy mechanism to mobile environments where filters on an intermediary, delay and transform data between mobile and fixed devices. The filters are part of the application making it difficult to support legacy applications. Multicasting (Kunz, 2002; Phan, 2002) has received considerable attention but much of the work revolves around either low-level communication protocols or groupware applications, which typically simulate multicast through a series of unicasts. Group based multicast systems such as described in (Tai, 2002) attempted to address the problems that face mobile devices that are intermittently attached to a network by building a hierarchy as receivers join the multicast group. The QoS-A protocol distributes multicast data through carefully selected nodes in a hierarchy, which are equipped to filter multimedia streams to reduce their demands on receiver (He, 2002). An MPEG-2 stream can be reduced to an MPEG-1 stream, or MPEG-1 could be reduced to contain only I-frames. These multicast based solutions only address network bandwidth; applications do not consider clients' hardware limitations and software incompatibilities. Moreover, they require modification of the software installed on Internet hosts (Kassler, 2001). A range of middleware technologies exist, including the common object request broker architecture (CORBA) (Hector, 2002), Globus (Foster, 2001), and DCOM (Knudsen, 2000). CORBA enables objects to interact in a language and platform independent manner through an interface definition language (IDL). A problem with CORBA is that the architecture adopts a traditional black box approach such that the platform implementation is hidden from the application (Pyarali, 2002).

Conclusion

This chapter had demonstrated how SOAP's platform and language independence can be used to overcome a common limitations such a bandwidth, memory capacity, as well as disparate programming environments. SOAP's handling of MIME attachments adds an extra dimension to SOAP by allowing non-text based files to be transported bi-directionally between client and server. SOAP also allows the client developer to register new data types which can, once registered, be used as RPC parameters. One criticism of Apache's SOAP implementation is that it forces the SOAP client to write the client code to call the remote procedure. MS SOAP overcomes this to an extent by providing a WSDL file describing the Web service and how it should be used. The SOAP architecture allows legacy applications to interface to the SOAP API, no matter what their native platform is. This is important to the wider success of SOAP, in that, companies do not need to spend money upgrading their systems just so they adopt SOAP. The VBScript client invocation of the Java Web service demonstrates how disparate application could potentially communicate with each other using an XML-based system such as SOAP.

References

Casner, S., & Jacobson, V. (1999, February). *Compressing IP/UDP/RTP headers for low-speed serial links* (RFC 2508).

Cheshire, S. (2000). *For every network service there's an equal and opposite network disservice.* Retrieved from http://rescomp.stanford.edu/~cheshire/rants/net-workdynamics.html

Curbera, F. (2005). *Web services platform architecture: Soap, WSDL, WS-policy, WSaddressing, WS-Bpel, WS-reliable messaging and more.* Prentice Hall PTR.

Foster, I., Kesselman, C., & Tuecke, S. (2001). The anatomy of the grid: Enabling-scalable virtual organizations. *International Journal of Supercomputer Applications, 15*(3), 2001.

He, D., Muller, G., & Lawall, J. (2002). Distributing MPEG movies over the Internet using programmable networks. In *Proceedings of the 22nd International Conference on Distributed Computing Systems* (ICDCS 2002) (pp. 161- 170). July 2-5, 2002

Duran-Limon, H., & Blair, G. (2002, January). Reconfiguration of resources in middleware. In *Proceedings of the 7th IEEE International Workshop on Object-Oriented Real-time Dependable Systems (WORDS 2002)*, San Diego, CA (pp. 219-226).

Huang, L., Horn, U., Hartung, F., & Kampmann, M. (2002, September 5-7). Proxy-based TCP-friendly streaming over mobile networks. In *Proceedings of the 5th ACM Workshop on Wireless and Mobile Multimedia (WOWMOM 2002)*, Atlanta, GA (pp. 17 - 24).

Kassler, A., Kucherer, C., & Schrader, S. (2001, September). Adaptive wavelet video filtering. In *Proceedings of the 2nd International Workshop on Quality of Future Internet Services (QofIS)*, Coimbra, Portugal (pp. 72-78).

Katz, R. (1994). Adaptation and mobility in wireless information systems. *IEEE Personal Communications, 1*(1), 6-17.

Knudsen, K. (2000). Building PerfMon support into applications using COM. *Microsoft Systems Journal (MSJ)*, February.

Kojo, M., Raatikainen, K., Liljeberg, M., Kiiskinen, J., & Alanko, T. (1997). An efficient transport service for slow wireless telephone links. *IEEE Journal on Selected Areas in Communications, 15*(7), 26-34.

Kunz, T., & Cheng, E. (2002, July 2-5). On-demand multicasting in ad-hoc networks: Comparing AODV and ODMRP. In *Proceedings of the 22nd International Conference on Distributed Computing Systems (ICDCS 2002)*, Vienna, Austria (pp. 40-52).

Matthur, A., & Mundur, P. (2003, September 24-26). Congestion adaptive streaming: An integrated approach. In *Proceedings of the 9th International Conference on Distributed Multimedia Systems (DMS 2003)*, Florida International University Miami (pp. 102-108).

Meggers, J. (1998, September 10-13). A multimedia communication architecture for hand-held devices. In *Proceedings of the 9th IEEE International Symposium on Personal Indoor and Mobile Radio Communications*, Boston (pp. 372-376).

Modi, T. (2001, March). *Clean up your wire protocol with SOAP*. JavaWorld. Retrieved from http://www.javaworld.com/javaworld/jw-03-2001/jw-0330-soap.html.

Phan, T., Zorpas, G., & Bagrodia, R. (2002, July 2-5). An extensible and scalable content adaptation pipeline architecture to support heterogeneous clients. In *Proceedings of the 22nd International Conference on Distributed Computing Systems (ICDCS 2002)*, Vienna, Austria (pp. 507- 516).

Pyarali, I., Schmidt, D., & Cytron, R. (2002, September 21-24). Achieving end-to-end predictability of the TAO real-time CORBA ORB. In *Proceedings of the 8th IEEE Real-Time Technology and Applications Symposium*, San Jose, CA (pp. 33-40).

Saber, M., & Mirenkov, N. (2003, September 24-26). A multimedia programming environment for cellular automata systems. In *Proceedings of the 9th International Conference on Distributed Multimedia Systems (DMS 2003)*, Florida International University Miami (pp. 437-448).

Snell, J., Tidwell, D., & Kulchenko, P. (2001). *Programming Web services with SOAP*. O Reilly.

Solon, T., McKevitt, P., & Curran, K. (2003, October 22-23). Telemorph: Bandwidth determined mobile multimodal presentation. In *Proceedings of the Information Technology and Telecommunications Conference (IT&T 2003)*, Donegal, Ireland: Letterkenny Institute of Technology (pp. 92-93.)

Stefanov, T., Lieverse, P., Deprettere, E., & Van der Wolf, P. (2000, October). Y-chart based system level performance analysis: An M-JPEG case study. In *Proceedings of the Progress Workshop*, Utrecht (NL) (pp. 134-146).

Wong, G., Hiltunen, M., & Schlichting, R. (2001, April 22-26). A configurable and extensible transport protocol. In *Proceedings of the IEEE Infocom 2001 Conference,* Anchorage, AK (pp. 319-328).

XML. (2002) *XML specification*. Retrieved from http://www.w3.org/XML/

WAP. (2002). Retrieved from http://www.wapforum.org/what/WAP_white_pages.pdf

Yoshimura, T. Yonemoto, Y., Ohya, T., & Wee, S. (2002, May 7-11). Mobile streaming media CDN enabled by dynamic SMIL. In *Proceedings of the 11ᵗʰ International World Wide Web Conference (WWW 2002)*, Honolulu, HI (pp. 651-661).

Endnote

[1]   http://xml.apache.org/soap/docs/index.html

Chapter V

Advanced Data Compression Techniques for SOAP Web Services

Christian Werner, University Lübeck, Germany

Carsten Buschmann, University Lübeck, Germany

Stefan Fischer, University Lübeck, Germany

Abstract

A major drawback of using SOAP for application integration is its enormous demand for network bandwidth. Compared to classical approaches, like Java-RMI and Corba, SOAP messages typically cause more than three times the network traffic. In this chapter we will explore compression strategies and give a detailed survey and evaluation of state of the art binary encoding techniques for SOAP. We also introduce a new experimental concept for SOAP compression based on differential encoding, which makes use of the commonly available WSDL description of a SOAP Web service. We not only conduct a detailed evaluation of compression effectiveness, but also provide the results of execution time measurements.

Introduction

Like all other XML protocols, SOAP suffers from the fact that only a very small part of the transmitted message contains real payload. The rest of it is XML markup and protocol overhead. Comparisons on different approaches for realizing remote procedure calls (RPC) have shown that SOAP, over HTTP, uses significantly more bandwidth than competitive technologies (Marahrens, 2003; Tian et al., 2003). For our experiments, we implemented a simple RPC server and client on different platforms (MS .Net, Apache Axis, Corba, JavaRMI, RMIIIOP). Then, we measured the resulting network traffic for each case using the Ethereal network analyzing utility.

Figure 1 summarizes the results. For all implementations the number of transmitted bytes increases with the number of transmitted RPC messages in an almost linear way (all values do not include overhead for protocols on network layer and below). There is virtually no difference in the number of transmitted bytes between Microsoft's SOAP Implementation and Apache Axis. Both cause three times more network traffic than JavaRMI and Corba.

For the case of only one message ($n = 1$) the SOAP implementations cause the smallest amount of traffic: 1,972 bytes (Java), 1,976 bytes (SOAP .Net), 2,626 bytes (RMI), and 2,887 bytes (Corba). For all cases with more than one message the two SOAP implementations perform worse than RMI, RMIIIOP and Corba. The reason for this is, that unlike SOAP, these implementations exchange information about naming service before sending the first RPC message, causing a relative high traffic offset.

Figure 1. Transmission of random strings (l = 250 Bytes)

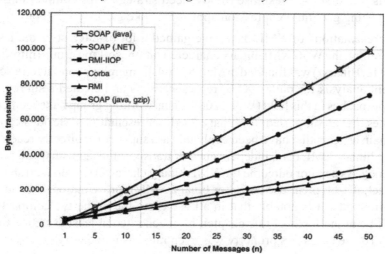

Though today's wired networks are powerful enough to provide sufficient bandwidth even for very demanding applications, like media streaming, there are still some fields of computing where bandwidth is costly. In cellular phone networks (GPRS, UMTS), for example, it is quite common to charge according to the transmitted data volumes. Also, dialup connections, via modem or ISDN are still rather common in enterprise networks. Third, communication in energyconstrained environments, such as sensor networks, calls for economical use of resources such as bandwidth. In these domains powerful compression strategies for SOAP could be useful to minimize costs and ensure best possible performance by saving bandwidth.

The SOAP specification does not explicitly define strategies for compressing SOAP documents, but states that there is no need for the underlying transport protocol to use the XML 1.0 serialization of the SOAP message's XML information set for transporting SOAP documents "on the wire." Also compressed representations are allowed. So, compression is generally out of focus of SOAP but is located on transport level.

Since HTTP is by far the most widely used protocol for transporting SOAP messages, it is no surprise that nearly all practically used approaches for compressing SOAP documents are based on HTTP's compression mechanisms. Well-known SOAP toolkits (respectively their underlying HTTP implementations) like Apache Axis and Microsoft .NET do already offer support for the gzip HTTP-content-encoding as defined in (Deutsch, 1996; Fielding et al., 1999).

By using gzip compression for HTTP requests as well as for responses we could reduce the network traffic by roughly 26% for all cases (illustrated in Figure 1). This is still worse than JavaRPC, RPCIIOP and Corba.

In this chapter we will discuss different strategies for compressing SOAP messages more efficiently than gzip does. Since SOAP messages are always written in XML, we can—as a first step—make use of advanced strategies for compressing XML rather than using general compression approaches like gzip.

Binary representations of XML data have gained a lot of interest in the last two years. Therefore, the W3C XML binary characterization working group (http://www.w3.org/XML/Binary/) was founded in March 2004. Its members conducted a detailed requirement analysis for binary XML representations and created a survey of the existing approaches in this field (W3C, 2006). This working group has specified a set of properties that are important for binary XML representations. Besides compactness the main aspects that have been evaluated are support for directly reading and writing the binary XML data, independence of transport mechanisms, and processing efficiency. As a major outcome the XML binary characterization working group created a set of 18 typical-use cases for binary XML representations and analyzed their requirements. It is notable that in all use cases the property "compactness," which will be in the focus of this chapter, has been rated at least as a nice-to-have feature. In 10 use cases this property was even rated as mandatory.

In December 2005 another W3C working group was established that focuses on the interoperability of binary XML: The Efficient XML Interchange Working Group (http://www.w3.org/XML/EXI/).

Up to now both of the W3C working groups in this field have not drafted any recommendations. Currently they are still discussing the requirements of interoperable binary XML representations.

In this chapter we will introduce a highly specialized way of XML compression, which is custom-tailored for SOAP: differential SOAP encoding. The idea behind this is the following: Rather than transmitting the whole SOAP message, we only transmit the differences between the SOAP message and a SOAP skeleton which is generated out of the service's WSDL description.

The remainder of this chapter is structured as follows: After an introduction on the theoretical basics of data compression, we will give a survey of XML compression with a focus on SOAP. Then, we will present our approach of differential SOAP compression. We will finally make a conclusion and discuss some future work.

Theoretical Background

There are basically two different approaches for data compression. The first one is entropy encoding. Compression algorithms using this approach exploit the fact that not all symbols of a message have the same frequency. Short codes are assigned to symbols with high frequencies and longer codes are assigned to symbols with lower frequencies. Shannon found that there is a fundamental limit for the gain of this encoding scheme (Shannon, 1948). Each symbol has certain information content, called entropy, which is determined by its frequency.

The idea behind entropy encoding is to minimize the redundancy of a message by coding all symbols according to their entropy. It is crucial for entropy encoding that no other characteristics of the data source are taken into account than the statistical characteristics of its symbols. Entropy encoding is always lossless.

In computer science practice it is common to use octets as symbols. Due to the different probabilities of the 256 different octets in binary files we can compress all kinds of binary data with various entropy encoding algorithms. A very well known approach is the Huffman algorithm (Huffman, 1952), which is used in many compression programs including gzip.

Another way for data compression is called source encoding. Here, certain characteristics of the data source are exploited. Example: If we know that a binary file is a black and white image where every black pixel is encoded as "0" and every white pixel as "1," we can use the fact that a "0" is normally followed by other "0"s and vice versa (because a black and white image has normally large areas which are solid black or white). So, we can encode a block of n "0"s as "n times 0" instead of writing n "0"s into the output file.

Beside the technique explained in this example, which is known as run length encoding, there are many other occurrences of source encoding. Some of them, like motion compression and spectral encoding, are limited to applications in signal and image processing, but others are more universal. One very important concept here is called "differential encoding." Here, we do not transmit the message itself, but only the difference between this message and a previous one. If a block of similar messages is sent, the resulting compression rates are very high. In computer networking differential encoding is used, e.g., for compressing RTP headers (Casner & Jacobson, 1999). Source encoding can be lossy or not and commonly achieves much higher compression rates than plain entropy encoding.

In practice it is quite common to use combinations of entropy and source encoding for even better compression rates.

Survey on XML Compression

Since XML finds wide use today as a general data format for storing semistructured information, many authors proposed algorithms for compressing XML. Especially in the field of XML databases researchers investigated strategies for storing very large XML Documents efficiently. We will not discuss these approaches here in detail, but will give a short overview with a strong focus on the specific advantages and disadvantages in conjunction with SOAP. SOAP documents are special in the way that they are typically:

- Not larger than a few kilobytes
- Not described by XML schema instances or DTDs, but by WSDL documents (which may however contain XML schema definitions)

Text Compression

The first idea for XML compression that comes to mind is to use general text file compressors, because XML documents can be stored as text files and pure entropy encoding mechanisms such as those implemented in gzip do perform quite well here. Unfortunately, this approach has bad side effects. The XML file is compressed and uncompressed as a whole (or at least in fixed size blocks) ignoring the XML structure completely. This makes it impossible to parse or change a compressed XML file without uncompressing and recompressing it completely.

Using SAX Events

The first thing that is important to understand when talking about XML compression is that there is usually no need for encoding the XML text file, but only the underlying XML information set (W3C, 2001). In almost all cases there is no need for preserving indentations, and thus they should not be encoded. Also, most of the CR (carriage return) and LF (line feed) characters might be unnecessary.

A smart way of separating the significant parts from unimportant ones is to use a SAX (Simple API for XML) parser. It interprets the XML structure and fires events which can be interpreted by the compressor. This approach has been taken for all implementations of XML specific compressors. It obviously leads to a kind of source encoding, because it relies on the specific property of XML documents to be SAX-parsable. Also, encoding using SAX events can be seen as lossy if we think of compressing text representations of XML documents, since things like indentations might be lost.

XMILL

Liefke and Suciu (2000) introduced XMILL as a universal XML compressor. Here, SAX events are evaluated by a so-called path processor. This processor separates the XML document's structure from its content and stores all isolated tokens in separate containers. There is one special container exclusively for the document's structure, which holds integer encoded references to start and end tags as well as to attributes and text node values. These references point to other containers which hold the actual data. The big advantage of this approach is that values in the data containers do not have to be stored as strings, but can be encoded with respect to their specific characteristic using semantic compression. For example, IP addresses can be stored as a sequence of four bytes. Such encoding rules are not determined automatically by XMILL, but have to be specified manually using command line options. Each container is entropy encoded using gzip compression and is then stored in the binary output file.

XMILL is probably the most versatile of all currently available XML compressors, its behavior being adaptable to special use cases. XMILL performs quite well also on very small files, which is very important when compressing SOAP messages. Versions of XMILL (newer than the one described in Liefke & Suciu, 2000) also have support for entropy encoders other that gzip, which lead to even better results. Nevertheless, one major drawback of using XMill for encoding SOAP is that for best results (with semantic compressors) compressing options must be adjusted for each service. This is probably not feasible in practice.

In Ghandeharizadeh et al. (2002) the benefits of using binary encoding for XML network messages instead of plain text encoding are discussed. The authors compare zip and XMILL compression. XMILL is slower than zip but achieves better compression rates even without semantic compression. The authors propose an adaptive middleware that is capable of determining which encoding style is the best one with respect to parameters like message size or available network capacity. XMILL is available as open source at http://www.sourceforge.net/projects/xmill.

ESAX and Multiplexed Hierarchical Modeling

Cheney (2001) introduced the concept of ESAX, which stands for "Encoded SAX" events. Here a symbol table is maintained that translates SAX events directly into binary format. Then, the resulting binary stream is passed to an entropy encoder for eliminating remaining redundancy. This simple approach works surprisingly well. The author compared the ESAX compressor with XMILL and found out that compression rates are only 1% to 7% worse, depending on the used entropy encoder.

Cheney also discussed the use of prediction by partial match (PPM) in conjunction with ESAX for further improvements. PPM is a generic algorithm for text compression and was introduced by Cleary and Witten (1984). It makes use of the fact that a symbol in a text does often occur in the same context of preceding symbols. The algorithm maintains statistics of which symbol has been seen in what contexts and uses this information for finding optimal encoding rules for each symbol.

Cheney conjectured that this approach can be used for XML compression more effectively if the hierarchical structure of an XML document is taken into account when applying the PPM algorithm. This technique is called multiplexed hierarchical modeling (MHM). He implemented different algorithms for identifying suitable context symbols for the PPM. One important result of his experiments is that it is very efficient to keep separate symbols statistics for elements, attributes and (text node) characters.

This approach is also very efficient for compressing small XML files. A free XML compressor called xmlppm, which makes use of multiplexed hierarchical modeling, is available at http://sourceforge.net/projects/xmlppm/.

WBXML and Millau

Another approach for binary XML encoding is WAP binary XML (WBXML). It was standardized by the W3C in 1999 and was originally meant for use in narrowband wireless networks, especially in conjunction with wireless markup language (WML). WML is comparable to HTML but custom-tailored for mobile devices. Unlike HTML, WML is a wellformed XML and thus parsable with any XML parser. In order to reduce WML file sizes for transmission over wireless phone networks, WML documents are recoded on the Web server to a much more compact binary WBXML representation. To ensure high performance on serverside and low usage of computing resources on the mobile clients, WBXML encoding is not based on sophisticated entropy and source encoding strategies such as those in XMILL and xmlppm. Instead, WBXML encoders split up the XML document in predefined tokens that are binary encoded using standardized coding tables (called code spaces). As an example, the token charset="UTF8" is encoded as the byte value 0x6A. There is no need to include the coding tables when transmitting the WBXML message, because all WBXML parsers are aware of these encoding rules.

In fact, WBXML is not limited to be used for encoding WML, but is a general approach for all XML languages. For implementing WBXML encoding rules for other languages, language-specific tag and attribute code spaces are needed. Currently, there are implementations for various languages used in the field of mobile communication, that is, SyncML (2001) and digital rights management rights expression language (DRMREL, 2002).

Characters that can not be found in the predefined coding tables (e.g., text node values) are always encoded inline (i.e., they are directly written to the binary file, enclosed by a predefined I_STRING escape token and a termination symbol specific to the character set).

A major benefit is that a WBXML aware SAX parser can interpret the binary encoded file directly and very quickly. Decoding is basically done by using lookup tables; no expensive arithmetic computations are needed. Girardot and Sundaresa (2000) introduce the Millau compression approach which is based on WBXML but adds two further improvements.

The first additional feature is that in Millau character data is not encoded inline, but in a separate stream. This is comparable to what is done in xmlppm and XMILL. This separation makes it possible to apply entropy encoding mechanisms efficiently in order to achieve higher compression ratios for files with a high amount of character data.

The second improvement concerns the code spaces. In WBXML the number of entries in the code spaces for tags and attributes is very limited. For complex languages these value ranges might be too small and so, the WBXML grammar was slightly modified in Millau enabling more table entries.

We are not aware of any publicly available Millau implementation. Thus we could not make any performance evaluations for Millau. Since it is an improved version of WBXML, it should achieve even higher compression rates than WBXML. As we will see in the next section, the compression results of WBXML on small files are very promising. For WBXML there are several implementations. In addition to various versions for mobile devices there is a free WBXML library that also includes some conversion tools for WBXML experiments on Windows and Unix Systems.

The authors are not aware of a SOAP compressor based on the WBXML or similar approaches. It is surely impossible to adopt WBXML or Millau directly for SOAP compression, because in SOAP it is common to use custom data types, which cannot be predicted when defining coding tables. In this way SOAP is much more dynamic than languages with a quite limited number of possible elements such as SyncML.

Compression Performance on Small Files

Many authors already evaluated the compression techniques described above in different contexts (Cheney, 2001; Liefke & Suciu, 2000). Nevertheless, most of these experiments were done with rather large files (> 100k bytes) and the efficiency of a compressor can vary for smaller files: Here it is very important that the compression algorithms do not reserve much space in the output stream for large tables mapping symbols to their bit codes. For very small files these coding tables might need more space than the encoded data itself, whereas for larger files, the added overhead for symbol tables becomes more and more irrelevant. Hence, compression results for large files are not necessarily transferable to small files which are typical for SOAP messages.

In order to evaluate the compression techniques described above with small files, we set up a test bed with 182 files of eight different languages. All files were taken from the test suite of a freely available WBXML library at http://wbxmllib.sourceforge. net/. We used these files because we want to include WBXML in our evaluation and, as previously described, WBXML does only work for some selected languages.

Table 1. Compression results for small XML files

Encoding	S_{total} [Bytes]	$S_{smallest}$ [Bytes]	$S_{largest}$ [Bytes]	$S_{average}$ [Bytes]	λ_{best}	λ_{worst}	$\lambda_{average}$	s_{λ}
XML (text, uncompr.)	191,856	129	6,645	1,054.15	1.00	1.00	1.00	0.00
XML (text. bzip2)	80,296	157	1,253	441.19	0.16	1.22	0.62	0.31
XML (text, gzip)	73,439	153	1,202	403.51	0.16	1.19	0.58	0.30
XMILL (bzip2)	87,646	195	1,282	481.57	0.18	1.51	0.73	0.43
XMILL (gzip)	72,720	153	1,085	399.56	0.16	1.19	0.58	0.32
XMILL (ppm)	68,981	145	1,064	379.02	0.15	1.12	0.55	0.30
xmlppm	62,598	75	1,099	343.95	0.14	0.70	0.43	0.14
wbxml	28,664	7	1,164	157.49	0.05	0.25	0.14	0.03

The results of this experiment are shown in Table 1. We compared the compression characteristics of two generic text compressors (gzip and bzip2) and three XML compressors (XMILL, xmlppm and WBXML). As described above, XMILL has support for different entropy encoders for compressing the different XMILL containers. This, of course, does also affect compression results. Hence we made different test series with gzip, bzip2 and a ppm compressor in the backend of XMILL. The performance of the different compressors is compared to the values within the line "XML (text, uncompressed)" in Table 1, which represents the normal, uncompressed XML encoding as a text file.

For all encoding variants we measured the total size of all 182 files stored in that encoding (S_{total}). The values for $S_{smallest}$ and $S_{largest}$ indicate the sizes of the smallest/largest file (also separately for each encoding). $S_{average}$ is the average file size (which is simply $S_{total}/182$). We then compared the file size of each file with its size encoded as text (uncompressed). The quotient $S_{text}/S_{encoding}$ yields the compression ratio λ. Table 1 shows the best, the worst, and the average compression rate. The average compression rate is not weighted by file size and thus different from the quotient of the S_{total} values for text and compressed encoding. The standard deviation s_λ indicates, if the compression rates are more or less constant for all file (small values for s_λ) or if they are spread over a wider range (larger values for s_λ).

The two text compressors perform quite well, their compression rates on small files are comparable with the XMILL compressor. In all test cases the gzip compression is more effective than bzip2, but XMILL (ppm) outperforms both. Nevertheless, xmlppm compresses even better. Using this tool even very small files could be further compressed ($\lambda_{worst} < 1$). Also, s_λ is very small for xmlppm's compression algorithm. That means that it performs well on most of the files, irrespective of certain file characteristics like a high amount of markup or repetitive structures.

This comparison shows clearly that WBXML is the most effective compressor for small files available. As outlined above there is no need to include the coding tables in the WBXML binary output, because for supported XML languages these tables are static and thus an identification tag for the compressed language is enough to find the right decoding rules for decompression or parsing. This makes WBXML compression more than twice as effective as xmlppm compression and also the s_λ value of 0.03 is very good. Enhanced variants of this approach, like Millau, should even perform better.

The drawback of WBXML compression is of course that only selected XML languages can be compressed and hence, this compression technique is not directly relevant for compressing SOAP. Nevertheless, these results are surely important for future work in this research area.

Differential SOAP Compression

Unlike the compression approaches described in the last section, which are usable for various kinds of text and XML files, we will now have a look at a new source encoding technique specifically designed for SOAP messages. We developed this approach out of the observation that SOAP messages that are sent by or sent to a Web service are in most cases very similar. In such cases, it is quite common to use differential encoding, which basically means that only the difference between a message and a previous one is sent over the wire. The documents, describing only the differences, are typically much more compact.

Architecture

When applying differential encoding to SOAP messages, there is one major problem. Since commonly used transport protocols like HTTP, and also SOAP itself are stateless, we cannot use previously sent messages to calculate the difference. Hence we use the commonly available WSDL description of a Web service to generate skeleton SOAP messages for all service operations (input and output). Then, the differences between a SOAP message and its corresponding skeleton file are calculated and sent over the wire. Each skeleton file contains a "generic" SOAP request or response in the sense that there are no data values in it but only markup. These skeleton files are then used for SOAP differencing (senderside) and SOAP patching (receiverside). SOAP patching here means to patch the SOAP difference

Figure 2. Differential encoding and decoding of SOAP requests

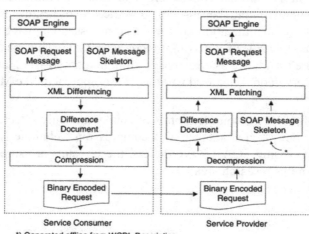

file into the SOAP skeleton to reconstruct the original message. To ensure that the original SOAP message can be reconstructed at the receiver-side, it is important that service consumer and service provider apply the same algorithm for skeleton generation and work with the same WSDL service description.

A prototypical architecture for differential SOAP encoding and decoding is illustrated in Figure 2. Here a service consumer sends a SOAP request to a service provider. At first, its SOAP engine produces a SOAP request message. Then the difference between this message and a previously generated SOAP request skeleton is calculated. The resulting difference document is then passed to an entropy encoding stage in order to remove the remaining redundancy. It produces a binary representation of the difference document which is finally sent to the service provider. Here the request skeleton is patched with the (previously decompressed) difference document. The patching process reconstructs the original SOAP message, which is then passed to the service provider's SOAP engine. For SOAP response messages this process would work vice versa.

The effectiveness of this approach depends on one important factor: The better the generated skeletons match with the SOAP messages generated by the used SOAP implementation, the smaller the resulting difference documents. A fundamental issue is here that a WSDL description (unlike pure XML schema) does not describe exactly one valid SOAP document structure for the input and output messages of a certain service operation. Hence, the SOAP document structure may vary between different SOAP implementations resulting in varying compression rates.

Fortunately it is not important for the overall performance that the document structure predicted by the algorithm for SOAP skeleton generation and the structure of the SOAP message to be sent *always* match very closely. The better the matching the smaller the resulting difference files are: It is important that this prediction works reliable in *the common cases* resulting in a good overall compression performance.

It is important that the calculation of a difference document is always possible, even if the SOAP message document is completely different from the predicted skeleton. This happens for example if a SOAP fault element is returned in the body of a SOAP response. In such cases the differential encoding does of course not provide any benefits in comparison with directly encoded SOAP messages.

Implementation

For implementing a differential SOAP compressor as outlined in the previous section, three main components are needed:

- A tool generating SOAP skeletons from WSDL files
- Tools for differencing and patching SOAP documents

- A common data format for representing differences between two SOAP documents

For generating the SOAP skeletons we are currently using an XSLT program. It is currently limited to work with RPC-encoded services and provides only support for simple data types like strings and integers.

For the last two items listed above, we can again make use of the fact that SOAP messages are written in XML and that such components have already been developed for XML in general.

Within the last years, tools for XML differencing became more and more popular. But, not all implementations are suitable for SOAP differential encoding, because most tools only provide functionalities for XML differencing, but not for patching. A main aspect here is that a machine readable output format must be produced instead of just highlighting the differences between two files.

The authors tested two free implementations of XML differencing tools which provide output in a machine-readable format that can be interpreted by a patching utility.

The first one, diffxml (Mouat, 2002) uses the so-called delta update language (DUL) as an output format. DUL is an XMLbased, proprietary language, which is currently exclusively used for this project. In this project also a patch utility for processing DUL documents has been developed. Diffxml is available at http://diffxml.sourceforge.net/.

The second tool, xmldiff, provides functionalities only for differencing and is available at http://www.logilab.org/projects/xmldiff. It can output the differencing results in two formats: a proprietary nonXML text format (no patching processor is available), and XUpdate, which is an industry standard developed by the XML:db initiative (Laux & Martin, 2000). For patching XML files with XUpdate documents, we used another utility called 4xupdate. It is based on the programming language python and included in the free XML processing library 4Suite (http://sourceforge.net/projects/foursuite/).

Example

To illustrate how SOAP differencing and patching works, we will demonstrate the whole process with a simple example. We implemented an RPC Web service providing a concatString(String0, String1, String2) procedure that returns a concatenation of the three input parameters. Both the SOAP server and the according client were implemented with the Apache Axis SOAP engine.

In a first step, the automatically generated WSDL description is processed with a short XSLT program for generating SOAP skeleton messages. This program gen-

Figure 3. Request skeleton (a), SOAP request (b), DUL (c) and XUpdate (d) difference documents

a)	```<?xml version="1.0" encoding="UTF8"?><soapenv:Envelopexmlns:soapenv="http://schemas.xmlsoap.org/soap/envelope/"xmlns:xsd="http://www.w3.org/2001/XMLSchema"xmlns:xsi="http://www.w3.org/2001/XMLSchemainstance"><soapenv:Body><ns1:concatStringxmlns:ns1="http://somename.test/concat"soapenv:encodingStyle="http://schemas.xmlsoap.org/soap/encoding/"><in0 xsi:type="xsd:string"/><in1 xsi:type="xsd:string"/><in2 xsi:type="xsd:string"/></ns1:concatString></soapenv:Body></soapenv:Envelope>```
b)	```<?xml version="1.0" encoding="UTF8"?><soapenv:Envelopexmlns:soapenv="http://schemas.xmlsoap.org/soap/envelope/"xmlns:xsd="http://www.w3.org/2001/XMLSchema"xmlns:xsi="http://www.w3.org/2001/XMLSchemainstance"><soapenv:Body><ns1:concatStringsoapenv:encodingStyle="http://schemas.xmlsoap.org/soap/encoding/"xmlns:ns1="http://somename.test/concat"><in0 xsi:type="xsd:string">foo</in0><in1 xsi:type="xsd:string">bar</in1><in2 xsi:type="xsd:string">foo</in2></ns1:concatString></soapenv:Body></soapenv:Envelope>```
c)	```<?xml version="1.0" encoding="UTF8"?><delta><insert charpos="1" childno="1" name="#text" nodetype="3"parent="/node()[1]/node()[2]/node()[2]/node()[2]">foo</insert><insert charpos="1" childno="1" name="#text" nodetype="3"parent="/node()[1]/node()[2]/node()[2]/ node()[4]">bar</insert><insert charpos="1" childno="1" name="#text" nodetype="3"parent="/node()[1]/node()[2]/node()[2]/ node()[6]">foo</insert></delta>```
d)	```<?xml version="1.0"?><xupdate:modifications version="1.0"xmlns:xupdate="http://www.xmldb.org/xupdate"><xupdate:append select="/soapenv:Envelope[1]/soapenv:Body[1]/ns1:concatString[1]/in0[1]" child="first()"><xupdate:text>foo</xupdate:text></xupdate:append><xupdate:append select="/soapenv:Envelope[1]/soapenv:Body[1]/ns1:concatString[1]/in1[1]" child="first()"><xupdate:text>bar</xupdate:text></xupdate:append><xupdate:append select="/soapenv:Envelope[1]/soapenv:Body[1]/ns1:concatString[1]/in2[1]" child="first()"><xupdate:text>foo</xupdate:text></xupdate:append></xupdate:modifications>```

erates two skeletons: one for concatString request messages and one for responses. The request skeleton is exemplarily shown in Figure 3a. If the Web service would provide any other operations than this, the XSLT program would also produce input and output skeletons for them. This process has to be done only once at client and at server side.

For each RPC, the client's SOAP engine generates a SOAP request document, an example is shown in Figure 3b. This document and the request skeleton are compared and the differences are written to a file.

The output format depends on the used differencing utility. Figure 3c shows an example for DUL output, which can be compared to output in XUpdate format shown in Figure 3d. But, of course, also other formats might be used here.

The output document in text format is obviously not much smaller than the original SOAP message. Hence, a compression utility (for example xmlppm) is used to create a smaller binary representation of this difference document. As we will see in the next section, the regular structure of XUpdate and DUL documents can be compressed very effectively.

This binary representation is then transmitted to the service provider. In practice, additional information must be transmitted: An unambiguous reference to the used WSDL instance for skeleton generation and also an unambiguous reference to the service's operation for identifying the correct skeleton to be used for patching. With these parameters, the service provider can restore the original SOAP request. Their encoding depends on the used transport protocol and is not in the focus of our work.

As already shown, the compressed difference document is then unpacked at server-side, merged with the request skeleton during a patching process and then passed to the server's SOAP engine. The SOAP response is then returned to the client—possibly also differentially encoded.

Compression Effectiveness

In order to compare the effectiveness of differential encoding with other compression approaches, we implemented a SOAP RPC test server and a client with three different remote procedures, which yield SOAP messages with different amounts of payload: void doNothing(), String echoString(String) and String concatString(String0, String1, String2, String3, String4). We saved SOAP requests (using random strings with five characters as request parameter) and responses for each operation to files. Then, we compressed these SOAP files using xmlppm, the most effective encoder for such small files. We also created skeleton messages for all operations and generated difference documents by using diffxml (for DUL output) and xmldiff (for XUpdate output). These documents were also compressed with xmlppm.

Figure 4. Effectiveness of different encoding techniques

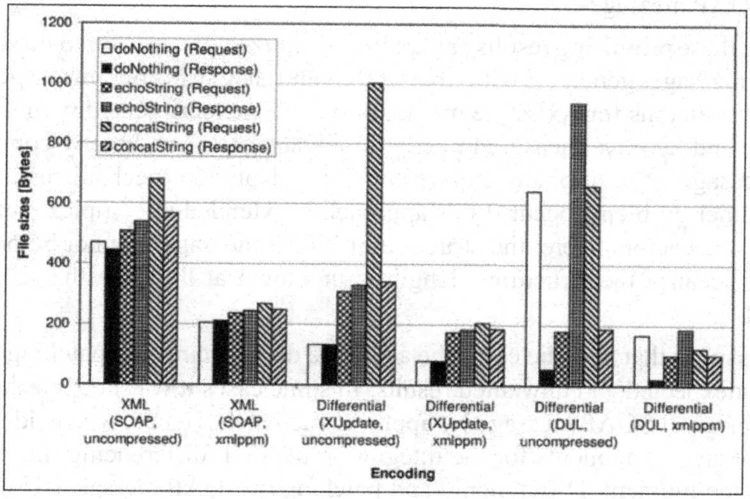

The results are shown in Figure 4. The skeletons generated for doNothing requests and responses match the SOAP request and response nearly perfectly (because no request or response values are exchanged with void doNothing(void)). There are only few differences at the syntactical level (different positions for parameters and namespace declarations in the XML file), but the semantics are the same. Hence, we get an empty XUpdate document without any update instructions. File size is 133 bytes as text file and 79 bytes when compressed with xmlppm. The difference document for encoding the request in DUL format is much larger here. This is because the diffxml did not detect the semantic equivalence of SOAP request and skeleton file for some reasons and various update actions are unnecessarily encoded here.

As for echoString and concatString, requests and responses carry real payload in the form of string parameters. These cannot be predicted during skeleton generation and therefore the difference files are bigger compared to doNothing messages. In the XUpdate and DUL documents for the concatString request the insertion of five strings is encoded. The DUL document for the concatString response is again much larger than needed. Probably this is due to certain heuristics in diffxml for speeding up the differencing process but decreasing the accuracy (which might be useful with much larger files).

In all cases the xmlppm compressed difference documents are not only significantly smaller than the text encoded but also more compact than the xmlppm compressed SOAP messages. The advantage of using differential encoding is largest if the SOAP messages are only predictable markup (doNothing). If the amount of payload increases, the sizes of compressed difference documents get closer to directly compressed SOAP messages.

Of course, these promising results cannot be generalized. We measured these values for SOAP messages generated with Apache Axis and an XSLT program that generates optimized skeletons for Axisstyle messages. We also experimented with .Netstyle messages, and here we measured nearly no advantages over directly compressed SOAP messages. So, in practice quite complex adaptation mechanisms might be needed. Other problems occur if this approach is extended to complex data types, like arrays or vectors. Here, the structure of SOAP messages cannot be predicted precisely, because the structure's length is unknown at the time the skeleton is generated.

Another issue is that in some cases the available differencing and patching utilities produce unexpected and unwanted results. In some cases it was not possible to restore the original SOAP message by applying the patch. Hence, we decided not to implement any components for the integration of XML differencing into a SOAP engine at the moment. Differencing and patching of SOAP messages is possible, but only with user interaction. But, we expect the needed tools to become more reliable in the near future. We are also exploring possibilities to integrate differencing components specially adapted to SOAP directly into the transport handler chain of the SOAP engine.

Algorithmic Complexity and Execution Speed

As already stated in the architecture section, the proposed scheme consists of the four steps:

1. Differencing   } at the sender-side
2. Compression
3. Decompression } at the reciever-side
4. Patching

Compared to the SOAP communication commonly known, these steps are additional ones that don't have to be taken if no differential encoding is employed. Thus, the time it takes to execute them must be considered as overhead. Especially with servers answering many requests per time unit, fast execution is important.

First, we want to shed light on the theoretical algorithmic complexity of the involved algorithms. Considerations on runtime complexity of these kinds of algorithms are commonly based on tree structures because XML (and SOAP) is generalized to hierarchically structured information.

As for the step of differencing, implementations for two different algorithms are publicly available (Mouat, 2002). Whereas the fast match edit script algorithm (FMES) uses a heuristic to find a compact difference document, the extended Zhang and Shasha algorithm (EZS) always finds a minimum difference document. This accuracy is paid by taking a runtime of $O(n^2log^2n)$, where n is the number of leaves in a balanced tree, while FMES is done in $O(ne+e^2)$, where n is the number of leaves and e is a constant representing the degree of difference between the two trees. Even though SOAP documents are typically not balanced, we believe that this assumption is still close to the average case because total disequilibrium is extremely rare.

As for compression and decompression, we experimentally evaluated the runtime complexity of xml(un)ppm. Experiments showed that it exhibits linear behavior with regard to the number of nodes regardless of tree disequilibrium for both.

Patching is possible in $O(m \, log \, n)$, where m is the number of patching operations applied to a balanced tree with n nodes. We experimentally confirmed the linear dependence on m by measuring insertion time into documents of constant size. With regard to a single insertion, $\frac{1}{2}h$ comparisons are needed to find the position where to insert the new node, with h being the height of the tree ($log \, n$).

Table 2. Execution time results of different tools in milliseconds

		doNothing		echoStr		concatStr	
		Req.	**Resp.**	**Req.**	**Resp.**	**Req.**	**Resp.**
1. **Differencing**	FMES Java	3.6	3.1	3.6	4.0	4.9	3.6
	FMES Java Native	2.3	2.0	2.4	2.7	3.5	2.5
	FMES Python	3.1	3.1	3.8	3.8	6.5	3.8
	EZS Python	∞	∞	40.8	41.7	180.8	40.2
2. **Compression**	xmlppm(DUL)	1.3	1.2	1.5	2.0	1.9	1.5
	xmlppm(Xupdate)	1.4	1.4	2.0	2.0	2.6	2.0
	gzip(DUL)	1.0	1.0	1.0	1.0	1.0	1.0
	gzip(Xupdate)	1.0	1.0	1.0	1.0	1.0	1.0
3. **Decompression**	xmlunppm(DUL)	1.1	1.1	1.3	1.7	1.6	1.3
	xmlunppm(Xupdate)	1.2	1.2	1.7	1.7	2.2	1.7
	gzip(DUL)	0.9	0.9	0.8	0.9	0.8	0.8
	gzip(Xupdate)	0.9	0.9	0.9	0.9	0.8	0.9
4. **Patching**	Java	2.8	3.2	6.2	17.2	15.3	6.4
	Python	3.6	3.7	4.8	4.9	9.1	4.9

Apart from these theoretical considerations, we also conducted runtime measurements using the SOAP messages resulting from doNothing, echoString and concatString. Table 2 depicts the results in milliseconds. We explored the different available alternatives for all four steps on a machine powered by an Intel Xeon 3GHz HT CPU with 1.5 GBytes of memory, running a Debian 3 Linux. Runtime measurements were carried out by calculating the average over 5000 executions.

We compared three differencing implementation variants of the FMES algorithm with the EZS algorithm using the tools referenced in the implementation section. Two major conclusions can be drawn: First of all, the EZS algorithm is hardly suitable for real world SOAP differencing due to its extremely low execution speed. For the doNothing messages, the algorithm did not terminate at all, which hints on implementation errors. The FMES algorithm works between 10 and 50 times faster, the Java implementation runs fastest if static linking into native code is used (http://gcc.gnu.org/java/).

For compression as well as decompression, g(un)zip runs up to three times faster than xml(un)ppm, but yields significantly lower compression rates. Because difference documents expressed in XUpdate are larger than the DUL ones, compression takes longer due to more expensive I/O-operations.

We finally compared two patching tools implemented in Java and Python (described in the implementation section), finding that the Java variant runs faster for the short messages corresponding to doNothing but slower for the longer messages generated by echoString and concatString. This hints that the Python tool needs to be longer for initialization but is than more effective with regard to documents length.

In total, differentially encoded doNothing requests can be processed on the server side in 7.9 ms if xmlunppm(DUL) decompression and Python patching are used for the request and FSME Java Native differencing and xmlppm(DUL) are used for the response. This combination is also optimal in terms of compression effectiveness (see Figure 4). echoString and concatString take 10.8 ms and 14.7 ms respectively. On the client side, processing takes 8.4ms, 10.5ms and 11.6ms. However, we are convinced that a significant speedup can be achieved if differential encoding is implemented directly into the input and output streams of servers and clients, saving I/O operations due to not having to read and write the message from and to the hard disk.

Conclusion and Future Work

For clients with poor network connectivity, the high network traffic caused by encoding SOAP messages as text is a severe issue. In such environments, application performance can be improved by using binary encoding styles for SOAP message transport. This is totally transparent to the SOAP engine and therefore the typical benefits of XML Web services are not affected.

Today the most common approach for binary encoding SOAP messages is gzip in conjunction with HTTP. Nevertheless, gzip is not always the best choice for SOAP compression, because it is designed as a generic text compressor unaware of the hierarchical XML structure found in SOAP messages.

The contribution of this chapter is twofold. In an evaluation study of state of the art XML compressors with focus on small files as they are typical for SOAP, we showed that WBXML produces the best results, but is too limited in its applicability. Thus, as for today, the best available solution for SOAP compression is to use xmlppm.

Second, we presented a new compression approach based on differential encoding. Instead of sending the entire SOAP message only the difference between the message and a skeleton, which is previously generated from the WSDL service description, is transmitted. First tests presented by the authors indicate that it yields promising performance. Thus, this approach might be interesting for future work, including especially the development of more robust tools for SOAP message differencing resulting in compact binary output.

We are currently working on another approach that veers more towards WBXML. Here encoding rules are generated from the WSDL description (so that they are not generally static for SOAP, but static per service). First results of this compression approach will be presented in Werner et al. (2006b).

Another important issue concerns the transport protocol itself. As mentioned by Tian (Tian et al., 2003), not only SOAP but also HTTP adds significant overhead to the payload. Hence, the development of lightweight transport mechanisms for mobile Web services might also be very interesting. A first prototype of such a specialized transport binding for SOAP has been presented in Werner et al. (2006a).

All in all, SOAP compression is a field with a lot of open problems. We think that it is possible to improve compression rates if we take the step from generic XML compressors to language specific ones. As shown in this chapter, the step from generic text compressors to XML aware encoders has already considerably improved compression results.

References

Casner, S., & Jacobson, V. (1999). *Compressing ip/udp/rtp headers for lowspeed serial links* (RFC 2508).

Cheney, J. (2001, March 27-29). Compressing XML with multiplexed hierarchical PPM models. In *Proceedings of Data Compression Conference (DCC '01),* Snowbird, UT (pp. 163-173).

Cleary, J. G., & Witten, I. H. (1984). Data compression using adaptive coding and partial string matching. *IEEE Transactions on Communications, 32*(4), 396-402.

Deutsch, L. P. (1996). *GZIP file format specification, Version 4.3* (RFC 1952).

Fielding, R., Gettys, J., Mogul, J. C., Frystyk, H., Masinter, L., Leach, P. J., & BernersLee, T. (1999). *Hypertext transfer protocol: HTTP/1.1* (RFC 2616).

Ghandeharizadeh, S., Papadopoulos, C., Cai, M., & Chintalapudi, K. K. (2002). Performance of networked XMLdriven cooperative applications. *Concurrent Engineering: Research and Applications, 12*(3), 195-204.

Girardot, M., & Sundaresan, N. (2000, May 15-19). Millau: An encoding format for efficient representation and exchange of XML over the Web. In *Proceedings of the 9th international World Wide Web Conference on Computer Networks* (pp. 747-765). Amsterdam, The Netherlands.

Huffman, D. A. (1952). A method for the construction of minimumredundancy codes. In *Proceedings of the Institute of Radio Engineers* (Vol. 40, pp. 1098-1101).

Rights Expression Language, Version 1.0. (2002). Retrieved from http://xml.coverpages.org/OMA-DRMRELv10-20020628p.pdf

Laux, A., & Martin, S. (2000). *XUpdate working draft.* Retrieved from http://xmldb-org.sourceforge.net/xupdate/xupdate-wd.html

Liefke, H., & Suciu, D. (2000). *XMill: An efficient compressor for XML data* (Tech. Rep. No. MSCIS 99-26). Philadelphia: University of Pennsylvania.

Marahrens, I. (2003). *Performace- und EffizienzAnalyse verschiedener RPCVarianten.* Diploma thesis, Technical University of Braunschweig, Germany.

Mouat, A. (2002). *XML diff and patch utilities.* Cs4 dissertation, HeriotWatt University, Edinburgh, Scotland.

Shannon, C. E. (1948). A mathematical theory of communication. *Bell System Technical Journal, 20*, 379-423.

SyncML specification, Version 1.0.1. (2001). Retrieved from http://www.openmobilealliance.org/syncml/

Tian, M., Voigt, T., Naumowicz, T., Ritter, H., & Schiller, J. (2003, July 3-4). Performance considerations for mobile web services. In *Proceedings of the IEEE Communication Society Workshop on Applications and Services in Wireless Networks*, Berne, Switzerland.

W3C. (2001, October 24). *XML information set* (W3C recommendation). Retrieved from http://www.w3.org/TR/2001/REC-xml-infoset-20011024/

W3C. (2006). *XML binary characterization* (W3C working group note). Retrieved from http://www.w3.org/TR/2005/NOTE-xbc-characterization-20050331/

Werner, C., Buschmann, C., Jäcker, T., & Fischer, S. (2006a). Bandwidth and latency considerations for efficient SOAP messaging. *International Journal of Web Service Research*, *3*(1), 49-67.

Werner, C., Buschmann, C., Brandt, Y., & Fischer, S. (2006b, September 18-22). Compressing SOAP Messages by using pushdown automata. In *Proceedings of IEEE International Conference on Web Services (ICWS'06)*. September 18-22, 2006. Chicago.

Chapter VI

Mobile Agents Meet Web Services

Cristian Mateos, ISISTAN, UNICEN-CONICET, Argentina

Alejandro Zunino, ISISTAN, UNICEN-CONICET, Argentina

Marcelo Campo, ISISTAN, UNICEN-CONICET, Argentina

Abstract

Web services standards provide the basis for interoperability, discovery and integra-
tion of distributed applications. Web services will enable mobile agents to better
use and exploit Web accessible applications and resources. However, there is a
lack of tools for integrating mobile agents and Web services. This chapter presents
MoviLog, a novel programming language for enabling mobile agents to consume
Web services. The most interesting aspect of the language is its reactive mobility
by failure mechanism that allows programmers to develop mobile agents without
explicitly providing code for handling mobility or Web services invocations.

Introduction

Many researchers envision the Web of the future as a global community where people and intelligent agents interact and collaborate (Hendler, 2001). Unfortunately, today's Web has been designed for human interpretation and use (McIlraith et al., 2001), generally for reading and browsing HTML pages and online form filling. However, there is a need for automating the interoperability of B2B (business-to-business) and e-commerce applications. Until now, this interoperation has been handled by using programs that interact with Web accessible services to obtain and then parse HTML content for extracting data. This approach is very weak since it depends on the format of the HTML pages, and the interfaces for accessing services (e.g., CGI or RMI). In order to achieve a truly automatic interoperability between programs and Web accessible resources, new technologies aim at creating a *Semantic Web* (Berners-Lee et al., 2001), where information and services offered by any site are described in a nonambiguous and computer-understandable way.

In the scenario of the Web consisting of sites with highly dynamic content, mobile users, unreliable links and small portable devices such as personal digital assistants (PDAs) and cellular phones, mobile agents will play a fundamental role (Hendler, 2001). A mobile agent is a computer program that represents a user in a computer network and is able to migrate autonomously from site to site to perform task on behalf of the user (Tripathi et al., 2002). This feature is particularly interesting when an agent makes sporadic use of a valuable shared resource located at a remote site. In addition, efficiency can be improved by moving agents to a host to query large repositories and then return with the results, thus avoiding multiple interactions with the data over network links subjected to delays or interruptions of services.

Mobile agents exhibit a number of properties that make them suitable for exploiting the potential of the Web, because they add mobility—the capacity to migrate across sites of a network (Fuggetta et al., 1998)—to common capacities of ordinary intelligent agents such as reaction, perception, deliberation and autonomy. Some of the most significant advantages of mobile agents are their support for disconnected operations, heterogeneous systems integration, robustness and fault-tolerance (Lange & Oshima, 1999; Milojicic et al., 1999).

Despite the number of applications that can be benefited from the usage of mobile agents (Kotz & Gray, 1999), this technology has shown difficulties when used for interacting with Web content (Hendler, 2001). Agents' inability to understand concepts required for invoking and using Web accessible services and resources requires the creation of a Semantic Web, where content is described according to precise semantics. In this sense, we claim that there is a need for a mobile agent development tool for solving these problems which preserve, at the same time, the key benefits of mobile agent technology.

A step towards the widespread adoption of mobile agents is MoviLog (Zunino et al., 2002). MoviLog is a platform for building Prolog-based (Bramer, 2005) intelligent mobile agents for the Web that provides a novel mechanism for handling mobility named reactive mobility by failure (RMF). This mechanism allows the programmer to exploit the advantages of mobility without explicitly programming mobile code.

In order to take advantage of the features of mobile agents for building Web applications, we have extended MoviLog to invoke Web services. This offers a great opportunity for building distributed applications based on intelligent mobile agents that access Web information and resources in an automatized form. For example, it will be possible to automate classic e-commerce applications such as e-shops, e-malls and e-actions, allowing automatic interaction between participating entities at both sides of each transaction, along with a minimal programming effort.

This chapter is structured as follows: The next section introduces Web services and the Semantic Web. Next, we describe the most relevant work. Then, MoviLog is briefly introduced. After that, we explain our approach for integrating MoviLog and Web services. Then, an agent implemented with MoviLog is described. Finally, conclusions and future work are presented.

Web Services and the Semantic Web

Unlike the current Web, Web services (Vaughan-Nichols, 2002) (i.e., Web accessible programs and devices) can be seen as a set of programs interacting in a network without human intervention. In order to enable programs to interchange data, it is necessary to define communication protocols, formats for data transfers, and specific points on which the communication will be established. Such definitions must be made in a rigorous way, preferably by using a computer-understandable language with well defined semantics.

Web services are a natural consequence of the evolution of the Web into a more open medium that facilitates complex and systematic interactions between applications (Curbera et al., 2001). A fundamental goal of Web services is to provide a common representation of the applications that use different communication protocols and interaction models. A natural approach to cope with this is to decouple the abstract descriptions of application functionality from the interaction model involved, and then representing such descriptions in a common language that can be interpreted by every single application.

The technological backbone of Web services is based on standardization efforts centered on extensible markup language (XML) (W3C Consortium, 2000). XML is a markup language for handling structured data that extends and formalizes HTML. Additionally, the W3C Consortium have developed simple object access protocol

(SOAP) (W3C Consortium, 2003a), a communication protocol entirely based on XML. Nowadays, SOAP has become the most ubiquitous protocol for applications that interact with Web services.

One of the most-used languages for Web service representation is WSDL (W3C Consortium, 2003b). WSDL is an XML-based language that allows developers to create Web service descriptions as a set of functions that operate with SOAP messages. From a WSDL specification, a program can autonomously determine the services of a Web site and how to invoke and use these services. As a complement to WSDL, universal description, discovery and integration (UDDI) (OASIS Consortium, 2004) has been developed. UDDI provides mechanisms for publishing and searching service descriptions written in WSDL. The weak point of this infrastructure is that it does not take into account the semantics of each service. Some languages for solving these problems are resource description framework (RDF) (W3C Consortium, 2004) and ontology Web language (OWL) (Horrocks, 2005). RDF can be used to bind attributes to Web accessible resources and to link these resources between them. OWL extends RDF support for high-level resource descriptions. A step towards the creation of a standard service ontology is OWL-S (DAML Coalition, 2006).

Related Work

Web services are a suitable model for the systematic interaction of Web applications and the integration of legacy platforms and environments. A few years ago, technology for supporting automatic interactions between Web applications has started to emerge, first with the development of automated e-commerce and B2B transactions, and more recently, with the creation of large-scale resource sharing infrastructures for grid computing (Foster & Kesselman, 2003).

Grid computing is mainly centered around the *computational Grid* concept (Foster et al., 2001): A distributed computing infrastructure whose goal is to provide safe and coordinated computational resource sharing between organizations. In this context, Web services play a fundamental role, since they give a satisfactory solution to the problem of heterogeneous systems integration, which is a fundamental requirement of almost every grid-based application.

Another good solution to tackle down heterogeneous systems integration problems in grid applications is to employ mobile agents. This technology, besides being heterogeneous by nature, also makes for efficient use of hardware and software resources, due to location awareness capabilities of mobile agents. Moreover, mobile agent technology represents a powerful paradigm for developing heterogeneous applications that use Web resources, especially when these applications are designed as a set of agents interacting with the various services offered by the Semantic Web.

Many agent-based tools for programming the Semantic Web can be found in the literature. Some examples relevant to our work are ConGolog (McIlraith et al., 2001), IG-JADE-PKSLib (Martínez & Lespérance, 2004) and CALMA (Chuah et al., 2004). Roughly speaking, these tools aim at simplifying the development of intelligent agents which interact with Web services. However, ConGolog and IG-JADE-PKSLib do not support agent mobility. Furthermore, neither IG-JADE-PKSLib nor CALMA provide facilities for handling ontological information about Web services. In addition, IG-JADE-PKSLib agents present serious performance and scalability problems, as we have shown in (Mateos et al., 2006a).

A lot of work has also been concerned with providing frameworks and platforms for materializing Web services as mobile agents. For instance, Ishikawa et al. (2004) propose a framework for implementing mobile Web services, which run on a JAVA-based mobile agent platform named Bee-Gent. However, Bee-Gent lacks support for common agent requirements such as knowledge representation, reasoning and high-level communication. On the other hand, proposals like (Bellavista et al., 2005) and (Adaçal & Bener, 2006) are more focused on interfacing mobile agents with Web services standard technology. The first one is concerned with achieving interoperability of legacy mobile agent middlewares, whereas the latter one aims at adapting server-side Web services for mobile devices by using mobile agents. In either case, it is not clear to what extent implementation of mobility and service-agent interaction functionality is done automatically by the framework. Finally, another interesting work is the one presented in (Zahreddine & Mahmoud, 2005), where an agent-based approaches to leverage composite mobile Web services to mobile devices is proposed.

As we will explain, the utmost goal of MoviLog is to simplify the construction of Web-aware mobile agents. Unlike previous work, MoviLog exploits the notion of RMF for seamlessly integrating mobile agents with Web resources, while providing scalability, flexibility and ease of programming. The next section takes a closer look at the MoviLog language.

MoviLog

MoviLog (Zunino et al., 2002) is a platform for building intelligent mobile agents, based on a strong mobility model (Fuggetta et al., 1998), where agents' execution state is transferred on migration. MoviLog is an extension of JavaLog (Amandi et al., 2005), a framework for agent-oriented programming.

MoviLog takes advantage of the benefits of both Java and Prolog since it is built as an extension of JavaLog. At one hand, Prolog is an adequate alternative for representing agents' mental states, and building reasoning algorithms (Amandi et al., 2005). On the other hand, Java has good features for supporting low-level code migration, such as platform independence, multi-thread support and object serialization (Wong et al., 1999).

In order to provide mobility across sites, each MoviLog host has to execute a MARlet (mobile agent resource). A MARlet is a Java servlet (Hunter & Crawford, 2001) that encapsulates a Prolog inference engine and provides services to access it. In this way, a MARlet represents an execution environment for mobile agents, or *brainlets* in MoviLog terminology. Additionally, a MARlet is able to provide intelligent services under demand, such as modifying the content of the main inference engine logic database or perform logic queries. In this sense, a MARlet can be used as an inference server for agents and external Web applications.

Besides providing basic strong mobility primitives to Brainlets, the most important aspect of MoviLog is the notion of reactive mobility by failure (RMF) (Zunino et al., 2005), a mechanism not exploited by any other tool for programming mobile agents. This mechanism states that when certain predicates previously declared in the code of a Brainlet fail, MoviLog transparently moves the Brainlet and its execution state to another site that contains definitions for that predicate, thus making local use of those definitions later. For instance, the following code implements a Brainlet whose behavior is programmed by the rules included in the CLAUSES section:

PROTOCOLS

protocol(a, 2)

CLAUSES

b(Y):- ...

?- a(X,Y), b(Y).

The section "Protocols" states that every clause whose functor is a and arity is 2 will be treated by RMF.[1] In this way, when the evaluation of $a(X,Y)$ fails, the agent will be transferred to a site that contains definitions for the clause. Then, in case of a successful evaluation at the remote site, the algorithm will try to solve $b(Y)$, according to the standard Prolog evaluation algorithm; otherwise the evaluation of ?- will fail, due to the failure of $a(X,Y)$.

The next example presents a simple brainlet whose goal is to first collect temperature values generated at different measurement sites, and then calculate the average of these values. Each measurement point is represented by a MoviLog site running a process which store on a regular basis its measure T in the local Prolog database, in the form of a *temperature(T)* predicate. The code that implements the brainlet is:

PROTOCOLS

protocol(temperature, 1)

CLAUSES

```
average(List, Avg):- ...
getTemp(Curr, List):- temperature(T), thisSite(S),
            M = measure(T, S), not (member(M, Curr)),
            getTemp([M|Curr], List).
getTemp(Curr, Curr).
average(Avg):- getTemp([], List), average(List, Avg).

?- average(Avg).
```

The idea of the program is to force the brainlet to visit all the measurement sites, asking the temperature to each one of them, and then computing the average of those values. The potential activation point of RMF has been highlighted in the code. As the reader can see, the "Protocols" section defines that *temperature(T)* must be evaluated by RMF. As a consequence, if the evaluation of that clause fails at a site S (the brainlet has already obtained the measure) MoviLog will transfer the brainlet to a site that contains another temperature. The evaluation of *getTemp* will end successfully once all sites offering clauses *temperature(T)* have been visited.It is worth noting that the example shows two clear limitations of MoviLog. First, it only uses mobility for evaluating non-local clauses. This may cause performance problems and inefficient usage of system resources. Consider for instance the situation of a large brainlet that requires a small Prolog clause. Clearly, moving the clause to the site where the Brainlet executes requires less bandwidth usage than the opposite approach. In addition, protocols let the programmer to specify the points of the code that will be treated by RMF. Nevertheless, it is necessary to extend the current protocol mechanism to instruct RMF to use some remote invocation mechanism for accessing resources in addition to mobility. In the next section, we expose an approach for solving the mentioned problems.

MoviLog and Web Services

MoviLog is based on RMF, a novel mobility model that reduces the effort for developing mobile agents by automating decisions about mobility, such as when and where to migrate (Zunino et al., 2005). Despite the advantages RMF has shown, it is not adequate for developing Web enabled applications where a mix of mobility and remote invocation is required. This section shows an approach to overcome these issues.

Basically, RMF and its runtime support have been adapted to provide integration with the Semantic Web. This support enables MoviLog agents to interact with Web resources to perform their tasks, which makes MoviLog more useful as a mobile agent programming language. Nevertheless, to accomplish this adaptation the following problems were solved:

- **RMF extension:** It was necessary to extend the resource description mechanism used by MoviLog in order to describe Web resources and the way an agent accesses to a certain resource instance. In this sense, proper methods for accessing Web resources (apart from mobility) has been added, such as remote invocation, for the case of Web services, and copy of resources between sites, for the case of Web information retrieval.

- **Automated resource access:** MoviLog should provide an environment for agent execution which automates certain decisions related to resource access and, at the same time, let the programmer define policies for making these decisions. Custom decisions are made based on system metrics, such as network traffic, distance between sites, CPU load or available RAM at a site, among others. In this way, the programmer is able to specify *intelligent* decision mechanisms for accessing resources, thus potentially improving the usage of system resources.

- **Web Service semantics:** To achieve a truly automated interaction of agents and Semantic Web services, each agent has to understand the *meaning* of a Web Service. To do so, we have extended MoviLog to handle ontologies expressed in OWL.

Each one of the items exposed is essential for an effective integration of MoviLog to the Semantic Web. In the next three subsections, we will explain the approaches used in each case.

RMF Extension

In MoviLog, a protocol defines the format of the prolog clauses (i.e., functor and arity) which will trigger the migration of an agent when the site where the agent is currently executing does not contain a definition for any of those clauses. The protocol definition mechanism has been extended to describe more classes of resources that an agent might need to accomplish its goals. Particularly, a single prolog clause can be considered as a resource that agents access on a certain point of their execution. In fact, (Zunino et al., 2005) defines *failure* as the impossibility of an executing agent to obtain some required *resource* at the current site.

A MoviLog resource is composed of a name, and a set of properties, which vary on each resource (for example, functor and arity for a clause-like resource; user, password and database name for a database connection). As we saw, the programmer declares the need for accessing a resource (in a certain point of an agent's code) by adding a protocol into a special section of the program. This protocol contains the mentioned resource name and properties.

The first version of MoviLog (Zunino et al., 2002) proposes to move a brainlet every time an agent requests access to a resource unavailable at the current site. Although mobility is an effective method for accessing resources, performance of agents may suffer if migration is not performed in an intelligent way. For example, consider the case where the size of a brainlet is greater than the size of a requested resource. Clearly, it would be more convenient to get a copy of the resource from the remote site instead of moving the agent to that site. In this case the requested resource is a Web service, the proper access method is to remotely invoke the service, thus transferring only the (potentially small) service arguments and results. Finally, the interaction of an agent with a large remote database can be accomplished only by moving the agent to the remote site, and then locally interacting with the resource. In this case, database access by copy is unacceptable due to the great transfer cost over the network.

The ideas previously discussed show the need for adding extra mechanisms for accessing resources (apart from mobility) to MoviLog. As a consequence, performance can be improved by selecting the most adequate access method for the required resource (see section titled "Automated Resource Access"). Moreover, the methods that can be used for accessing a particular resource may depend on specific characteristics of it, such as its size, permissions, availability, and so forth. To solve this problem, each MoviLog resource is tagged with a type that allows agents to know what access methods can be used to obtain that resource.

Additional Mechanisms for Accessing Resources

In RMF, every time a resource required by an agent is not present at the current site, RMF transfers the agent and its execution state to any site that contains definitions for that resource. This process is performed iteratively along the agent lifetime.

As we mentioned earlier, it is necessary to consider other resource access methods in addition to mobility to avoid performance problems in the execution of brainlets and to make the best usage of network resources. In this sense, the MoviLog evaluation algorithm has been redesigned to support a number of new methods for accessing non-local resources (Figure 1). The goal of this task was to decouple an agent resource access request from the selected method to obtain that resource. The three access methods defined for enhancing MoviLog are:

- **Move:** Moves the agent to the site owning the resource. This implies to serialize the agent execution state and then send it to the remote site. At the remote site, the agent is restored from its serialized form and its execution continues. Let us consider, for instance, the case of an agent that interacts many times with a large remote database. In order to better access the database, it is convenient to migrate the agent to the remote site and use the data locally, thus avoiding wasting valuable bandwidth and time caused by numerous remote interactions with the database.

- **Fetch:** Transfers a resource from a remote site to the local site by copying it to a shared repository accessible by the agent. For example, if an agent needs a sorting algorithm, the code implementing this algorithm can be copied from a remote site to the current location of the agent.

- **Invoke:** Accesses the resource by sending a request to a server agent located at a remote site, then waiting until the results are received, and finally resuming the normal execution flow. This is the proper method to access Web services in MoviLog. This works as follows: The agent sends the name of the service and input parameters to a remote server agent; then this agent locally invokes the service and returns the results back to the client.

Figure 1 shows the steps that MoviLog performs for accessing resources. First, based on a protocol that describes a resource, the algorithm asks the MoviLog platform the list of sites offering that resource. Second, an effective access to the resource must be carried out, first selecting a candidate site from the resulting list of the previous step, and then performing the specific retrieval operation (copy, remote request or agent migration). Third, the agent execution state is updated according to the new conditions after successful access to the resource.

Figure 1. MoviLog non-local resource access mechanism

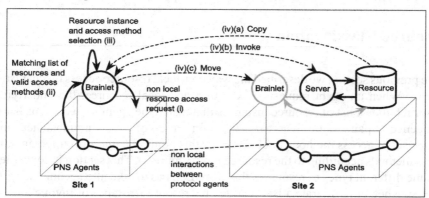

The brainlet evaluation algorithm works as follows: After a failure, the agent queries the platform for sites offering the required resource, thus obtaining a list of properties (resource type, availability, size, etc.) of the matching resource instances. Taking this list as an input, the algorithm creates a list of pairs $L=<a,b>$, where a represents the information associated to a resource instance and b, the valid methods for accessing that instance. For example, the platform does not consider the *fetch* method to access a large database. Based on the list L, the following actions are performed:

- **Select the specific instance to access:** The algorithm selects from the input list the source site from where the resource will be retrieved. In other words, the algorithm selects an element from the list of instances, leaving the remaining items as backtracking points to ensure completeness.

- **Select the access method:** The algorithm selects the access strategy that best adapts to current execution conditions (site load, available memory, network traffic, etc.), particular characteristics of the application (many or few interactions with the same remote resource) or even custom policies specified by the programmer (see section titled "Automated Resource Access"). Depending on these factors, the platform decides the method for accessing the resource.

Note that, in Figure 1 a new type of agent named protocol name server (PNS) is introduced. Basically, PNSs are stationary agents (i.e., nonmobile) whose goal is to help brainlets to handle failures.

Each host capable of hosting brainlets has one or more PNS agents. PNSs are responsible for managing information about protocols offered at their owner's site, and for returning the list of resource instances matching a given protocol under demand. A site offering resources register with its local PNSs the protocols associated with these resources. As a consequence, PNS agents announce the new protocols by broadcasting this information to other MoviLog-enabled sites of the network.

The next section describes further details of the approach.

Resource Classification

In the previous section we described the way non-local resource access mechanisms operate. When an agent requests access to a non-local resource, the underlying platform builds a list of resource instances that match the agent's needs. This list is a sequence of pairs <a,b>, where a is the information of a matching instance, and b is the set of access methods to obtain a. At this point, the platform filters invalid access methods according to the resource type (Figure 2). This section is concerned with the different types of resources that MoviLog has to take into account in order to select whether to migrate a Brainlet, fetch a resource instance or invoke it.

A resource can be classified as either *transferable* or *non-transferable*. A transferable resource can be freely copied from one site to another (e.g., a file or an environment variable), whereas a non-transferable resource remains in a site and cannot be transferred (e.g., a printer or a scanner). There are two kinds of transferable resources: *free* and *fixed*. Free resources can be moved across different sites; fixed resources represent data and devices whose transfer is non-viable (a large database) or undesired (private files, passwords, etc.). Unlike the former case, this last subdivision is done at the application level, and does not depend on the resource type at all.

In MoviLog, a Web service is a resource which represents a service invocation and access support through the Web. This support is composed of Java code that associates an executing Prolog clause requesting access to a Web service with the corresponding low-level SOAP request. In other words, such a Java code maps the service name and input parameters, which are Prolog data types, to their counterparts expressed as SOAP data types. Notice that this invocation support may not be present in every MoviLog site (i.e., every site is not capable of invoking Web services). Moreover, a MoviLog Web service is a non-transferable resource, since the Java code, which performs parameter mapping and low-level SOAP calls, is not copied between sites.

Prolog clauses represent free-transferable resources, since they are basically code that in most cases can be migrated. However, a MoviLog site may deny the transfer of a set of clauses; in this case, these clauses are viewed as fixed-transferable resources. The denial of a transfer could be as a result of one or more of the following reasons:

- If the estimated size of the set of clauses to transfer is too large, its transfer can be inefficient. For example, the transfer of a group of clauses that represents a long Prolog algorithm may not be allowed because of network traffic limitations.

- Some of the clauses have variables that are instantiated with non-serializable objects (i.e., values that are not translatable into a network-transferable format). In this case, the transfer of the resource is impossible.

Figure 2. Classification of resources accessible by mobile entities (Source: Vigna, 1998)

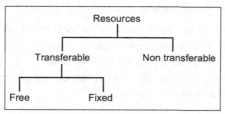

- The remote site has established security restrictions for the transfer of certain resources. Despite the set of clauses is free of the previous problems, there could be security limitations that yield in a denial of fetching-like operations on those clauses.

The MoviLog runtime system has been extended with built-in *classification policies* for dynamic categorization of resources, which are configured statically on each server. Thanks to this support, it is possible to specialize as much as is needed for the policy that categorizes a specific resource. At present, the basic MoviLog support for categorizing resources includes fixed policies, where the resource type is configured statically and do not vary along time, and variable policies, where the resource type is computed dynamically. In this sense, a MoviLog Web service resource has an associated fixed policy (i.e., the resource is always non-transferable), whereas a Prolog clause associated policy will determine the type dynamically (e.g., by running a code size estimation algorithm).

Automated Resource Access

The introduction of resource access policies to MoviLog evaluation algorithm bring some benefits that help automating agent execution. First, MoviLog can establish default policies for accessing resources in an efficient way. In addition, a flexible support for programming policies allows the agent developer to declare his own access decisions based on the requirements and characteristics of his application. The way MoviLog defines default access policies is similar to the way a programmer does (i.e., by picking the *best* resource from a list of candidate instances). The main difference is that programmers need some standard directives or commands to indicate to the platform what to do when accessing resources.

The basic elements upon which complex access rules are built are system metrics. MoviLog offers the programmer a number of prolog predicates that return the current value for a certain metric (CPU load, available memory, network traffic, proximity between sites, etc.). For example, the invocation to $freeMemory(Site, R)$ executes instead a prolog predicate which instantiates R with the amount of free memory at $Site$. Based upon this predicate, the programmer is able to create more complex policies. This is the case, for example, of an access rule which retrieves a required resource from the site with the highest amount of available RAM.

MoviLog's approach for access policies specification has two major benefits. On one hand, Prolog's declarative nature represents a great flexibility for declaring rule-based policies. On the other hand, it is possible for an agent to modify its access policies in a dynamic and intelligent way, since each policy is in fact a Prolog rule contained in the agent's private knowledge base.

Profiling

Having measures about different aspects of system performance suggests the need that every site on the MoviLog network must be able to manage this information. In this sense, each MoviLog site is responsible for getting and maintaining up-to-date values of system metrics, and also providing a profiling service interface according to programmers' needs. In short, each site provides precise measuring mechanisms for the following metrics:

- **CPU load:** It means the percentage of CPU utilization at some site. It is a useful measure under certain circumstances. For example, if a given resource can be obtained by both *fetch* and *move* methods, and the local CPU load is twice as the CPU load of the site of the resource, move method could be used, thus providing a simple strategy for balancing load across sites.

- **Remote CPU load:** It represents the CPU load at some remote site. Clearly, it is very difficult to have up-to-date values of CPU utilization from other sites, due to the highly dynamic nature of this metric and the potential delays on information transfer over the network. To solve this problem, every MoviLog site broadcast, on a regular basis, average information about CPU local utilization.

- **Free RAM:** It represents the percentage of RAM available for allocation at some site. Furthermore, remote free RAM metric (i.e., available memory at a remote site) is computed similarly to remote CPU load.

- **Transfer rate:** This metric means the current speed of the outcoming communication links, and can be obtained by using typical operating system commands (e.g., Unix *ping*). Having measures about network transfer speed is crucial to decide whether migrating agents or fetching resources, or even invoking services remotely. In most cases, this latter will generate the least amount of data to be transferred, consequently improving agent execution performance.

- **Communication reliability:** It represents the percentage of the information lost during transfer through the network.

- **Proximity between sites:** It is a metric mostly related to network topology, and computes the distance (measured in number of hops) from the local host to some node of the network. Basically, this metric gives an approximated value of the transfer delay of information over the network.

- **Number of executing agents:** It is closely related to CPU load, especially when each agent is doing CPU intensive work (i.e., it is neither blocked nor waiting for some notification or signal). This value, which can be obtained by asking the local agent execution engine, gives an approximate idea of the CPU and memory utilization. Also, the number of executing agents at some site can be estimated in a similar way in which remote CPU load is computed.

- **Agent size:** This metric represents the estimated size in bytes of the allocated memory space for an executing agent (i.e., the allocated RAM for the agent code and execution state). It is a useful metric to help making decisions on whether or not to migrate an agent, depending of its size and the current network transfer speed. Similarly, this metric can be applied to estimate the size of a resource. In this way, complex access policies that decide whether to migrate an agent or fetch a resource based on each one's size can be declared.

Table 1 summarizes the metrics described previously. The programmer is allowed to use predefined predicates, which compute the metrics in order to declare complex decision rules for accessing resources. These rules have to be included in a special section of the Brainlet code with a unique name and the decision behaviour concerning what instance to select, given a candidate list, and what access method to apply to get that instance. In order to activate a rule, one or more declared protocols have to be associated with the rule name. Then, when the access to the protocol fails, MoviLog searches for similar resources and picks one of them according to the decision made by the rule configured for the protocol.

Web Services Semantics

The effective use of Web services requires both agents and applications to be integrated with legacy Web infrastructure. Nevertheless, the implementation of this integration would be impossible, unless those services are represented in an agent-understandable semantic language (Kagal et al., 2003).

Table 1. System metrics supported by MoviLog

Category	Metric name
Processor and memory	CPU load
	Remote CPU load
	Free RAM
	Remote free RAM
Network	Transfer rate
	Communication reliability
	Proximity between sites
Agent-related	Number of executing agents
	Agent size

A solution to the problem of interoperation between intelligent agents and Web services is to use structured descriptions of the concepts included in a service. These descriptions specify *what* functionality the service provides but not *how* to do it. In this way, agents interact with Web services at the application level, by understanding abstract descriptions that are enough to express services functionality and intended purpose.

The use of Web content description languages offers some advantages for functionality-based discovery of Web services, which permits automatic interaction between agents and services. Service discovery is an inherently semantic problem, because it must abstract the superficial differences between the offered services and the requested ones, so semantic similarities of these two can be recognized. To cope with this problem, utilization of OWL-S over UDDI has recently been proposed, thus creating a powerful infrastructure for Web Service discovery based on the functionality they provide (Srinivasan et al., 2004; Srinivasan et al., 2006).

In order to provide a truly automated interaction with the Semantic Web, each MoviLog agent has to understand the exact meaning of a Web service. To make this possible, we have extended MoviLog to handle ontologies written in OWL Lite, a dialect of OWL for metadata annotation. The most interesting aspect of OWL Lite for our work is that it is easily translatable to Prolog, since it has description logic equivalent semantics, which is a decidable fragment of first-order logic (Baader et al., 2003). Consequently, it is possible to make automatic inferences from a translated OWL Lite ontology and using traditional theorem provers. The reader should remember here that MoviLog agents identify resources through protocols, which are Prolog rules, thus inferences with respect to an OWL Lite ontology expressed as prolog rules can be done.

From this line of research we have already obtained encouraging results. Particularly, we have integrated MoviLog with Apollo (Mateos et al., 2006b), an infrastructure for semantic matching and discovery of Web services. Apollo includes a prolog-based reasoner implemented as a set of rules for computing semantic likeness between OWL Lite-annotated services. This support is used by MoviLog agents in order to determine the set of Web services which best suit their service request.

An Example

In this section we describe in detail an application coded in MoviLog. The application consists of a travel agent whose responsibility is to arrange an itinerary across a number of cities, making the necessary bookings for hotel rooms and airplane tickets to complete the overall trip. The application scenario is situated at a tourism company that sells different tourist packages and manages all these sellings with a mobile agent-based system. Every time a client wishes to buy a package, an agent is asked to plan an adequate itinerary between the requested origin and destination, along with the corresponding hotel rooms and airplane tickets reservations. It is assumed that both hotel and airline companies involved in the process provide support for Web services for booking rooms and tickets, respectively.

A high level view of the tasks performed by each actor involved in the selling process is shown in Figure 3. Upon receipt of a new request, the travel agent construct an itinerary based on the client preferences such as the desired intermediate cities and the number of days he plans to stay at each one of them. For every stopover of the resulting itinerary, the agent books a flight on any airline according to planned dates in advance. Similarly, the agent books the necessary hotel rooms. Finally, the entire schedule and reservations are returned back to the client, and the transaction is recorded in a database.

From Figure 3 we can see that the travel agent interacts with two kind of resources along its lifetime. First, the agent books rooms and tickets by invoking *Web services* published by hotel and airline companies. Once the request has been successfully served, the agent must register the transaction in a specific company database, so it will need to establish a *connection* to the mentioned database and then store the data. The words in italic represent resources that the agent needs to achieve its goal. In others words, when an executing agent fails to access a *Web Service* or a *database connection* at the current site, RMF will automatically handle this failure, trying to locate and access similar resources owned by other sites.

The code implementing the travel agent is shown in the "protocols" portion. For simplicity, date and time-related information are not taken into account during the

Figure 3. A tourist package construction process

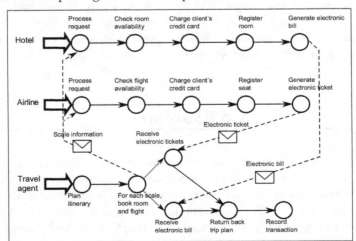

reservation process. For the same reason, the program does not handle exceptions that might be thrown by a Web service, such as insufficient credit card balance, unavailability of rooms or tickets, and so on.

PROTOCOLS

```
protocol('data-base-connection,' [dbName('sellings')], 'dbPolicy').
protocol('web-service,' [name('bookFlight')], 'wsPolicy').
protocol('web-service,' [name('bookHotelRoom')], 'wsPolicy').
```

POLICIES

```
accessWith('dbPolicy,' [ResourceID, Site], 'move', _, 'move'):-
    CPULoad(Site, Load), Load <= 50.
sourceFrom('wsPolicy', [ID1,Site1], [ID2,Site2], Result):-

    leastCPUUsage(Site1, Site2, Result).
```

CLAUSES

```
leastCPUUsage(Site1, Site2, Site1):-
    CPULoad(Site1, Load1),
    CPULoad(Site2, Load2),
    Load1 <= Load2, ! .
leastCPUUsage(_, Site2, Site2).
scheduleCircuit(Origin, Destination, Cities, Schedule):- ...
bookFlightsAndHotelRooms([Destination], [], 0).
bookFlightsAndHotelRooms([C1Info,C2Info|Cities],[SchInfo|Sch],Cost):-
    C1Info = city-info(City1, DaysAtCity1),

    C2Info = city-info(City2, DaysAtCity2),

    web-service([name('bookFlight'), input([from(City1),to(City2)])], FlightInfo),
    web-service([name('bookHotelRoom'),
                    input([location(City2),days(DaysAtCity2)])], HotelInfo),
    FlightInfo = [cost(TicketCost), ticket(Ticket), airline(Airline)],
    HotelInfo = [cost(RoomCost), number(RoomNumber), hotel(Hotel)],
    ScheduleInfo = [FlightInfo, HotelInfo],
    bookFlightsAndHotelRooms([City2Info—Cities], Schedule, SubCost),
    TempCost is SubCost + TicketCost,
    Cost is TempCost + RoomCost.
storeTransaction(Schedule, Cost):-
    data-base-connection([dbName('sellings')], Connection),

    storeTransaction(Schedule, Cost, Connection),
    closeDBConnection(Connection).
storeTransaction(Schedule, Cost, Connection):- ...
```

```
closeDBConnection(Connection):- ...
? -doService(Origin, Dest, Cities, Schedule, Cost):-
    scheduleCircuit(Origin, Dest, Cities, Circuit),
    bookFlightsAndHotelRooms(Circuit, Sch, Cost),
    storeTransaction(Sch, Cost).
```

The code is composed of three sections. The section "Protocols" declares the agent protocols (i.e., descriptions) of those resources whose failure may trigger RMF. Three protocols have been declared: A connection to the company's database (whose name is *sellings*), a service for flight booking (*bookFlight*) and a service for hotel booking (*bookHotelRoom*). Notice that the last two protocols are declared in a way that they are independent from the particular airline or hotel providing those services.

The "Policies" section defines the strategies for accessing the resources. Two policies for accessing database connections and booking services, namely *dbPolicy* and *wsPolicy*, have been declared. The first one states that an agent will move to any site *S* providing database connections only if the CPU load at *S* is less or equal than 50%, otherwise any other alternative method for accessing the resource will be used. On the other hand, *wsPolicy* adds restrictions about the source to be contacted for invoking Web services. In this case, given two different sites with Web services invocation support, the one with the least current CPU usage will be chosen. It is worth mentioning that *CPULoad* is a profiling predicate that returns the current CPU usage at some site. Both policies could have been implemented by using other profiling predicates such as those related to the performance and transfer rates of the outcoming communication links.

Finally, the section "Clauses" implements the travel agent's behaviour as a set of Prolog rules. The rule *?-doService* constructs an itinerary across different cities (code not shown), then makes the reservations, and finally stores the results. The lines of code in bold are potential activation points of RMF. When the execution of the code reaches a clause whose functor and first argument match any declared protocol, that clause is not further evaluated according to the standard prolog evaluation algorithm. In such case, the clause is interpreted as a request to access some resource that is described by the mentioned protocol.

At this point, the reader may be wondering how MoviLog can access a resource from just a simple Prolog call. In other words, how MoviLog maps a call of the form *resource-name*($[property_1, property_2, ..., property_n], arg_1, arg_2, ..., arg_m$) to the desired resource instance. Every protocol published by a MoviLog site is composed of a name, a unique identifier, a list of properties and a local Prolog clause, the last of which implements the resource access functionality. In the case of a Web service resource, this clause performs the service invocation itself and then returns the results back, whereas for a database connection resource its associated clause will create an object that represents that connection (e.g., a JDBC object), check if the agents have permissions, and finally return the connection. In other words, each one of these kinds of clauses implements the access tasks that depend on the type of the specific resource instance described by the associated protocol. Also, each protocol defines the way a runtime instantiated Prolog clause maps to its resource access clause. Therefore, effective resource access is fully transparent to the programmer, due to the fact that the MoviLog platform binds at runtime each argument arg_i of the current executing clause with the results given by the specific resource access clause.

Conclusion and Future Work

Web services enable the construction of new types of applications characterized by their ability to interact with Web-accessible services through standard protocols. The extensions of Web services with semantics aim at realizing a dream where programs autonomously use the vast amounts of resources present on the Web. In this complex, rich computational environment, intelligent mobile agents will have a fundamental role due to their capacity to infer, learn, act and move.

Our research aims at providing tools for building intelligent agents that autonomously interact and live within the WWW. JavaLog is a programming language that supports the basic bricks for constructing intelligent agents. MoviLog adds flexible and usable support for reactive mobility to JavaLog. We have described in this chapter an approach for integrating MoviLog with Web services.

The main difference between MoviLog and others platforms for mobile agents is twofold. First, its support for reactive mobility by failure dramatically reduces development effort by automatizing agent and resource mobility decisions. Second, it permits to transparently invoke Semantic Web services, which enables the construction of Semantic Web-aware mobile agents with little coding effort.

We are currently working on improving the way MoviLog sites manage protocol and profiling information in order to achieve better scalability. Until now, we have experienced some problems when the number of sites or even the amount of interchanged information increase. A step towards addressing this issue is GMAC (Gotthelf et al., 2005), a multicast-based communication protocol specially designed for MoviLog. It is important to note that this idea is still being explored.

Finally, although the description of the RMF support for agent and resource mobility were circumscribed to MoviLog, the mechanism can be further applied to other programming languages and contexts. In fact, we have implemented a prototype RMF-based mobile agent platform for the Java language. The middle-term goal from this line of research is to isolate as much as possible RMF from the programming language involved, so to provide mobility at the middleware level in other contexts besides the Semantic Web, such as those related to grid computing.

References

Adaçal, M., & Bener, A. B. (2006). Mobile Web services: A new agent-based framework. *IEEE Internet Computing, 10*(3), 58-65.

Amandi, A., Campo, M., & Zunino, A. (2005). JavaLog: A framework-based integration of java and prolog for agent-oriented programming. *Computer Languages, Systems and Structures, 31*(1),17-33.

Baader, F., Calvanese, D., McGuinness, D., Nardi, D., & Patel-Schneider, P. (2003). *The description logic handbook: theory, implementation, and applications.* Cambridge University Press.

Bellavista, P., Corradi, A., & Monti, S. (2005). Integrating Web services and mobile agent systems. In *Proceedings of the 1ˢᵗ International Workshop on Services and Infrastructure for the Ubiquitous and Mobile Internet (SIUMI) (ICDCSW 2005)* (Vol. 3, pp. 283-290).

Berners-Lee, T., Hendler, J., & Lassila, O. (2001). The Semantic Web. *Scientific American, 284*(5), 34-43.

Bramer, M. (2005). *Logic Programming with Prolog*. New York: Springer-Verlag.

Chuah, S. H, Loke, S. W., Krishnaswamy S., & Sumartono, A. (2004, July 20). CALMA: Context-aware lightweight mobile BDI agents for ubiquitous computing. In *Proceedings of the Workshop on Agents for Ubiquitous Computing (UbiAgents 2004)*. NY: Morgan-Kaufmann Publishers.

Curbera, F., Nagy, W. A., & Weerawarana, S. (2001). Web services: Why and how. In *Proceedings of the Workshop on Object-Oriented Web Services (OOPSLA 2001)*, Tampa, FL. ACM Press.

DAML Coalition. (2006). *OWL-S 1.2 pre-release*. Retrieved from http://www.daml. org/services/owl-s

Foster, I., Kesselman, C., & Tuecke, S. (2001). The anatomy of the grid: Enabling scalable virtual organization. *The International Journal of High Performance Computing Applications, 15*(3), 200-222.

Foster, I. & Kesselman, C. (2003). *The grid 2: Blueprint for a new computing infrastructure*. Morgan-Kaufmann Publishers.

Fuggetta, A., Picco, G. P., & Vigna, G. (1998). Understanding code mobility. *IEEE Transactions on Software Engineering*, *24*(5), 342-361.

Gotthelf, P., Mendoza, M., Zunino, A., & Mateos, C. (2005, September 1-2). GMAC: An overlay multicast network for mobile agents. In *The 34ᵗʰ JAIIO Proceedings of the VI Argentine Symposium on Computing Technology (AST)*, Rosario, Santa Fé, Argentina.

Hendler, J. (2001). Agents and the Semantic Web. *IEEE Intelligent Systems*, *16*(2), 30-36.

Hunter, J., & Crawford, W. (2001). *Java servlet programming*. O'Reilly & Associates, Inc.

Horrocks, I. (2005). OWL: A description logic based ontology language. In P. Beek (Ed.), *Principles and Practice of Constraint Programming (CP 2005)* (LNCS 3709, pp. 5-8). Springer.

Ishikawa, F., Yoshioka, N., Tahara Y., & Honiden, S. (2004). Behavior descriptions of mobile agents for Web services integration. In *Proceedings of the IEEE International Conference on Web Services* (pp. 342-349).

Kagal, L., Perich, F., Chen, H., Tolia, S., Zou, Y., Finin, T., et al. (2003). Agents making sense of the Semantic Web. In W. Truszkowski, C. Rouff, & M. G. Hinchey (Eds.), *Innovative concepts for agent-based systems* (LNCS 2564, pp. 417-433). Springer.

Kotz, D., & Gray, R. S. (1999). Mobile agents and the future of the Internet. *ACM Operating Systems Review*, *33*(3), 7-13.

Lange, D. B., & Oshima, M. (1999). Seven good reasons for mobile agents. *Communications of the ACM*, *42*(3), 88-89.

Martínez, E., & Lespérance, Y. (2004, July 19-23). IG-JADE-PKSlib: An agent-based framework for advanced Web service composition and provisioning. In *Proceedings of the Workshop on Web Services and Agent-Based Engineering* (pp. 2-10). NY: Morgan-Kaufmann Publishers.

Mateos, C., Zunino, A., & Campo, M. (2006a). Extending MoviLog for supporting Web services. *Computer Languages, Systems and Structures* (in press). Elsevier Science.

Mateos, C., Crasso, M., Zunino, A., & Campo, M. (2006b). Adding Semantic Web services matching and discovery support to the MoviLog platform. In M. Bramer (Ed.), *Artificial intelligence in theory and practice, IFIP International Federation for Information Processing*. Springer.

McIlraith, S., Son, T. C., & Zeng, H. (2001). Semantic Web services. *IEEE Intelligent Systems, Special Issue on the Semantic Web*, *16*(2),46-53.

Milojicic, D., Douglis, F., & Wheeler, R.(1999). *Mobility: Processes, computers, and agents*. Reading, MA: Addison-Wesley.

OASIS Consortium. (2004). *UDDI, Version 3.0.2.* Retrieved from http://uddi. org/pubs/uddi_v3.htm

Srinivasan, N., Paolucci M., & Sycara, K. (2004). An efficient algorithm for OWL-S based semantic search in UDDI. In J. Cardoso & A. Sheth (Eds.), *Semantic Web Services and Web Process Composition: Proceedings of the First International Workshop (SWSWPC 2004)*, San Diego, CA (LNCS 3387, pp. 96-110). Springer.

Srinivasan, N., Paolucci M., & Sycara, K. (2006). Semantic Web service discovery in the OWL-S IDE. In *Proceedings of 39th Hawaii International Conference on Systems Science* (Vol. 6, p. 109b).

Tripathi, A. R., Karnik, N. M., Ahmed, T., Singh, R. D., Prakash, A., Kakani, V., et al. (2002). Design of the ajanta system for mobile agent programming. *Journal of Systems and Software, 62*(2), 123-140.

Vaughan-Nichols, S. J. (2002). Web services: Beyond the hype. *Computer, 35*(2), 18-21.

Vigna, G. (1998). *Mobile code technologies, paradigms, and applications.* PhD thesis, Politecnico di Milano, Milano, Italy.

W3C Consortium. (2000). *Extensible markup language (XML), Version 1.0* (W3C recommendation, 2nd ed.). Retrieved from http://www.w3.org/TR/2000/REC-xml-20001006

W3C Consortium. (2003a). *SOAP: Primer, Version 1.2, Part 0* (W3C recommendation). Retrieved from http://www.w3.org/TR/2003/REC-soap12-part0-20030624/

W3C Consortium. (2003b). *Web services description language (WSDL), Version 1.2* (W3C working draft). Retrieved from http://www.w3.org/TR/2003/WD-wsdl12-20030303/

W3C Consortium. (2004). *RDF primer* (W3C recommendation). Retrieved from http://www.w3.org/TR/rdf-primer

Wong, D., Paciorek, N., & Moore, D. (1999). Java-based mobile agents. *Communications of the ACM, 42*(3), 92-102.

Zahreddine, W., & Mahmoud, Q. (2005). An agent-based approach to composite mobile Web services. In *Proceedings of the 19th International Conference on Advanced Information Networking and Application* (pp. 189-192). IEEE Computer Society.

Zunino, A., Campo, M., & Mateos, C. (2002). Simplifying mobile agent development through reactive mobility by failure. In G. Bittencourt & G. Ramalho (Eds.), *Advances in Artificial Intelligence: Proceedings of the 16th Brazilian Symposium on Artificial Intelligence (SBIA 2002)*, Brazil (LNCS 2507, pp.163-174). Springer.

Zunino, A., Campo, M., & Mateos, C. (2005). Reactive mobility by failure: When fail means move. In G. Tayi & S. S. Ravi (Eds.) *Information Systems Frontiers, Special Issue on Mobile Computing and Communications: Systems, Models and Applications* (pp. 141-154). Kluwer Academic Publishers

Endnote

1   For a comprehensive introduction to Prolog see http://www.coli.uni-saarland. de/~kris/learn-prolog-now

Chapter VII

RAWS & UWAS:
Reflective and Adaptable Web Services Running on the Universal Web Application Server

Javier Parra-Fuente, Oxford University, UK

Salvador Sánchez-Alonso, University of Alcala, Spain

Marta Fernández-Alarcón, Pontifical University of Salamanca, Spain

Abstract

Reflection is a powerful technology that allows us to produce auto-adaptable soft-ware. RAWS is a reflective, multilevel Web service architecture aimed at allowing a Web service to transform its structure and behaviour without the need of human intervention to change the source code, compile it or deploy it again on the applica-tion server. Using RAWS, the Web service can change itself automatically. Current application servers have a very important limitation: The deployment platform (J2EE, .NET, etc.). Using current servers, a Web service or application can only be deployed on a server which runs with the same technology. To solve this drawback, we have developed universal Web application server (UWAS), a platform capable of deploying Web services or applications written in any object-oriented language or for any platform. This is possible thanks to the fact that UWAS internally uses a language-independent object-oriented Web server markup language (OOWSML) representation based on XML. Altogether, RAWS & UWAS make it possible to deploy a Web service on the server regardless of its implementation technology, providing the flexibility to automatically adapt or transform the Web service structure and/or behaviour.

Introduction

Web services are programmable components of applications that use SOAP (Gudgin et al., 2003) as an access protocol, regardless of their client and component technology (a drawback in DCOM) and regardless of the language in which both communication ends are written (a drawback in RMI). SOAP generally uses the HTTP transport protocol over the port 80 for request/response, thus crossing corporate firewalls (a drawback in CORBA or DCOM) and facilitating the interoperability of applications that work with different technologies.

Currently, the modification of a Web service implies the availability, edition, recompilation and redeployment of the source code. Depending on the application server, the deployment can either be a simple task or a very complicated work. If the application server supports the dynamic load of applications, then the deployment will be simple task; but if that is not the case, it will imply to stop the execution of the Web service, replacing the old version with the new one, and deploying the new version.

Reflection is a property of computational systems that allows them to reason and act by themselves and to modify their behavior (Maes, 1987). Although this concept has been successfully applied to other fields, such as distributed systems (Ledoux, 1999; McAffer, 1995), concurrent programming (Masuhara, Matsouka, & Yonezawa, 1993), aspect-oriented programming (Pawlak, Duchien, & Florin, 1999; Tanter et. al., 2003), its application to Web services design has not been addressed yet. Reflection can be applied to Web services in order to enhance their adaptability and flexibility. We propose in this chapter a Web service reflective architecture, RAWS, which dynamically modifies a Web service during its execution.

In this chapter, we introduce the basic concepts of reflection that will be applied to Web services (the introspective characteristics and the analysis of the structural and behavioral reflection of the Web service), the architecture model of a reflective and adaptable Web service, and the automatic generation mechanism to obtain the reflective infrastructure needed for a Web service to be dynamically adaptable.

Nowadays, J2EE and .NET are the most commonly used platforms to code Web services or applications. Web application/service servers are J2EE or .NET servers. A J2EE-coded Web service must be recoded to be able to be deployed on a .NET server.

In this work, we introduce UWAS, a universal Web application server model which makes it possible to deploy Web applications/services regardless the Web technology for which those applications/services were developed.

Reflective and Adaptable Web Services

In general terms, reflection in a system can be classified into three groups, depending on the information that the system can reflect:

- **Introspection:** The system is capable of observing and reasoning on the system elements, but it is incapable of modifying those elements (Foote, 1992).

- **Structural reflection:** The system is capable of enquiring and modifying its structure at runtime (Foote, 1989).

- **Behavioral reflection:** The system is capable of manipulating and modifying its behavior (Ferber, 1989).

The RAWS architecture will prove how all the aforementioned kinds of reflection can be successfully applied to Web service design. Reflection is usually represented, as in Figure 1, by a two-level architecture: A base level that contains the modules that solve the problem, and a metalevel containing the representation of the base level. An application is represented in the base level and can be manipulated by the

Figure 1. Reflective system architecture

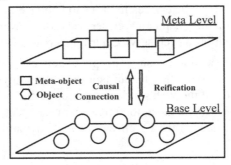

metalevel. Both levels are joined together by a causal connection (Smith, 1984), so that the changes brought about in the base level are reflected in the metalevel.

On the other hand, in order to manipulate the information of the metalevel, the computational behavior of the base level object is transformed into data. This process is called reification (Smith, 1982). The reificated information makes up the metainformation, thus allowing the reflective behavior.

The association of both the base and metalevels and the implementation of reflection can take place in two ways: (a) *explicitly*, if the base level object activates the reflection, or (b) *implicitly*, if the system activates the metaobject.

The abovementioned architecture can be applied to Web service design in order to enhance flexibility and adaptability. In the case of Web services, the base level will contain the Web service itself, while the metalevel will contain the metarepresentation of the Web service.

The Introspective Nature of Web Services

Although introspection allows to consult the structure of a given system, the way it communicates, etc., yet it does not allow its modification. Web services basically use three XML standards: simple object access protocol (SOAP), Web service description language (WSDL) and universal description, discovery and integration (UDDI). XML documents have a hierarchical structure of elements, attributes and entities, using document type definition (DOM) (Stenback, Le Hégaret, & Le Hors, 2003) or schemas (Fallside, 2001) to describe the grammar of each specific document. This hierarchical structure facilitates the introspection in XML documents.

Introspective Description of a Web Service

WSDL documents (Christensen et al., 2001) describe the way in which the business methods and the physical location of a Web service can be accessed. These documents contain five introspective characteristics of Web services: types, message, port type, binding and service.

It is possible to gather information about the structure of the Web service and the way it works by introspecting its WSDL document. As an illustration, let us think of a temperature Web service that has been located by a client. The client needs to know both how to use it and the structure of its business methods before the temperature Web service can be used. An introspective temperature Web service would allow the client to ask for directions on how to be able to fully use it.

Introspective Communication of a Web Service

SOAP documents describe the format of the messages to be sent among the various Web service participants (provider, client and broker). These messages can be classified into the following types: Request, response, error and data transfer.

In some given situations, either the client or the Web service itself needs to know about the contents of a certain SOAP message. SOAP messages are based in XML, which makes it easier to design interfaces that handle these message contents. In this way, several Java-based APIs like JAXM and JAX-RPC have been proposed.

Introspective Location and Publication of a Web Service

UDDI (Bellwood, Clément, & Von Riegen, 2003) is a service for locating Web services for clients as well as an advertising mechanism for Web service brokers. The advertisement of a Web service is made by means of information models that are defined using XML. There are four types of introspective information: business entity, business service, binding template and tModel.

Among all the aforementioned Web service standards UDDI is the one that more clearly addresses introspection, since it is aimed at the publishing and discovering of Web services. The introspective features of UDDI registries make it possible to know about the broker company, the binding points, ways of accessing the Web service, and other relevant info.

Structural Reflection of a Web Service

The structural reflection of a Web service allows for the modification of its structure at runtime. Although structural reflection has been described in general terms and used in several projects (Gudgin et al., 2003; Kiczales, Des Rivières, & Bobrow, 1992; Maes, 1987), Web service structural reflection has not explicitly been addressed yet. A reflective Web service presents two types of reflection: structural reflection of the Web service definition, and structural reflection of the Web service implementation.

Figure 2. Partial class diagram of JR-WSDL API

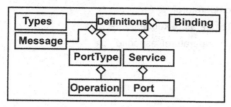

Structural Reflection of a Web Service Definition

Every Web service is self-describable due to its WSDL document, which describes its structure, business methods and location, among other features. In order to modify the structure of this description, and consequently the structure of the Web service itself, a metalevel that contains a representation of the Web service should be designed. We will refer to it as the Web service meta description level (WSMDL). This metalevel contains the representation of the Web service declaration (Meta-WSDL) and it does not depend on the programming language in which the Web service has been implemented.

In order to be able to work with Meta-WSDL representations we have developed a Java reflective WSDL (JR-WSDL) API, made up of 24 classes and interfaces. Each of these classes represents the corresponding part of the actual structure of the Web service in the metamodel. Figure 2 shows of the most significant classes in this API.

In this model, as in a WSDL document, a Web service definition has a type, and it is composed of one or more messages, bindings, port types and services. Port types and services are in turn made up of operations and ports respectively. This API allows to dynamically modify the Web service description characteristics, regardless of its implementation. In this model, each API class represents a tag in the WSDL document, while the sub-tags are represented by attributes of such class.

In the temperature Web service, this could be attained by representing each WSDL tag by a JR-WSDL class like the following:

```
<definitions>
<message name="getTemperatureRequest">
 <part name="city" type="xsd:string"/>
</message>
<message name="getTemperatureResponse">
 <part name="getTemperatureReturn" type="xsd:string" />
</message>
```

```
<portType name="Temperature">
  <operation name="getTemperature"...>
    <input message="getTemperatureRequest".../>
    <output message="getTemperatureResponse".../>
  </operation>
</portType>
</definitions>
```

Which makes use of the following classes:

```
class PortType{
  private String name;
  private Vector operations;
  ...
  public String getName()
  public void setName(String)
  public Vector getOperations()
  public void setOperations(Vector)
  public void addOperation(Operation)
  public void removeOperation(int)
}

class Operation{
  private Vector messages;
  ...
  public void addInputMessage(Message)
  public void addOutputMessage(Message)
}
```

And corresponds to the code:

```
Message m1=new Message("getTemperatureRequest");
Message m2=new Message("getTemperatureResponse");
Operation op=new Operation("getTemperature");
op.addInputMessage(m1);
op.addOutputMessage(m2);
PortType pt=new PortType("Temperature");
pt.addOperation(op);
```

Structural Reflection of a Web Service Implementation

The structural reflection of a Web service implementation allows to modify the code structure of the Web service at runtime (names of business methods, types of attributes, access permissions, etc.). Following the model already described for a structural reflection of the Web service definition, we have developed a metalevel called Web service meta implementation level (WSMIL) for the design of structural reflection. This metalevel contains metaWeb services that are the representation of the Web services.

MetaWeb services are automatically generated from the Web service, and they contain the reflective operations that can be run on the Web service code. In order for the metaWeb service to be capable of modifying the Web service structure, it needs to access its metacode, which holds the representation of the Web service code being executed. This metacode is language independent, and it is aimed at working on a virtual machine with a dynamic class loader. Although some specific implementations for other languages and platforms such as .NET or Smalltalk can be developed, we intentionally focus our work on Java.

In a Java-based model, the metacode of a Web service can be automatically obtained from the Web service itself by using the Java reflection API and a structural and behavioral reflective API (i.e., BCEL) (Dahm, 1999). In a reflective system like this, reification of the base level on the metalevel is needed to generate metacode from the original Web service. Authorized clients will invoke the metaWeb service, which will in turn execute the reflective operation by using the metacode of the Web service. On the other hand, in order for the metacode to manifest the changes in the original Web service, a causal connection must be established in order to transfer the new code to be loaded from the metalevel to the base level. In our system, the new code is dynamically loaded by means of a user-defined class loader of the Java virtual machine. This implies that a custom user-defined class loader has to be created, and that the former, which contains the old version, has to be destroyed.

Behavioral Reflection of a Web Service

Behavioural reflection is the Web service ability to dynamically modify its behavior. This can be observed from two different points of view: the modification of the code to be executed by the Web service, and the extension of the code to be executed, keeping part of the original code. A Web service can be modified through two different deployment approaches:

- **Static:** Involves editing the existing code, recompiling it, and then redeploying it on the application server. This model assumes that the source code is available, which constitutes one of its major disadvantages. Another important shortcoming is the difficulty of automating the modification process, because most code editions need human intervention.

- **Dynamic:** Entails the transformation of the original Web service into a pair Web service—metaWeb service, where the Web service can access its metaWeb service in order to modify either its structure (structural reflection) or its executable code (behavioral reflection) or both. The dynamic deployment (among other advantages) automates the modification process. At the same time, source code availability is not a need since a metarepresentation of the code in execution is always loaded in memory.

In the temperature Web service example, the original service is transformed into two abstraction layers: The temperature base Web service and the temperature metaWeb service, as it is shown in Figure 3.

Let us suppose that our original temperature Web service is a local service aimed at providing information on temperatures in Spanish cities. Consequently, the response message returned by a query on a city temperature is written in Spanish. If we want this service to provide information in English, we accordingly need to modify the method getTemperature(). As in:

```
public class Temperature{
    public String getTemperature(String city)
throws java.rmi.RemoteException{
    // SELECT into DataBase
    return "La temperatura en "+city+" es "+temp;
    }
    }
```

Figure 3. Transforming a Web service into a reflective Web service

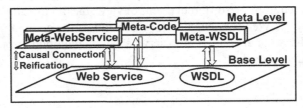

This original Web service will be transformed into a base Web service:

```
public class Temperature{
private Repository repository;
private Vector methods;
...
public String getTemperature(String city)
                throws java.rmi.RemoteException{
  Method m=methods.getMethod("getTemperature");
  return m.execute();
}
public boolean modifyMethod(String name, byte code[]){
  Method m=methods.getMethod("getTemperature");
  m.setCode(code);
  ClassFile cf=reify();
  repository.destroyWSClassLoader("Temperature");
  repository.createWSClassLoader(cf);
  return true;
}
}
```

This base Web service uses several metaclasses:

```
public class Method{
  private String name;
  private String returnType;
  private Vector parameters;
  private Code code;
  ...
  public void setCode(Code){...}
  public Code getCode(){...}
  public void excecute(){...}
}
```

Finally, the client can modify the Web service source code by sending the following message in a SOAP request:

```
<modifyMethod soapenv:encodingStyle="http://schemas.xmlsoap.org/
soap/encoding/" xmlns:ns1="operation">
```

```
<name xsi:type="xsd:string">
  getTemperature
</name>
<code xsi:type="soapenc:Array" soapenc:arrayType="xsd:byte[200]"
  xmlns:soapenc="http://schemas.xml soap.org/soap/encoding/">
  New code to update the original one
  <item>99</item>
  .....
  <item>104</item>
</code>
</modifyMethod>
```

Figure 4. Dynamic generation of reflective infrastructure

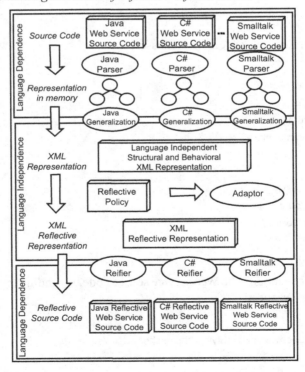

The Dynamic Generation Process

To have an adaptive behaviour, a Web service needs a reflective infrastructure. In order to simplify the transformation from a "regular" Web service to an adaptable Web service, this task can be automated. The design of the automatic transformation shown here is platform-independent, has two main advantages:

- Interoperability between metaWeb services
- Web service automatic translation from a computer language to another

Figure 5. Parser API for the recognition of the structure

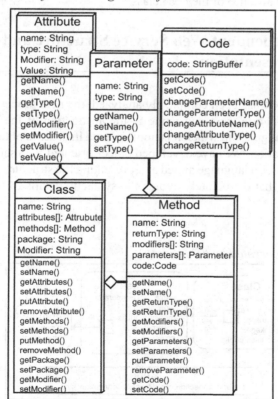

Parsing Web Services

A source code parser has to be designed to identify the structure and behavior of the Web service. This parser depends on the implementation language of the service, because the syntax of each language is, of course, different. Thus, we would have a parser for Java, another one for C#, Smalltalk, and so forth. The parser includes an API that reflects the structure of the Web service. Some representative classes of this API are those in Figure 5.

For example, the temperature Web service described before has a business method called getTemperature() that returns the temperature of the parameter city. The structural parser analyzes each different word in the source code, identifying the different syntactic elements and consequently generating an object, attribute, and so forth, of the parser API for each one. When this analysis is finished, the structural parser generates a Class object containing the class name in the name attribute and the get-Temperature method features in the method attribute. This getTemperature object has a public value in the access attribute, a string value in the return attribute, a Parameter object with the characteristics of the parameter city, and the method code is stored in a buffer that is an instance of the Code class.

Language-Independent Web Service Structure and Behavior Representation

When the source code has been completely analyzed, the next process is what we call "generalization," a process consisting in the abstraction of the Web service source code of the language in which it is implemented in order to obtain language-independent information. We have developed object-oriented Web service markup language (OOWSML), a language aimed at representing the structure and behavior of the Web service that deliberately avoids the syntactic details of the particular

Figure 6. Objects generated by the parser

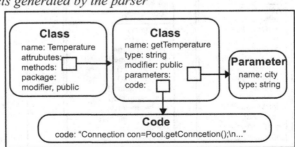

Table 1. Elements and attributes of OOWSML

Elements	Attributes
application	name
package	name
import	name
class	name, visibility, abstract, static, final, extends
method	name, visibility, abstract, static, final, returnType, constructor
argument	name, type
attribute	name, type, value, visibility, static, final
block	—
simpleSelective	condition
else	—
multipleSelective	expression
case	value
loop	type, initial, condition, increment
var	name, type, value, static, final
assignment	var, value
methodCall	object, method
parameter	name
operation	opl, operator, op2
new	class
return	expression
break	—
continue	—

programming language used. Table 1 shows the main elements and attributes that form the grammar of this language.

Using the temperature Web service analyzed above, its structure and behavior can be transformed so as to be language-independent. As a result of this process, the following document written in OOWSML would be generated:

```
<application name="Temperature">
 <class name="Temperature" visibility="public">
   <method name="getTemperature" visibility="public"
returnType="String" constructor="false">
     <argument name="city" type="string"\>
     <block>
```

```
    ... // SELECT into DataBase
    <return expression="The temperature in "+city+" is "+temp />
   </block>
  </method>
 </class>
</application>
```

Adding Reflective Features to a Web Service

The reflection level to implant in a Web service can be personalized by making use of the Web service adaptive policy document. Using the objects returned by the Web service code analyzer as the starting point, the desired reflective infrastructure is subsequently introduced depending on the adaptive policy document. The following table shows the reflective capabilities that can be added to a Web service.

This table relates the properties of the Web service and the actions that can be done regarding those properties. When an "X" appears in the table, it must be read as: "It is allowed to perform the action in this column for the property in this row." In particular:

- **get:** It is allowed to consult the value of the property
- **set:** It is allowed to modify the value of the property
- **add:** It is allowed to add to a new element to the property
- **delete:** It is allowed to eliminate an element of the property

A class has a name, it can be included into a package, and it has an access modifier, attributes and methods. All of them can be consulted or modified by the service creator. In addition, it is possible to be granted to add or delete class attributes and

Table 2. Reflective features of a Web service

Action / Property	get	set	add	delete
Name	X	X		
Package	X	X		
Access	X	X		
Attributes	X	X	X	X
Methods	X	X	X	X

methods. The attribute properties can be managed at a global level, by using the attributes property if all the attributes have the same properties, or at individual level, if each attribute has different properties. In this case, each particular attribute will have the following reflective capabilities.

It can be consulted or modified, for each attribute, its name, type, access modifier and/or initial value. In the same manner as with the attributes, methods can be dealt with at a global level by using the methods property, or at individual level, if it is allowed that methods have their own reflective properties:

The name, return type, parameters, access modifiers and code of the methods can be consulted or modified, and in the same way, its parameters or access modifiers can be added or eliminated.

Dynamically changing these properties will sometimes imply remaking the WSDL document of the Web service to ensure the integrity between that document and the Web service. When the reflective methods are added to the Web service, all the necessary functionalities to regenerate its WSDL document are automatically added to ensure the integrity of the Web service in future dynamic changes.

Table3. Reflective features of a Web service attribute

Property \ Action	get	set	add	delete
Name	X	X		
Type	X	X		
Access	X	X		
Value	X	X		

Table4. Reflective features of a Web service method

Property \ Action	get	set	add	delete
Name	X	X		
Return	X	X		
Parameters	X	X	X	X
Access	X	X	X	X
Code	X	X		

Regenerating the Reflective Source Code

Reflective source code regeneration is made by using the OOWSML document, which represents the Web service. This regeneration is carried out by a reifier, which depends on the desired programming language of the final code. We should remark that the reflective Web service language could be different from the language of the original source code, thus transforming Web services automatically from one language to another. The reifier uses XSLT to generate the new reflective source code.

RAWS Architecture

In this work, we introduce the RAWS architecture (Parra-Fuente et al., 2004), a multilevel reflective architecture integrated by different levels that communicate by means of causal connection and reification. These levels are:

*   **MetaWeb service level:** It contains a metarepresentation of the Web service. This representation, written in OOWSML, is programming language-independent.

Figure 7. RAWS architecture

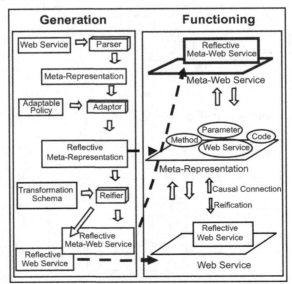

- **Metarepresentation level:** It contains the metarepresentation of the Web service and includes both the necessary reflective methods to communicate the Web service with the metaWeb service, and a reflective interface to remotely access/modify the Web service.

- **Web service level:** It contains the Web service with the code modifications to be able to communicate with its metarepresentation.

Then, if a Web service can behave like a reflective and adaptable Web service, it will be necessary to transform it by generating its reflective infrastructure, as it was explained in the previous section.

Shortcomings of Current Web Application/ Service Servers

The main disadvantage of current Web application/service servers is the limitation of platform, due to the fact that a server can only deploy software developed with the same technology of the Web application server.

It is possible to deploy several services, written in different languages, on different Web service servers. All services could communicate with each other by using SOAP, but there is a problem of maintenance in this approach, as it is necessary to manage several servers, which use different technology, deployment, administration, and so forth, with the maintenance problems that it supposes.

To solve the abovementioned shortcomings of current application servers, we propose the development of a UWAS that allows to deploy, in the same server, applications composed of modules implemented with different technologies. The main characteristics of this server are:

- **Multilanguage and multiplatform server:** The UWAS would be capable of deploying and running applications implemented with different languages regardless of the platform on which the application will run. This will allow it to run on the same server modules implemented with different technologies, like J2EE, .NET, and so forth.

- **Language-independent code representation:** The server would use a language-independent representation based on XML, what would allow the execution and cooperation of modules written in different languages.

- **Transformation from compiled code into language-independent code:** The server here proposed must be able to transform the original compiled code into language-independent code during the phase of the application deployment on the server. That common representation for all languages would allow the direct communication between the application modules implemented in different languages.

- **Semantic storage of the application deployment information:** It would be necessary to have a repository in which the deployed modules of the different applications would be published. The application modules could discover other modules or functionalities deployed on the same server and published in this repository.

- **Resource location:** The applications deployed on the UWAS and transformed into language-independent representations must be able to process the HTTP/ SOAP requests. The locator must look for the application and resource to be run into the semantic storage and give it to the run engine of the server.

- **Running platform translation:** The programming language-independent application code would have to be transformed into native code of the end platform where the application is going to be executed.

- **Direct interoperability:** Applications modules deployed in the same server should be capable of communicating to each other directly, even if they are implemented with different technologies, without the need of SOAP translations or HTTP communications.

UWAS Architecture

After analyzing the requirements that the UWAS has to achieve, we introduce the server architecture:

- **Multiplatform code parser:** A compiled code parser of each language in which could be written the Web modules deployable in the server. In order to transform the compiled code into language-independent code in a document based on XML.

- **Application repository:** Storage where semantic information about the applications and its modules deployed on the server is collected.

- **Application locator:** This module locates Web resources deployed on the server using the application repository.

- **Multilanguage interpreter:** A translator to convert the language-independent code into native code of the execution platform.

Figure 8. Universal Web application server architecture

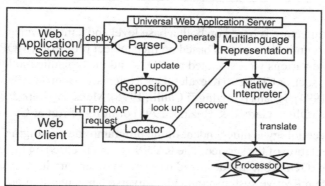

Figure 8 shows the relationships between the different modules of the server architecture. The Web application/service is deployed on the server. When it is deployed, the *parser* analyzes the code and transforms it into a multilanguage code representation document based on XML. The parser also updates the *repository* with the deployed application data. This repository will be used by the *locator* when the server receives a HTTP request from the Web client to run a resource of a specific Web application. Once the multilanguage code of the resource is located, it is transformed into native code by the *interpreter* and finally run by the processor.

UWAS presents several advantages compared with the conventional application servers, such as the following:

- **Universal server:** It provides a server capable of deploying applications, regardless the language in which the application is written. It will not be necessary to administrate, to have licenses, to know the operation, and so forth, of different servers, because all the Web application will be deployed in this server.

- **Direct interoperability:** The Web modules of the same application implemented in different languages will have more mechanisms to communicate to each other without SOAP communications.

- **Language-independent representation:** The applications/services are represented in a way that is independent of the implementation language used. This allows direct code generation obtained from the analysis and design phases, without the need to know multiple programming languages.

Related Work

The RAWS architecture is based on both a base level and a metalevel architecture, which has its origin in the systems based on meta object protocols (MOPs) (Maes, 1987). There are various works related to MOPs and the dynamic modification of their semantics, such as Clossete (Kiczales, Des Rivières, & Bobrow, 1992), Cognac (Murata et al., 1994), Iguana (Gowing & Cahill, 1996), MetaXa (Golm & Kleinöder, 1998), Guanará (Oliva, García, & Buzato, 1998) or nitrO (Ortín & Cueva, 2001).

Web services technology is independent of the programming paradigm that is used in the implementation of the service. The RAWS system is based on the object-oriented paradigm (OOP), but it is designed to work on other paradigms based on the study of diverse reflective systems applied to diverse languages and programming paradigms: procedural paradigm—3-LISP (Des Rivières & Smith, 1984), BROWN (Friedman & Wand, 1984), functional paradigm—TEIRESIAS (Davis & Lenat, 1982), SOAR (Laird, Newell, & Rosenbloom, 1987), logical paradigm—FOL (Weyhrauch, 1980), META-PROLOG (Bowen, 1986)—or OOP—3-KRS (Maes, 1987), Smalltalk (Rivard, 1996).

The UWAS has its theoretical basis on the multiplatform RAWS server (Parra-Fuente, 2005). This server deploys Web services and transforms them into reflective and adaptable Web services automatically, and it allows to modify dynamically the structure (e.g., business method's name, adding a parameter to the method, etc.) and the behaviour (changing the code that runs a business method) of the Web service.

Future Work

The RAWS Research Group, specifically created to develop the RAWS model, is currently working on a .NET extension of the proposed architecture. Another important research topic is the design of an intermediate level between the Web service and the metacode. This intermediate layer will provide the metalevel with paradigm-independence. Our interest in automating the Web service modification process is also an outstanding issue that is currently being addressed. The design of a communication prototype for the clients to be able to remote and dynamically modify the Web service is one of the priorities.

We are working on a multi-paradigm representation based on XML to develop a paradigm-independent server. A semantic representation of the Web application/service content is being developed with the aim to give semantic information to clients looking for a specific Web application/service.

Conclusion

In this chapter, the RAWS and the UWAS architectures was presented. RAWS is aimed at the dynamic design of reflective and adaptable Web services, and establishes a three-level model. The Web service level contains the conventional Web service and it is self-describable. The metarepresentation level contains the metarepresentation of the Web service, acting as an interface of reflective communication between the Web service and the metaWeb service. The metaWeb service level contains a platform-independent metarepresentation, what makes the interoperability between different metaWeb services possible.

The dynamic generation process of a metaWeb service has been introduced in order to show how any Web service can behave like a RAWS by modifying the original code. This process includes a parser to analyze the source code and to obtain the structure and behavior of the Web service, an adaptor to add the reflective characteristics specified by the Web service author in the adaptable policy document, and finally a reifier to generate both the reflective Web service and the reflective metaWeb service.

UWAS is a Web aplication/service server which capable of deploying and running applications implemented in different languages and with different technologies. Applications/services deployed on UWAS will have a common XML-based representation, which allow the direct communication among the different applications/services.

References

Bellwood, T., Clément, L., & Von Riegen, C. (2003). *UDDI, Version 3.0.1* (UDDI Spec Technical Committee specification). OASIS.

Bowen, K. (1986). Meta-level programming and knowledge representation. *New Generation Computing, 3*(4), 359-386.

Christensen, E., Curbera, F., Meredith, G., & Weerawarana, S. (2001). *Web services description language (WSDL), Version 1.1* (W3C note 15). World Wide Web Consortium.

Dahm, M. (1999). Byte code engineering. In *Proceedings of Java Informations Tage (JIT '99)* (pp. 267-277). Springer-Verlag.

Davis, R., & Lenat, R. (1982). *Knowledge-based systems in artificial intelligence.* McGraw-Hill.

Des Rivières, J., & Smith, B.C. (1984). The implementation of procedurally reflective languages. In *Proceedings of the 1984 ACM Symposium on LISP and Functional Programming* (pp.331-347). ACM Press.

Fallside, D. C. (2001). *XML schema* (W3C recommendation). World Wide Web Consortium.

Ferber, J. (1989). Computational reflection in class based object-oriented languages. In *Proceedings of the 4th International Conference on Object Oriented Programming Systems, Languages and Applications (OOPSLA '89)* (pp. 317-326). ACM Press.

Foote, B., & Johnson, R. E. (1989). Reflective facilities in Smalltalk-80. In *Proceedings of the 4th International Conference on Object Oriented Programming Systems, Languages and Applications (OOPSLA '89)* (pp. 327-335). ACM Press.

Foote, B. (1992). Objects, reflection and open languages. In *Proceedings of the Workshop on Object-Oriented Reflection and Metalevel Architectures (ECOOP '92).*

Friedman, D., & Wand, M. (1984), Reification: Reflection without metaphysics. In *Proceedings of the 1984 ACM Symposium on LISP and functional programming* (pp. 384-355). ACM Press.

Golm, M., & Kleinöder, J. (1998). MetaXa and the future of reflection. In *Proceedings of the Workshop on Reflective Programming (OOPSLA '98)* (pp. 1-5). ACM Press.

Gowing, B., & Cahill, V. (1996). Meta-object protocols for C++: The iguana aproach. In *Proceedings of the Reflection '96 Conference* (pp. 137-152).

Gudgin, M., Hadley, M., Mendelsohn, N., Moreau, J. J., & Frystyk, H. (2003). *Simple object access protocol, Version 1.2* (W3C recommendation). World Wide Web Consortium.

Kiczales, G., Des Rivières, J., & Bobrow, D. (1992). *The art of the meta-object protocol.* ACM SIGPLAN Notices.

Laird, J., Newell, A., & Rosenbloom, P. S. (1987). SOAR: An architecture for general intelligence. *Artificial Intelligence, 33*(1), 1-64.

Ledoux, T. (1999). OpenCorba: A reflective open broker. In *Meta-Level Architectures and Reflection: Proceedings of the 2nd International Conference on Metalevel Architectures and Reflection (Reflection '99)* (LNCS 1616, pp. 197-214). Springer-Verlag.

Maes, P. (1987). Concepts and experiments in computational reflection. In *Proceedings of the Conference on Object Oriented Programming Systems, Languages and Applications (OOPSLA '87)* (Vol. 22, pp. 147-155). ACM SIGPLAN Notices.

Masuhara, H., Matsouka, S., & Yonezawa, A. (1993). Design an OO reflective language for massive-parallel processors. In *Proceedings of the Conference on Object Oriented Programming Systems, Languages and Applications (OOPSLA '93)*. ACM Press.

McAffer, J. (1995). Meta-level programming with CodA. In *Proceedings of the 9th European Conference on Object-Oriented Programming (ECOOP '95)* (LNCS 952, pp. 190-214). Springer-Verlag.

Murata, K., Horspool, R. N., Yokote, Y., Manning, E. G., & Tokoro, M. (1994). Cognac: A reflective object-oriented programming system using dynamic compilation techniques. In *Proceedings of the Conference of Japan Society of Software Science and Technology (JSSS '94)* (pp. 109-112).

Oliva, A., García, I. C., & Buzato, L. E. (1998). *The reflective architecture of guanará* (Tech. Rep. No. IC-98-14). Institute of Computing, State University of Campinas, So Paulo, Brazil.

Ortín, F., & Cueva, J. M. (2001). Building a completely adaptable reflective system. In *Proceedings of the European Conference on Object Oriented Programming (ECOOP '01)*.

Parra-Fuente, J., Sánchez-Alonso, S., Sanjuán-Martinez, O., & Joyanes-Aguilar, L. (2004). RAWS: Reflective engineering for Web services. In *Proceedings of the 2004 IEEE Internacional Conference on Web Services (ICWS 2004)* (pp. 488-495). IEEE Computer Society.

Parra-Fuente, J., Sánchez-Alonso, S., Sanjuán-Martinez, O., & Joyanes-Aguilar, L. (2005). RAWS architecture: Reflective and adaptable Web service model. *International Journal of Web Services Research (JWSR), 2*(1), 36-53.

Parra-Fuente, J. (2005). *Reflective and dynamic adaptable Web services on application servers supported by virtual machines*. PhD thesis, Pontifical University of Salamanca.

Pawlak, R., Duchien, L., & Florin, G. (1999). An automatic aspect weaver with a reflective programming language. In *Meta-Level Architectures and Reflection: Proceedings of the 2nd International Conference on Metalevel Architectures and Reflection (Reflection '99)* (LNCS 1616). Springer-Verlag.

Rivard, F. (1996). Smalltalk: A reflective language. In *Proceedings of the Reflection '96 Conference* (pp. 21-38).

Smith, B. C. (1982). Reflection and semantics in a procedural language (Tech. Rep. No. MIT-TR-272). MIT Press.

Smith, B. C (1984). Reflection and semantics in LISP. In *Proceedings of the 11th ACM SIGACT-SIGPLAN Symposium on Principles of Programming Languages* (pp. 23-35). ACM Press.

Stenback, J., Le Hégaret, P., & Le Hors, A. (2003). *Document object model (DOM) specification, Version 1.0* (W3C recommendation). World Wide Web Consortium.

Tanter, E., Noyé, J., Caromel, D., & Cointe, P. (2003). Partial behavioral reflection: Spatial and temporal selection of reification. In *Proceedings of the 18th ACM SIGPLAN conference on Object-Oriented Programming, Systems and Languages (OOPSLA '03)* (pp. 27-46). ACM Press.

Weyhrauch, R. (1980). Prolegomena to a theory of mechanized formal reasoning. *Artificial Intelligence, 13*(1,2).

Chapter VIII

Metadata-Based Information Management Framework for Grids

Wei Jie, Institute of High Performance Computing, Singapore

Tianyi Zang, Institute of High Performance Computing, Singapore

Terence Hung, Institute of High Performance Computing, Singapore

Stephen Turner, Nanyang Technological University, Singapore

Wentong Cai, Nanyang Technological University, Singapore

Abstract

Information service is a key component of a Grid environment and crucial to the operation of Grids. This chapter presents an information management framework for a Grid virtual organization (VO). This information management framework is a hierarchical structure which consists of VO layer, site layer and resource layer. We propose different models of information data organization for information management in Grids and simulation experiments were conducted to evaluate the performance of these models. Based on the experimental results, we further introduce the data organization model for our information management framework. A performance evaluation conducted on a cross-domain Grid testbed indicates that our information management framework presents good scalability with large number of concurrent users and large amount of information aggregated. In this chapter some application experiences of using the information management framework are also presented.

Introduction

A Grid (Foster, 1999) is concerned with coordinated resource sharing and problem solving in dynamic, multi-institutional virtual organizations (VO) (Foster, 2001). The information service (Plale, 2002) is a key component in such a Grid environment. It provides fundamental mechanisms for information discovering and monitoring, and serves as an underlying service for other Grid services such as meta-scheduler, execution management service, and performance diagnosis. However, information management in a Grid environment is a challenging issue because the information belonging to different organizations is characterized as diverse, dynamic, heterogeneous, and geographically distributed. The autonomy of resource owners needs to be honored along with their local resource management and usage policies.

The open Grid services architecture (OGSA) (Foster, 2002) was presented to address the challenges in a dynamic, heterogeneous, and geographical Grid environment and it provides a universal resolution for the Grid information service. The Globus toolkit (Globus, 2004) provides the MDS (MDS, 2004), which is an OGSA based framework for information management for a Grid. The MDS provides interfaces for information operations like accessing, aggregating, generating, and querying of service data. The MDS also provides a standard mechanism for registration, polling, and notification/subscription of service data. However, the MDS lacks efficient mechanisms to organize and manage information that suits the hierarchical nature of the Grid VO structure. In addition, very few results have been published that quantitatively study the performance of the OGSA-based information services. Other typical works on Grid information service include GMA (Tierney, 2002), Hawkeye (2004) and MCS (Singh, 2003). Grid monitoring architecture (GMA) is a producer-consumer model for monitoring resource information in a Grid. Hawkeye uses the monitoring agents for automatic resource monitoring and problem detection within a distributed system. Metadata catalog service (MCS) introduces the metadata mechanism for information and data management in a data Grid environment.

In this chapter, we present a metadata-based information management framework within the OGSA framework for Grids. Firstly, the architecture of this information management framework is described. We proposed two models of data organization for information management in Grids. To evaluate the performance of these models, we designed and conducted a set of experiments. Based on the experimental results, we further introduce the data model for our information management framework. The performance of our information management framework is studied on a cross-domain Grid testbed. In addition, we share the application experiences of using our information management framework. Finally, we conclude the chapter and give our future research directions.

Architecture of the Information Management Framework

In this section, we will describe the overall structure of our information management framework and its running environment.

Structure of the Information Management Framework

Our information management framework is a VO-oriented Grid service with a hierarchical structure which consists of three component services (i.e., VO information service (VIS), site information service (SIS), and node information service (NIS)). These component services run on the VO layer, site layer and resource layer, respectively (as in the diagram shown in Figure 1):

- **Resource layer:** The resource layer has one or more node information services (NISs). Each Grid node to be monitored in a participating site of a Grid VO hosts one NIS. An NIS can collect information from information providers (IPs) which produce information sources.

- **Site layer:** There is typically one site information service (SIS) per site. An SIS collects information data from its registered NISs through the subscription/notification mechanism, and supplies these data to the VO layer which it registers with.

- **VO layer:** There is typically one VO information service (VIS) for a Grid VO. For a VO that consists of multiple sites, each site can run its own SIS that will index the various resources available at that site. Then, each of these SISs would be registered in the VIS. Similarly, a VIS collects information data from SISs through the subscription/notification mechanism.

Figure 1. Structure of the information management framework

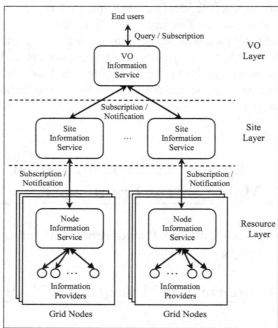

In the structure illustrated in Figure 1, the component services in each layer monitor their data sources for updates and/or provide notification under certain conditions such as data updates have been received, the client has requested notification on a time schedule, and so on. The interactions between the component services are asynchronous. The update may be performed entirely through event-driven notification.

Environment of the Information Management Framework

Figure 2 illustrates the environment of the information management framework. Users can access the framework through a Web-based Grid portal. Multiple users may connect to and access the framework at different locations through the same Grid portal. User requests are sent to a specific Web server and captured by Java servlet/Java server pages which routes the requests to service clients residing in the Web server. Each machine in a Grid environment may host component service(s) of the information management framework. The service clients will invoke component service(s) through Web services protocols (Curbera, 2002).

Figure 2. Environnent of the information management framework

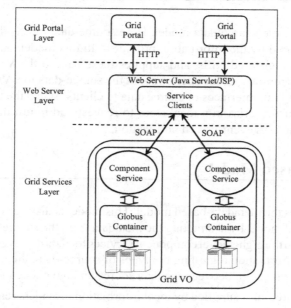

The component services of our information management are transient Grid services and we have a service factory for service instance creation. In the initialization of a Grid VO, the service factory creates an instance of the VIS for the entire VO, an instance of the SIS for each site, and an instance of the NIS for each Grid node. Thereafter, all instances are deployed on certain machines as per VO configuration. The instances will also register themselves with a publicly known Grid service registry. Service clients can query that registry to get the location of the service instances; after that the clients will directly invoke the service instances.

Model of Information Data Organization

In this section, we propose two models of data organization for information management in Grids (i.e., source-data-based model and metadata-based model). To evaluate the performance of these two models, we designed and conducted a set of experiments, and investigated the performance behavior of these two models.

Source-Data-Based Model

Figure 3 describes the source-data model. Here source-data means the raw information data captured by the information providers. In this model, an SIS collects
source-data from registered NISs, and supplies these data to the VIS it registers
with. VIS is the central target for queries about the source-data in a VO. It exposes
query and subscription interfaces of source data to clients. When the interfaces are
invoked, VIS issues queries in a local store to request and return the data to the
client, or/and generates event-driven notification.

Metadata-Based Model

Figure 4 describes the metadata-based model. This model is distinguished from the
source-data-based model by abstracting the metadata from the source-data and distributing them into the higher level component services for data discovery. Generally,
metadata is the information regarding the types of source-data, the information to
initiate the communication between the data source and the client and so forth.

In this model, source-data supplied by local information providers remains in NISs
instead of being collected to higher layer. An NIS offers metadata of collected
source-data to its registered SIS. Similarly, the metadata of SISs are collected by
a VIS to build an aggregate directory of metadata for a Grid VO. In other words,

Figure 3. Source-data-based model

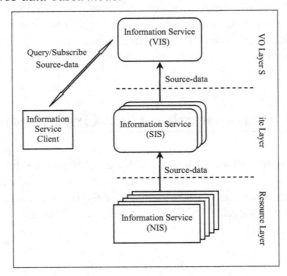

Figure 4. Metadata-based model

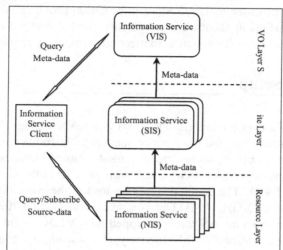

VIS supports publication and discovery of source-data and provides necessary information to initiate the communication between an NIS and a client. As Figure 4 shows, when requesting certain source-data of a VO, the client must first consult the VIS to locate the corresponding NIS capable of supplying the specific source-data. After that, the client issues new queries to the located NIS, and the source-data is transferred from that NIS to the client directly.

Performance Study

The performance study aims to evaluate and compare the scalability of our information management framework as well as its component services in terms of the two data organization models (i.e., source-data-based model and metadata-based model). In this performance study, we are concerned with the following issues:

- **How does the performance of a VO-oriented information management framework scale with the number of users?** This study is important because the number of users accessing the service will increase dramatically when a Grid grows in size.

- **How does a VIS or an SIS scale with the number of lower level component services it is aggregating?** The answer to this question will help us understand the capability of a VIS or an SIS.

- **How does the performance of an NIS scale with the amount of data it contains (the number of IPs)?** More information providers will be added to cater for various application requirements. An information management framework must have the potential to meet this scalability requirement.

Experimental Setup

We performed all the experiments (Zang, 2004) in a LAN setting (Zhang, 2003) to ensure the performance of the information management framework is affected primarily by the service components. The server-side testbed includes three Linux machines with hostname *faraday*, *newton* and *plato* on a 100 Mbps LAN. They all run a Linux kernel 2.4.18. The detailed configurations of these machines are: Machine *faraday* has two 1.4GHz AMD Opteron processors (with a 1024KB cache) and 1.0GB memory; machine *newton* is equipped with a 1.5GHz Intel Pentium 4 CPU (with a 512KB cache) and 754MB memory; machine *plato* is configured with a 1.5GHz Intel Pentium 4 CPU (with a 512KB cache) and 256MB memory. The client side testbed comprises two Linux machines on a 100Mbps LAN. They are equipped with one 1.5GHz CPU and 256MB memory.

Globus toolkit is deployed on both server side and client side as the hosting environments of the component services of the information management framework as well as the service clients. We simulated concurrent users by running individual Java threads on client side machines. For each user, two successive requests have 1-second time interval. In other words, after a user sends a query, he has to wait for one second before sending the next query.

Performance Metrics

Four metrics are used in our study: throughput, response time, and two load metrics. Throughput is defined as the average number of queries processed by a component service per second. The response time means the average time span (in seconds) starting from the instance that a client sends a query to a component service to the instance that the response from that component service is received by the client. The two load metrics used in our experiments are CPU_Usage and CPU_Load:

- **CPU_Usage** indicates the percentage of the CPU cycles spent in user mode and system mode, which is measured by averaging the sum of cpu_user and cpu_system captured by Unix command 'top.'
- **CPU_Load** is the average number of processes in the ready queue waiting to run over the last minute. This metric can also be captured by the 'top' command.

CPU_Usage may be high while CPU_Load is low if a machine is running a small number of compute intensive applications. CPU_Usage may be low while CPU_Load is high if the same machine is trying to run a large number of applications that are blocking on I/O. These two load metrics are collected every 5-second time interval.

In our experiments discussed later the values of the above performance metrics are obtained by averaging all the values recorded during a 10 minute time interval.

Experiment 1: Service Scalability with Number of Concurrent Users

This experiment aims to investigate the first issue mentioned earlier. For both source-data-based and metadata-based models, VIS, SIS and NIS use the same mechanisms to collect source-data or metadata. To simplify our experiment design, we performed experiments to test the scalability of VIS with respect to the number of users. The results will reflect the scalability of the information management framework.

In this experiment, machine *faraday* is put at the VO layer to host VIS. The resource layer is merged with the site layer, and the other two server side machines are on the site layer to host SISs. Each SIS has 10 local IPs to simulate the available resources on each site. We developed five IPs to collect various source-data (e.g., CPU load, memory usage, OS, etc) and one IP to collect metadata. We simulated up to 300 users on a client machine, and these users send queries asking for the data generated by all IPs in our experiments.

Figures 5 through 8 show the results of this set of experiments. When the number of concurrent users is below 100, we have the following observations:

- Figure 5 shows that the throughputs of both the source-data-based model and the metadata-based model increase slowly with the increase in the number of concurrent users. But, the throughputs of the source-data-based model are less than that of the metadata-based model.

- Figure 6 indicates that the response times of both models also increase gradually and have almost the same value.

- Figure 7 and Figure 8 reveal that the CPU_Load and CPU_Usage for both the models are almost unchanged. This means these two metrics are not affected with the increased number of users.

When the number of concurrent users becomes more than 100, the throughput of the source-data-based VIS begins to decrease, and that of the metadata-based VIS still keep rising. However, when the number of concurrent users is more than 150, the throughput of the source-data-based VIS drops dramatically. It nearly reaches zero

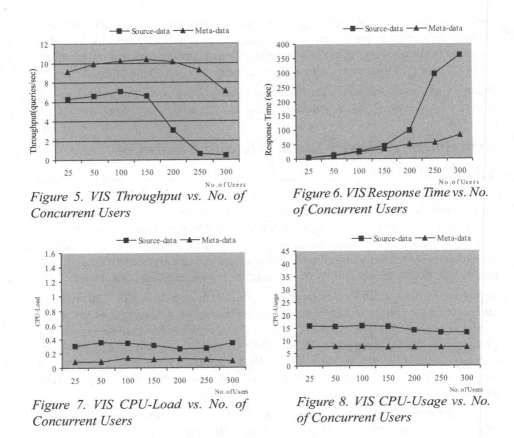

Figure 5. VIS Throughput vs. No. of Concurrent Users

Figure 6. VIS Response Time vs. No. of Concurrent Users

Figure 7. VIS CPU-Load vs. No. of Concurrent Users

Figure 8. VIS CPU-Usage vs. No. of Concurrent Users

when the number of users is more than 250. But, the throughput of the metadata-based VIS does not decrease so significantly. Similarly, when the number of users is greater than 150, the response time of the source-data-based VIS begins to increase significantly, but the response time of metadata-based VIS remains to increase slowly. This result reveals that the metadata-based model presents quite better scalability with the number of concurrent users than the source-data-based model.

Now, we examine the changes of CPU_Load and CPU_Usage when there is a big number of users. While the throughput is decreasing and the response time is increasing, the CPU-Load and CPU-Usage for the metadata-based VIS remain the same. For the source-data-based VIS, the CPU-Load has light fluctuation, but the CPU-Usage even falls when the number of users is over 250. This phenomenon tells us there are fewer queries waiting for the CPU and the CPU is not used up. But, now the question is why the throughput and response time for the source-data-based model become worse when the number of users reaches a big value? We believe that, with the increasing number of users, source-data-based VIS has to generate a great deal of SOAP messages for the communication with clients; these messages contain a bigger amount of source-data (compared with metadata). This causes heavy traffic, which blocks the further access of clients, and results in unsatisfactory throughput and response time.

The aforementioned analysis indicates the communication between clients and the source-data-based VIS can cause a bottleneck of performance when the number of concurrent users grows. Instead of duplication of VIS, the metadata-based model is a good solution to improve the scalability of the information management framework.

Experiment 2: Service Scalability with Number of Collectors

This experiment intends to investigate the second and third issues mentioned earlier. As discussed earlier, the NISs use the information provider mechanism, while the SISs and VISs use subscription/notification mechanism to collect information in both source-data-based and metadata-based models. In order to examine how the performance of component services scales with the number of collectors employed (for the information provider mechanism, collectors refer to the information providers; for the subscription/notification mechanism, they are service data subscribed), we conducted two experiments for the source-data-based model to evaluate and compare the scalability of the two mechanisms. The results are applicable to the metadata-based model as well.

- For the information provider mechanism, we configure an NIS to simulate the expanded local information providers with a refreshing interval of 30 seconds. The NIS is located on the machine *faraday*. Up to 80 IPs report five types of source-data to that NIS. On the client machine, 10 concurrent users send queries to the NIS for the information collected by all the IPs.

- For the subscription/notification mechanism, an SIS is also deployed on the machine *faraday*. It subscribes lower layer component services to collect the same type and amount of data as the provider mechanism. The refreshing interval of subscription is set to 30 seconds as well. Machine *newton* and *plato* are put on the lower layer, and each hosts an NIS with up to 40 IPs. Similarly, on the client machine, 10 concurrent users sent queries to the SIS for the information collected by the subscription/notification mechanism.

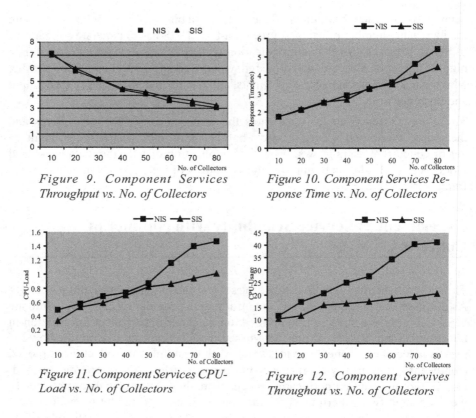

Figure 9. Component Services Throughput vs. No. of Collectors

Figure 10. Component Services Response Time vs. No. of Collectors

Figure 11. Component Services CPU-Load vs. No. of Collectors

Figure 12. Component Servives Throughout vs. No. of Collectors

The experimental results are illustrated in Figures 9 through 12. We observed that, for the two component services, both throughputs and response times are similar when the number of collectors are less than 50, and present a nearly linear relationship with the number of collectors. The CPU_Load and CPU_Usage for the two component services go up gradually, but the increase of CPU_Usage for NIS with the provider mechanism is faster than that for SIS with the subscription/notification mechanism. It indicates the amount of data collected is the key factor to affect the scalability of component services.

For the cases of more than 50 collectors, the difference in terms of CPU_Usage becomes more apparent. For SIS, the values of CPU_Usage grow steadily; but for NIS, those values increase significantly which causes a noticeable increase of response time. We believe it is because of too many Information Providers running in the local machine.

The above analysis reveals that, for NIS using the provider mechanism, too many IPs can become the performance bottleneck. An effective solution is abstracting the metadata from the source-data to reduce the amount of data aggregated. Using the metadata-based model, we can compound the metadata of each resource and supply them by one collector. In this way, both the amount of data collected and number of collectors is greatly reduced and the scalability of component services is improved significantly.

Hybrid Data Organization Model for the Information Management Framework

We can make a basic conclusion from the two experiment sets conducted: The metadata-based model has relatively better scalability with the number of users and the amount of data, while the source-data-based model has a shorter response time for a smaller number of users due to prefetching the source-data from the resource layer. Based on the conclusion, a hybrid data organization model is introduced in our information management framework to benefit from the advantages of both the source-data model and the metadata model.

In this hybrid model, the information for a Grid is further classified into two categories (i.e., static information and dynamic information). The static information is unchanged information in a Grid VO such as Grid service metadata, information on software and hardware configuration of computational resources, and so on.

Figure 13. Hybrid model

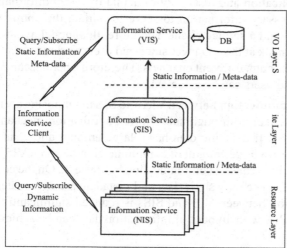

The dynamic information is the real time information about the usage and status of available resources, such as job status, CPU load, and so forth.

Static data and dynamic data are handled differently in the hybrid model: The static information is organized in the source-data-based model, and the dynamic information is organized in the metadata-based model as shown in Figure 13. In this model:

- Static information in an NIS is supplied to its registered SIS, and SIS in turn provides those data to a VIS. If a client is requesting static data, VIS may issue a query in its local database and return source-data to the client.

- Dynamic information will remain in NISs instead of being collected to higher layer. An NIS offers metadata of collected source-data to its registered SIS. Similarly, the metadata of SISs are collected by a VIS to build an aggregated directory of metadata for a Grid VO. If the client is requesting dynamic data, firstly, the VIS will be consulted to locate the corresponding NIS capable of supplying the specific source-data. Then, the client issues new queries to the located NIS to retrieve the real-time information. Regarding the metadata of dynamic information, it consists of its properties to locate and access the information source, including the type of information, the name of the corresponding Grid service data, the reference of the Grid service to hold the service data, and so on.

This hybrid model adopted by our information management framework brings the following benefits:

- **Avoid information access bottle neck at the VO layer:** In this model, VIS supports publication and discovery of actual dynamic information data and provides necessary information to serve to initiate the communication between an SIS and a service client. Therefore, this model avoids information access bottle neck at the VO layer since end users retrieve static and dynamic information through different channels. Therefore a better scalability with the number of end users can be achieved.

- **Reduce communication between VIS and SISs:** Supposing a VIS aggregates dynamic information through subscription/notification mechanism from its registered SISs. If dynamic data has a large amount and changes very frequently, there is a large amount of communication between VIS and SISs and thus very likely to cause a communication bottle neck. On the contrary, in this hybrid model, since only static data and metadata are aggregated to VIS, the communication between VIS and SISs is reduced significantly. Therefore a better scalability with amount of information data can be achieved.

- **Manage information for large scale Grid VO:** For a large scale Grid VO which typically comprises of large number of sites and large amount of information data, it is not practicable to aggregate all information to a VIS. Our hybrid model is capable of managing information for a large scale Grid because a VIS only contains a small amount of metadata and static data. Moreover, the size of metadata increases much slower with the increasing of actual information data. This implies a better scalability with amount of information can be achieved.

We have constructed a prototype information management framework that implements the architecture and model described above. The component services are implemented as Grid services that inherit the base services of the Globus toolkit. Service client is implemented as Java class and hides the complexity of the service client routines which implement the service invocation logic, access service data, perform error checking, and so on. Through a portal powered by the Jetspeed (2004), users can access our information management framework simply using a Web browser. User's requests are captured by the portal and further routed to the service client. The service client talks to the component services, and finally results are presented in the portal.

Our information management framework has been deployed in a small scale Grid VO testbed linking two administrative domains in Singapore (see Figure 14), that is, Institute of High Performance Computing (IHPC) and Nanyang Technological

Figure 14.   Cross-domain Grid testbed for the information management framework

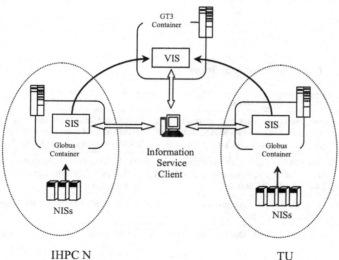

University (NTU). Both IHPC and NTU set up their own SIS server. A VIS server is also set up at IHPC. In addition, each side also put some resources into this testbed. The detailed configurations of these servers and resources are listed in Table 1.

We conducted experiments on the above Grid VO testbed to evaluate the performance of our information management framework. The main objective of these experiments is to study the scalability of this information management framework with the number of concurrent users and the number of information providers. To validate the simulation results presented earlier, we also compare the performance of our information management framework with the source-data-based model and the metadata-based model. In the source-data-based model, VIS aggregates both static data and dynamic data through subscription/notification mechanism from its registered SISs, and therefore VIS is the only target for queries about all information in a Grid. In the metadata-based model, VIS aggregates only the metadata through subscription /notification mechanism from its registered SISs.

In our experiments, the response time of the VIS is chosen as the main performance metric. The other experimental setups are similar to the simulation experiments discussed in earlier section. Figure 15 and Figure 16 show the response time of the VIS with the number of concurrent users and the number of information providers, respectively. Each curve in the graphs is normalized against the case of the source-data-based model. We observed that when the number of concurrent users and the number of information providers are getting bigger, the response time in the hybrid model based information management framework is shorter than that of both source-data-based and metadata-based models. This indicates that our information management framework scales well spanning from small Grids to large Grids, and it is capable of handling large number of queries and large amount of information.

Table 1. Grid VO testbed configuration

Domain	IHPC	NTU
Resources	Comprise 10 machines, each has one 1.5GHz Intel Pentium 4 processor with 512KB cache, 256MB memory, Linux kernel 2.4.18	Comprise 10 machines, each has one 1.5 GHz Intel Pentium 4 processor with 512 KB cache, 256MB memory, Linux kernel 2.4.18
SIS Server	Two 2.8GHz Intel Xeon processors with 512KB cache, 1.5GB memory, Linux Kernel 2.4.22, Globus toolkit 3.2	One 1.8GHz Intel Pentium 4 processor with 512KB cache, 768MB memory, Globus toolkit 3.2.
VIS Server	Two 2.8GHz Intel Xeon processors with 512KB cache, 2.5GB memory, Linux kernel 2.4.22, Globus toolkit 3.2	
Client	One 1.4GHz AMD Opteron processor with 1024KB cache, 1.0Gb memory, Linux kernel 2.4.18	

Figure 15. VIS response time with no. of concurrent users

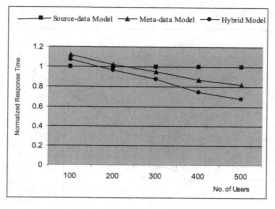

Figure 16. VIS response time woth no. of information providers

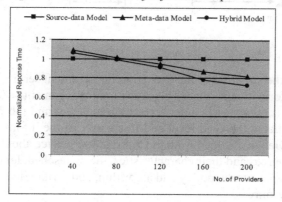

Application Experiences

Our information management framework has been integrated into a Grid application execution framework. This framework is a Grid architecture that comprises of software components and services to support the execution of large scale applications in a Grid environment. It allows various Grid resources to be discoverable, and provides mechanisms to execute various types of applications on appropriate resources. In this framework, there are two key services (i.e., the execution management service, and the information service which is based on our information management framework).

Figure 17. The execution management service and its interaction with the information service

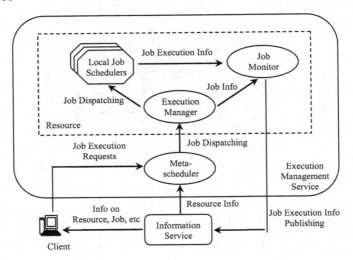

Figure 17 depicts the structure of the execution management service and its interaction with the information service. The execution management service has three main components (i.e., metascheduler, execution manager and job monitor). The metascheduler works at the Grid level and it is a user of the information service. Based on the knowledge obtained from the information service about the existence of appropriate resources and their characteristics, the metascheduler carries out resource selection as per certain policy and algorithm, and further dispatches clients' jobs across Grid resources.

The execution manager component of the execution management service works at the resource level. It is responsible for job execution upon receiving jobs from the meta-scheduler. The execution manager may also dispatch jobs to some local job schedulers such as LSF (2004), PBS (2004) and Condor (Condor, 2004) which can help to make full use of computational resources.

Each Grid resource also has a job monitor which keeps track of job execution. The job monitor may rely on local job schedulers to provide detailed job execution information (e.g., job status, resource consumption, etc.). This information can be published to job related information sensors which are plugged into the information service. Thus, users can learn job execution information through query/subscription to the information service.

Here we can see that the information service plays an important role in the entire Grid application execution framework and serves as a supporting service. It provides necessary information catering to the requirements of the execution management service. The information service also hides the complexity of a heterogeneous, distributed and dynamic Grid environment and presents Grid users comprehensive information about resources, jobs, and so on.

Conclusion and Future Work

The Grid is a promising infrastructure of science and engineering computation. Grid technologies are evolving toward OGSA which provides a uniform service-oriented architecture. In this chapter, we present a VO-oriented information management framework based on the OGSA framework for Grids. This information management framework is a three-layer structure supporting information generation, collection, update and accessing. The information management framework presents to users a global view of all the information within a Grid VO. Our framework introduces the metadata concept and presents an information data organization model for information management. The experimental results indicate that our information management framework presents good scalability with large number of concurrent users and large amount of information aggregated.

In our future work, more experiments will be conducted over a large scale Grid across different organizations, and we will further refine/extend the information architecture and model. We also intend to enhance the functionality of the information management framework to include the features such as historical data analysis, performance prediction, and fault-tolerance.

References

Condor. (n.d.). Retrieved May 2004, from http://www.cs.wisc.edu/condor/

Curbera, F., & Duftler, M. (2002). Unraveling the Web services web: An introduction to SOAP, WSDL and UDDI. *IEEE Internet Computing*, 86-93.

Foster, I., & Kesselman, C. (1999). *The Grid: Blueprint for a new computing infrastructure*. Morgan Kaufmann.

Foster, I., & Kesselman, C. (2001). The anatomy of the Grid: Enabling scalable virtual organizations. *International Journal of High Performance Computing Applications, 15*, 200-222.

Foster, I., & Kesselman, C. (2002). *The physiology of the Grid: An open Grid services architecture for distributed systems integration.* Retrieved May 2004, from http://www.globus.org/research/papers/ogsa.pdf

Globus toolkit. (n.d.). Retrieved May 2004, from http://www.globus.org/

Hawkeye. (n.d.). Retrieved May 2004, from http://www.cs.wisc.edu/condor/hawkeye

Jetspeed. (n.d.). Retrieved May 2004, from http://jakarta.apache.org/jetspeed/site/

LSF. (n.d.). Retrieved May 2004, from http://www.platform.com/products/LSF/

MDS. (n.d.). Retrieved May 2004, from http://www.globus.org/toolkit/mds

PBS. (n.d.). Retrieved May 2004, from http://www.openpbs.org/

Plale, B., & Dinda, P. (2002). Key concepts and services of a Grid information service. In *Proceedings of ISCA 15th International Parallel and Distributed Computing Systems.*

Singh, G., & Bharathi, S. (2003). A metadata catalog service for data intensive applications. In *Proceedings of Supercomputing Conference 2003.*

Tierney, B., & Aydt, R. (2002). *A Grid monitoring architecture.* Retrieved May 2004, from http://www.ggf.org

Zang, T. Y., & Jie, W. (2004). An OGSI-compliant Grid information service: its architecture and performance study. In *Proceedings of the 7th International Conference on High Performance Computing and Grid in Asia Pacific Region.*

Zhang, X., & Freschl, J. (2003). A performance study of monitoring and information services for distributed systems. In *Proceedings of the 12th IEEE International Symposium on High Performance Distributed Computing.*

Chapter IX

Architectural Foundations
of WSRF.NET

Glenn Wasson, University of Virginia, USA

Marty Humphrey, University of Virginia, USA

Abstract

State management has always been an underlying issue for large scale distributed systems, but it has only recently been brought to the forefront of Grid computing with the introduction of the Web services resource framework (WSRF) and its companion WS-notification. WSRF advocates standardized approaches for client exposure to and potential manipulation of stateful services for Grid computing; however, these arguments and their long term implications have been difficult to assess without a concrete implementation of the WSRF specifications. This chapter describes the architectural foundations of WSRF.NET, which is an implementation of the full set of specifications for WSRF and WS-notification on the Microsoft .NET framework. To our knowledge, the observations and lessons learned from the design and implementation of WSRF.NET provide the first evaluation of the WSRF approach. A concrete example of the design, implementation and deployment of a WSRF-compliant service and its accompanying WSRF-compliant client are used to guide the discussion. While the potential of WSRF and WS-notification remains strong, initial observations are that there are many challenges that remain to be solved, most notably the implied programming model derived from the specifications, particularly the complexity of service-side and client-code and the complexity of WS-notification.

Architectural Foundations of WSRF.NET

There is probably no single best approach with regard to state management in distributed systems. The fundamental issue is not whether state exists in the services that comprise the distributed system (most people believe that the description of a non-trivial distributed system must include some representation of state), but rather what a client can assume about the state of the particular service with which the client wants to interact. For years, architects and system designers have compared the relative virtues of *stateful* services and *stateless* services. Simplistically, on one hand, it is argued that *stateless* services scale better and are more fault-tolerant, while on the other hand *stateful* services support terser messages that are hence more efficient, can be more intuitive to design, and can indeed scale well due to recent advances in software support for services. The general theme regards the notion of *conversation*—specifically, what can and should a client say in its *next* request to the service?

Until recently, state management in Grid computing was not a first-class architectural concern. The Grid community largely relied on the Globus toolkit (Globus Project, 2006), which is a collection of tools for wide area, cross-domain computing. Prior to 2002-2003, Globus was not constructed as a collection of *services*, rather Globus was a collection of semi-independent tools that individually facilitated remote job execution, remote file transfer, and so forth. The Globus toolkit lacked a single architectural principle with regard to state management.

In 2002-2003, the open Grid services infrastructure (OGSI) (Tuecke et al., 2003), under the broader umbrella of the open Grid services architecture (OGSA) (Foster, Kesselman, Nick, & Teucke, 2002), synergized the traditional approach of performing Grid computing via Globus (Globus Project, 2006) or Legion (Grimshaw, Ferrari, Knabe, & Humphrey, 1999) with the emerging commercial approach of Web services. Web services would provide much of the underlying XML-based protocols for communication between services, while OGSI would provide a canonical rendering of such services. That is, OGSI constrained the appearance (to potential consumers) and behaviors of services, arguing that such constraints would make the overall service composition and subsequent execution more predictable and easier to assess and manage.

In January 2004, a team from IBM and the Globus Alliance introduced the Web services resource framework (WSRF) as an attempt to *re-factor* many of the concepts in OGSI to be more consistent with today's Web services (Czajkowski et al., 2004a). In contrast to early versions of the Globus toolkit, the central theme of WSRF is the manipulation of state. In the W3C's Web service architecture (WSA) (Booth et al., 2004), services are either stateless or any reference to state in the client-server protocol is an application-level concern. In WSRF, the argument is that there is great value in the canonical referencing and/or manipulation of state, paralleling the argument in OGSI was that there is great value to the canonical behavior and appearance of services. The difference between OGSI and WSRF is that WSRF requires no modification to Web services tooling. Of course, the significant research challenge for the community is to determine the extent to which WSRF and WS-notification adds value above the Web services approach. Almost immediately after the introduction of WSRF, a healthy debate emerged on this subject, particularly its similarities and differences with the Web services composite application framework WS-CAF (Little, Webber, & Parastatidas, 2004) and REST (Fielding, 2000).

WSRF.NET is an implementation of the WSRF and WS-notification specifications on the Microsoft .NET framework and is the first publicly-available implementation of the full set of specifications for both WSRF and its associated WS-notification (WSRF Project, 2005). In this chapter, we build upon and update our earlier assessment of WSRF.NET (Humphrey, Wasson, Morgan, & Beekwilder 2004). In creating WSRF. NET, we significantly leveraged our experience designing and implementing OGSI on .NET, OGSI.NET (Wasson, Beekwilder, Morgan, & Humphrey 2004). We describe how we have interpreted the WSRF and WS-notification suite of specifications and most importantly attempt to assess the resulting package, particularly in terms of the programming model. We do not claim that our programming model is the *only* programming model for WSRF and WS-notification, but we argue that it is a logical consequence of the implementation of the specifications on the .NET framework. Additionally, the difference between WSRF and WSRF.NET was difficult at times to discern. Overall, while the potential of WSRF and WS-notification remains strong, initial observations are that there are many challenges that remain to be solved, most notably the implied programming model derived from the specification, particularly the complexity of service-side code, client-side code, and WS-notification.

The outline of this chapter is as follows. The next section contains a brief overview of the WSRF approach as of the time of this writing. This is followed by a section containing a description of WSRF.NET, which is our open-source implementation of the WSRF suite of specifications. The subsequent section describes a use-case scenario for constructing and consuming a WSRF-compliant Web service in WSRF. NET. We discuss a traditional Grid scenario involving remote execution. The discussion section details the issues and concerns of the resulting implementation. The final section is the conclusion.

WSRF

The core of the WS-resource framework (WSRF) is the WS-resource, a "composition of a Web service and a stateful resource" (Czakowski et al., 2004a) described by an XML document (with known schema) that is associated with the Web service's port type and addressed by a WS-addressing EndpointReference (Box et al., 2004). WSRF defines functions that allow interactions with WS-resources such as querying, lifetime management and grouping. WSRF is based on the OGSI specification (Tuecke et al., 2003) and can be thought of as expressing the OGSI concepts in terms that are more compatible with today's Web service standards (Czakowski et al., 2004a). Arguably and simplistically, it is sometimes convenient when contrasting OGSI and WSRF to think of OGSI as "distributed objects that conform to many Web services concepts (XML, SOAP, a modified version of WSDL)," while WSRF is fundamentally "vanilla" Web services with more explicit handling of state. One artifact of this is that OGSI did not really support interacting with these base Web services and instead only interacted with "Grid services" (by definition these were OGSI-compliant); WSRF fully supports interacting with any Web service, whether WSRF-compliant or not (although the argument is made that client interactions with WSRF-compliant services are richer and easier to manage).

Currently, there are 4 specifications in the WS-ResourceFramework. WS-ResourceProperties defines how WS-resources are described by resource property (XML) documents that can be queried and modified. Note that the resource property document is a view or projection of the state of the WS-resource, but it is not equivalent to the state. WS-ResourceLifetime defines mechanisms for destroying WS-resources (there is no defined creation mechanism). WS-ServiceGroups describe how collections of Web services and/or WS-resources can be represented and managed. WS-BaseFaults defines a standard exception reporting format.

While notification is not technically a required part of the WSRF specifications, it is nevertheless an instrumental piece. Many of the WSRF specifications reference notification in a generic manner, so in all likelihood WS-notification will be implemented alongside WSRF. WSRF separates notification into three separate specifications which are conceptually separate, but which realistically tend to be grouped together (herein referred to collectively as WS-notification or simply notification). These pieces are WS-BaseNotification (the simplest form of notification possible); WS-BrokeredNotification, which allows for intermediaries as an extra level of abstraction between producers and consumers; and WS-topics, which is a description of how topics can be grouped and referenced hierarchically. WSRF and WS-notification are currently being standardized in OASIS (2006a, 2006b).

As mentioned earlier, the core issue regarding WSRF is whether or not state is important enough (and viewed/manipulated often enough by clients) that it should be given a canonical form in the service's interface (the WS-ResourceProperties document).

WSRF.NET

Our original motivation for OGSI.NET was to provide a familiar abstraction (the OGSI abstraction) for intra- and inter-enterprise Grids based solely on .NET. An equal motivation for OGSI.NET was to seamlessly interconnect with the Linux/UNIX OGSI world that would be supported by the Globus toolkit v3. Upon the introduction of WSRF in January, 2004, we immediately decided to implement WSRF on .NET for the same reasons; however, an additional reason was that we believed that we could not properly evaluate the core WSRF concepts without an implementation. In other words, we see an important contribution of WSRF.NET is as a means by which early adopters can evaluate the WSRF approach for themselves.

It is both positive and negative that, ultimately, we did not re-use as much code from OGSI.NET as we had hoped, in part because the WSRF.NET software architecture was more heavily utilized in the existing Microsoft tooling, as discussed below. That is, whereas OGSI.NET was forced to create separate infrastructure, WSRF.NET heavily utilizes the Microsoft applications and tooling such as IIS, ASP.NET (Microsoft's support for Web services/SOAP that is integrated with IIS), the Web services enhancements (WSE), and Visual Studio .NET (VS.NET). Note that we still had to write our own WSDL generator because Microsoft chose not to support extensibility attributes on certain WSDL elements that are utilized by the WSRF/WS-notification specifications. While this is not WSRF's fault, the requirement of an attribute on the portType to identify the resource property document's schema (for example) does make it impossible to comply with WSRF using current Microsoft's tools.

In this section, we give an overview of the design of WSRF.NET. More details can be found in the WSRF.NET Programmer's Reference (Wasson, 2005). Figure 1 shows how a request message is processed by WSRF.NET. A client request message is first received by IIS. IIS then sends the request to ASP.NET. Inside ASP.NET, a "wrapper" Web service receives the message. This wrapper was generated by static tooling

Figure 1. Information flow in WSRF.NET

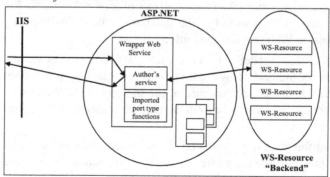

based on the Web service written by the service author. Its primary purpose is to provide an ASP.NET-friendly encapsulation for both code written by the service author and functionality they wish to import (such as WSRF spec-defined port types). ASP. NET performs its normal functions of message deserialization, including running the Microsoft Web services enhancements (WSE) (Microsoft, 2005) pipeline and invoking the correct service method.

Part of the functionality of the wrapper service includes the ability to automatically resolve the execution context specified by the EndpointReference (EPR) used in the request message and provide a programmatic interface to the appropriate resource. Although there are potentially many ways in which the execution context could be resolved and many different interfaces for a Web service programmer to interact with a resource, we chose to implement stateful resources using the Microsoft XML database support through ADO.NET (e.g., MS SQL server, or SQLServer express) or Xindice. Before the wrapper service begins execution of the appropriate method, the object specified by the reference properties element of the EPR is loaded from the database. It is then made accessible to the Web service method as if it were a data member of the Web service class. When the method invocation is complete, the wrapper service will save this member's value back into the database. The result of the invocation is then serialized into a SOAP message by ASP.NET and returned via IIS to the client.

WSRF.NET security is and will continue to be based on WSE, which supports WS-security, WS-SecureConversation and WS-policy as well as many other emerging specifications. Since WSRF.NET Web services are normal Web services running under ASP.NET, all WSE features are available.

Programming a WSRF.NET service involves the use of attributes (i.e., metadata that can be used to annotate variables, classes, methods, etc., in the .NET framework). The [resource] attribute is used in source code to programmatically declare which part(s) of the service state are to comprise the resource. This attribute is used on data members of the Web service class (both private and public). By definition, all annotated members are loaded/stored automatically on each method invocation using the supplied EPR as a key. As shown in Figure 3, processes can also be represented as WS-Resources by putting the [resource] attribute on WSRF.NET's *ProcessHandle* type. Information is then stored in the database to bind this handle to a running Win32 process on Web service invocations.

Whereas, WSRF does not define how to create new WS-resources, WSRF.NET provides a *Create*() library method. How the service exposes this is up to the service author. The first option is the direct exposure of the method in the Web service interface. The second option is to instead expose some other method, which then invokes the *Create*() operation.

After defining the state that makes up the resource, the service author must typically define the resource properties of the WS-Resource; the resource properties document is the "exposed view" of the resource. WSRF.NET allows an author to define elements of this document with the [ResourceProperty] attribute which can be placed on any .NET property. In .NET, properties are a mechanism for writing accessor functions for data stored in a class's fields. When the value of a resource property is to be computed dynamically, e.g., when it is a function of the resource state, the service author puts the attribute on any .NET property with a "getter" (see the CPUTime property in Figure 3). .NET properties can also have "setters." Such properties annotated with the [ResourceProperty] attribute will have their setter function executed when a client performs a SetResourceProperty call. The sum of all [ResourceProperty] annotations defines the resource property document (RPD). WSRF.NET automatically generates the RPD schema, which is an XSD document, and places it in the service's WSDL.

Services are composed of potentially many port types, as some are defined in the WSRF specifications, and some are defined by the service author and others. WSRF. NET provides implementations of the specification-defined port types, and the service author imports these port types into the service by using the [WSRFPort-Type] attribute. Composing port types into a service means composing functions, composing resources, and composing resource properties. WSRF.NET does this via three mechanisms. First, [WebMethod] annotated members become part of the service's port type (recall that services must have only one port type as per the WS-I Basic Profile). Second, [Resource] annotated members become part of the service's resource. Third, [ResourceProperty] annotated members become part of service's resource property document.

The configuration of a WS-resource is done using the WSE and ASP.NET *web.config* file, with a new WSRF.NET <config section> used for configuring certain specific WSRF port types. Most services need no WSRF.NET specific configuration.

Figure 2. Remote excution via WSRF.NET

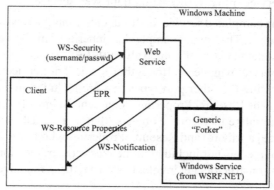

Using WSRF.NET: The Remote Execution Scenario

Figure 2 shows a scenario that we use to show how a person writes a service using WSRF.NET, and how a client subsequently uses the service. To support the traditional requirement of remote execution for Grids, in WSRF.NET, we have provided a generic "Proc Spawner," that when given an authorized username and password will spawn a process as that user (this is analogous to the procControl-D in Legion and the "fork" gatekeeper in Globus). In general, and in this scenario, a person might choose to expose the ability to execute a particular application via a Web service (as opposed to the ability to execute *any* application). This is shown at the right of Figure 3. In the code that follows, this application is called "Sample.exe" and the Web service is called "LaunchSample."

In this example, jobs are WS-resources and WSRF is used to expose their state via resource properties. That is, a client engages the remote service by securely passing the username and password on the target Windows machine via WS-security and receives an EPR back. This EPR represents the newly started job. To monitor the job, the client uses WS-ResourceProperties functions (i.e., GetResourceProperties). When the job completes, the client receives an asynchronous notification via WS-Notification. We now describe how the service author creates the WS-resource and then how the client is written.

Creating the WSRF-Compliant Web Service

The critical step in using any WSRF implementation is to first determine what comprises the state of the service, and then to determine what this state's projection (resource properties) should be to the clients. Then, to instantiate the service in WSRF.NET, a service author first creates the Web service using VS.NET just as they would any other Web service. The author then annotates the service logic with attributes that the WSRF.NET tools recognize and can use to transform the author's compiled Web service into a WSRF-compliant Web service.

Figure 3 shows the completed service for "LaunchSample," a representative WSRF-compliant Web service. The LaunchSample class inherits from "ServiceSkeleton" (line 4). The ServiceSkeleton class, off which all WSRF.NET services derive, provides the glue between the service wrapper and the author's code. The ServiceSkeleton provides a means for accessing the other port types that are included in the service. It also provides access to the ResourcePropertiesDocument. In lines 10-26, InitResource() lets a port type initialize its resource objects (that is, its class members annotated with the [Resource] attribute) and ResourceProperties when a new WS-Resource is created. InitResource() is not included in the class constructor for LaunchSample, because the class constructors get invoked when a request message first reaches IIS so the information needed from processing the message (e.g., the EPR in the WS-addressing headers) is not yet available at that point. A more important reason is because the class constructor is called every time a Web method invocation comes in and not just when a new WS-resource is created. We do not want to initialize the resource every time, just once. The InitResource method takes a hash table which contains the parameters used in initializing the various port types that make up the service. To prevent collisions we expect the keys of the hash table to be the fully qualified name of the class that implements the port type and it is up to the port type to know the type of the object to which its key refers. The only functionality exposed to clients is CreateJob (lines 28-62). This method first uses Microsoft's WSE to extract the username and password (lines 34-37, not shown). Next, in lines 39-49, we construct the parameters necessary to pass to the generic Proc Spawner included in WSRF.NET. The result of this invocation (line 50) is used in lines 52-59 to construct the EPR, which is returned to the client in line 61. Lines 64-69 contain the only resource property defined for this WS-resource, in this case returning the total milliseconds that the job has executed. Note the use of the "get" in line 66 as a means to implement GetResourceProperty.

Figure 3. WSRF-complaint "LaunchSample" Web service

```
1  [WebService]                                         36 // Assume outcome of this code is u = username (string)
2  [WebServiceBinding]                                  37 //      and p = password (string)
3  [WSRFPortType(typeof(GetResourcePropertyPortType))]  38
4  public class LaunchSample : ServiceSkeleton          39  Hashtable ht = new Hashtable();
5  {                                                    40  ht["Executable"] = @"C:\Sample\Sample.exe";
6                                                       41  ht["WorkingDir"] = @"C:\Sample";
7   [Resource]                                          42  ht["Arguments"] = new string[] { };
8    private ProcessHandle proc = null;                 43  ht["USERNAME"] = u; // see comments above
9                                                       44  ht["PASSWORD"] = p; // see comments above
10 public override void InitResource(Hashtable parameters) 45  ht["clientEPR"] = clientEPR;
11 {                                                    46
12   // start up the new process that corresponds to    47  Hashtable param = new Hashtable();
13   // a new WS-Resource                                48  param["LaunchSamplePortType"] = ht;
14   parameters =                                       49
15     (Hashtable)(parameters["LaunchSamplePortType"]); 50  string rp = ServiceBase.Create(null, param);
16  string executable = (string)parameters["Executable"]; 51
17  string workingDir =(string)parameters["WorkingDir"]; 52  // create the new EPR to return to the client
18  string []args = (string[])parameters["Arguments"];  53  EndpointReference epr = new EndpointReference(new
19  string username = (string)parameters["USERNAME"];   54      Uri("http://localhost/Sample/LaunchSample.asmx"));
20  string passwd = (string)parameters["PASSWORD"];     55  ReferenceProperties refProp =
21  EndpointReferenceType clientEPR =                    56      WSUtilities.createReferenceProperties(rp);
22      (EndpointReferenceType)parameters["clientEPR"]; 57  epr.ReferenceProperties = refProp;
23                                                       58  EndpointReferenceType eprT =
24  proc = ServiceBase.createProcess(username, passwd,   59      WSUtilities.convert(epr);
25          executable, workingDir, args, clientEPR);    60
26 }                                                     61  return eprT;
27                                                       62 }
28 [WebMethod]                                           63
29 public EndpointReferenceType                          64 [ResourceProperty]
30 CreateJob(EndpointReferenceType clientEPR)            65 public double CPUTime {
31 {                                                     66   get {
32   string u = null, p = null;                          67     return proc.TotalProcessorTime.TotalMilliseconds;
33                                                       68   }
34 // Get the username and password from SOAP headers    69 }
35 // Code not shown for brevity                         70
```

The normal compile-and-deploy mechanism of VS.NET is overloaded in WSRF. NET to also execute the PortTypeAggregator. The PortTypeAggregator pastes together all the port types that make up the service, to comply with section 4.4 of the WS-ResourceProperties specification. The PortTypeAggregator will automatically invoke the WSDL generator. If the VS.NET add-in has been installed, the Port-TypeAggregator runs, as part of the build process, over any ASMX file marked as containing a WSRF service.

Creating the WSRF-Compliant Client

Figure 4 shows the client that interacts with the service from Figure 3 in order to execute the Sample.exe application. Line 4 instantiates a proxy to the WSRF-compliant Web service. The proxy code itself was generated via the "Add Web Reference" option in VS.NET. Note that this is a significant improvement over OGSI.

Figure 4. WSRF-compliant client for "LaunchSample" WSRF-complaint Web service

```
1  static void Main(string[] args)
2  {
3     // create a proxy for the job launching service
4     localhost.LaunchSampleServiceWse proxy =
5          new localhost.LaunchSampleServiceWse();
6     // create the security tokens for the WSE headers
7     X509SecurityToken token =
8          GetSecurityToken(null);
9     EncryptedData ed = new EncryptedData(token);
10    SoapContext reqContext =
11         proxy.RequestSoapContext;
12    reqContext.Security.Elements.Add(ed);
13    // use the username and password
14    UsernameToken nt = new
15         UsernameToken("Fred", "passwd",
16         PasswordOption.SendPlainText);
17    reqContext.Security.Tokens.Add(nt);
18    reqContext.Security.Elements.Add(new
19         MessageSignature(nt));
20    EncryptedData ed2 = new EncryptedData(token,
21         "#"+nt.Id);
22    reqContext.Security.Elements.Add(ed2);
23
24    // create a notification listener
25    AsynchnonousNotificationListener listener = new
26         AsynchronousNotificationListener();
27    listener.start();
28    EndpointReferenceType myEPR =
29       new EndpointReferenceType(new
30          AttributedURI(null,
31          string.Format("http://localhost:{0}/Listener",
32             listener.ListeningPort)),
33          null, null, null, null);
34    TopicExpression te =
35       WellknownDialects.SIMPLE.createExpression(
36          new XmlQualifiedName("JobDone",
37          "http://gcg.cs.virginia.edu"));

38    te.addHandler(new TopicExpressionListener(
39         HandleJobDone));
40    listener.registerExpression(te);
41
42    // call the service's CreateJob method to launch the job
43    localhost.CreateJob cj = new localhost.CreateJob();
44    cj.clientEPR = myEPR;
45    localhost.CreateJobResponse cr = proxy.CreateJob(cj);
46    EndpointReferenceType eprT = cr.CreateJobResult;
47
48    // stop encrypting and sending Username token
49    //   now that the job launch is finished
50    reqContext.Security.Elements.Clear();
51    reqContext.Security.Tokens.Clear();
52
53    // set the EPR for the proxy's <To> header to be the
54    // EPR returned by the CreateJob call
55    WSUtilities.setEPR(proxy, eprT);
56    localhost.GetResourcePropertyResponse grpr = new
57         localhost.GetResourcePropertyResponse();
58    grpr = proxy.GetResourceProperty(new
59         XmlQualifiedName("CPUTime",
60         "http://gcg.cs.virginia.edu"));
61    Console.WriteLine(grpr.Any[0].OuterXml);
62    // continue application work
63  }
64  private void HandleJobDone(topic t,
65       NotificationMessageHolderType msg)
66  {
67    // handle the fact that the job completed
68    // e.g. retrieve output and start next job in sequence
69  }
```

NET, in which the generic Microsoft tooling had no such ability. Line 5 shows the use of WSE, in this case to securely pass the username and password from the client to the server (lines 6-22). Note that while line 16 implies that we are sending the password in cleartext, we are actually using our X.509 certificate to encrypt the password (see line 7). Lines 24-40 are used to create the notification listener that will be used to receive the "job done" event. Note that the HandleJobDone function is set as the callback to be called when the notification message on the "JobDone" topic is received. Line 43 instantiates the data structure—and line 44 places the EPR of the notification listener in the data structure—that will be passed to the CreateJob method of the Web service in Line 45. Lines 50-51 turn off encryption, specifically for the GetResourceProperty invocation of lines 55-60 (Line 61 writes it on the screen). When the notification message on the "JobDone" topic is received, the HandleJobDone function is called (lines 64-69). This function could inspect the contents of the message to see if the job completed successfully and either restart it or move on to the next job.

It should be noted that we have experienced difficulties using the WSDL from the specifications with the Microsoft tooling. That is, arguably incorrect proxy code is generated from the WSDL in the specifications. Certain issues are inherent in the Web services model (for example, every service used the EndpointReference type and so a new version of this type is defined in each service's different, and therefore incompatible, namespace) and not specific to WSRF but it does cause some problems in that we have to hand-patch the proxy code.

Discussion

There are a number of interrelated observations/concerns we made during the implementation of WSRF.NET:

- **Design of state:** The most important issue for a service author is clearly: What is the appropriate state for a service to expose? How this state is rendered via WSRF (and WSRF.NET) is secondary. With regard to WSRF, it is true that a client does not care about the real (private) service state, but to what extent will a client ever care about the projection of that state (resource properties)? Further, fundamentally, does there need to be a canonical way of asking for those projections of multiple, independent services? These are very difficult questions that cannot be answered at this time.

- **Client/Service coupling:** There are four tenants to the Microsoft view of a service-oriented architecture: Boundaries are explicit; services are autonomous; services share schema and contract, not class; service compatibility is determined based on policy (Box, 2004). WSRF arguably makes the client and service more tightly coupled, potentially violating these tenants. Policy assertions will certainly play an important role in WSRF (and all Web services), but, intuitively it seems as if WSRF-based clients and services share a tighter implicit bond than in generic Web services. In many WSRF usage scenarios, clients are responsible for the creation, destruction, and maintenance (via, for example, SetResourceProperties) of WS-resources. The fact that the client is maintaining (or mirroring) this state associated with a service creates this tighter bond. The question is whether or not this coupling is really any stronger than similar usage scenarios based on "pure" Web services and whether or not the WS-Resource abstraction provides enough utility to compensate. New specifications for "pure" Web services such as WS-transfer (Alexander et al., 2004) define a CRUD (create, read, update, delete) interface that can be used for Web services. It also defines that the entities being created are "resources." If this specification (and subsequent ones built upon it such as WS-management (Arora et al., 2004)) are to be embraced, the same issues must be dealt with. It could also be argued that part of the tightness of the client-service coupling comes not from WSRF, but from the programming model provided by vendors. All major vendors (including Microsoft) provide an object-oriented model for programming Web services in which methods are invoked on services by invoking methods on a local "proxy" object. While such proxy object fit nicely into current programming practices, they imply that Web services are to be treated like any other distributed object technology (e.g., J2EE [Sun Microsystems, 2005] or Corba [Object Management Group, 2005]). It can be argued that object lifetime management and conversational (typically synchronous) method invocation are not in the spirit of service-oriented architectures (SOAs) and therefore an improper use of Web services. As more advanced Web service programming tools and models become available, hopefully these issues will be diminished for all Web services (including WSRF-based services).

- **Complexity of service-side code:** First, it is not clear to what extent the service writer must understand the hosting environment. For example, *when* and *how* the state is saved/loaded will greatly impact the semantics of the WS-Resource, which inevitably is important to the service writer. This is exacerbated by the composition model, where a service author may import a port type that contains its own resource state, and therefore *what* the state of their service's WS-resource actually is may not be obvious to the service author. This is a property of WSRF, not WSRF.NET. Second, because by definition a WS-ResourceProperty is a *projection* of the state, and not the state itself, there is a decoupling between a service author declaring something to be a WS-resource and its appearance (or projection), via WS-ResourceProperty. So, a service author has to take *two* steps: Declaration of the state, and then declaration of the ResourceProperty. This can lead to a situation in which the service author forgets one of the steps altogether, or more likely forgets to change one (e.g., the ResourceProperty) after having changed the other (the state). Having to do something *twice* in a programming language is never desired. Arguably, this is not unique to WSRF.NET. In the future, some fundamental link between resources and resource properties (i.e., change one and the other should automatically change) would be part of a higher level, application-specific programming model. While some have advocated that a more direct link between resource state and resource properties is desirable because of its straight-forward mapping onto language/environment specific constructs (e.g., EJBs), others have argued that the lack of explicit linkage is, in fact, desirable. Ultimately, WSRF should be viewed as a set of specifications on which application logic is built. The flexible connection between state and resource properties allows many different application-specific connections to be developed. Third, and perhaps most importantly, it is not clear to what extent the WSRF rendering of state management results in an unintuitive interface between client and server. Consider a service that performs online tracking of packages. The non-WSRF rendering might have an operation with the following signature: *public bool CheckPkgIn (package pkg, string location)*. The WSRF rendering might look like: *public bool CheckPkgIn (string location)*. The package is *not* an explicit parameter of the WSRF service, because the package itself is part of the resource, so the "package" is referenced in the SOAP headers via a particular EPR. Arguably, as the state of a Web service becomes more complex in a particular WSRF-compliant Web service, more parameters will seem to disappear in the signature of operations, leaving an unintuitive interface. Note that this does have the advantage of making the message smaller, thus faster to sign and/or encrypt and send.

- **Complexity of client-side code:** First, implicitly there is a notion of persistence in WS-resources, but unfortunately the semantics of persistence are not precise. What guarantees does the service provide to the client with regard to state? What should the client do when the service has an error saving/restoring state other than abort the potentially long, complex sequence of operations? Since the definition of persistence is again, application specific, WSRF is arguably not the place for it. However, any service will have to answer this question and potentially complex clients must be built with this understanding. There is also the related issue regarding whether or not and how the client saves the EPRs that it has acquired. Must every client treat EPRs as being analogous to Kerberos tickets, which are stored in the user's file system—knowing that if the EPRs are lost, the client has no way to reengage the WS-resource? Of course, resource discovery will be used to allow clients to find (and re-find) service EPRs, but the question is whether in any practical application (e.g., the remote job execution scenario in Wasson & Humphrey, 2004) will require the discover/indexing infrastructure to prevent the client from having to maintain large amounts of state. Second, by definition, clients must treat EPRs as opaque data structures. EPRs cannot be tested for equality, that is, it cannot be determined if two EPRs refer to the same WS-Resource. An EPR is not a persistent name, because the service can arbitrarily change it and still have it refer to the same "state." For example, assume that a client gets a service group membership list (SG1). Later, a service S leaves SG1, so the same client gets a notification of an updated list (SG2). While it would seem that SG1 – S = SG2, it could be the case that SG1 and SG2 have *no members in common*, by the definition of EPRs. In this case, should the client stop doing everything with regard to EPRs in SG1, because it has no guarantee that whichever service it had previously engaged is still in the service group (perhaps S was kicked out of the service group because it is no longer trusted)? Similarly, a client could create a WS-resource and get EPR1 back. Subsequently, the client could receive a notification containing EPR2 stating "the WS-resource is no longer valid." How does the client know if: (a) EPR2 and EPR1 are the same resource, or (b) the client was never supposed to receive this message? More abstractly, it seems that "names" can change arbitrarily, and the client must handle it. Many of these issues may be resolved as both the WSRF and WS-addressing specifications progress.

A related, seemingly application-specific issue is the handling of errors. WSRF is silent on failures (except to define the WS-BaseFaults messages that carry fault information) preferring to have WSRF-based applications define their own error semantics. However, it is an open question whether stateful resources assist or inhibit systems architects in handling faults. On one hand, properly persistent WS-resources represent a recoverable entity, allowing a service to return to an appropriate state in the event of a server crash (client crashes and EPR discovery are still an issue as mentioned above). However, the very fact that a client interacts with a projection of a service's state precludes a set of failure recovery mechanisms that might address the problem by changing internal service operations. In other words, the service must continue to expose its state through the same WSDL-defined schema that the WSRF client was built against. Any additional information that a service must expose limits its ability to change its internal function. As large-scale systems are built on WSRF and traditional Web services, these issues will become increasingly important.

- **Discovery:** The service group is overloaded, in that it supports discovery of WS-resources but it also supports general grouping. How this may or may not interact with other Web services discovery mechanisms (e.g., UDDI) is not clear. Also, we note that there may be scalability issues with service groups because they *must* support the "list" operation.

- **Reliability in WS-notification:** Reliability is not required in the WS-Notification specifications, instead relying on the (optional) WS-ReliableMessaging

(Ruslan et al., 2005). Every other asynchronous messaging framework that we have worked with has touted reliable messaging as its best and most important feature, for example, JMS (Hapner, Burridge, Sharma, Fialli, & Stout 2002). An example of problems that arise because of this is the use or reference to WS-notification in specifications like WS-ResourceLifetime, where it is all but stated that death notifications can be used for cleanup. Without reliability, clients must be more complex to determine when WS-resources have been destroyed. With reliability, clients are much simpler to write. While it is certainly true that not all notification messages need to be reliable (and so requiring reliability would be too heavy weight), it is not clear how clients determine what deliver guarantees can be expected from various WSRF-compliant services they might wish to interact with or whether a client's design is even appropriate for the reliability model of the service they are using.

- **Interoperability in WS-notification**: Two issues in WS-notification significantly impact the potential for interoperable implementations. First, the raw method delivery of a notification message is particularly problematic as the specifications states: "In this case the NotificationConsumer referred to in the wsnt:ConsumerReference element MUST implement all the NotificationMessages associated with the topic or topics referred to by the Topic Expression, and include corresponding operations in its portType definition." (Graham, Hull, & Murray, 2004). However, the "NotificationMessages associated with the Topic or Topics" is ambiguous. One can assume that this refers to messages which, via some well-defined pattern matching scheme, are of well-known name and type in the consumer's interface. Even if this pattern is assumed to be extremely straight-forward, for example, the name of the method is the name of the topic and in the same namespace, etc., then the question of parameters is still undefined. To our knowledge, none of the specifications state the information passed with a notification, thus making interoperable raw message delivery challenging. Second, interoperability will be difficult to achieve given the lack of sufficient definition for the SubscriptionManager and PublisherRegistrationManager port types in the WS-notification specification (and indeed, this problem also crops up in other specs such as WS-Service-Group). These two port types store, manipulate, and reference subscriptions that consumers have made to producers, and registrations of publishers to brokers respectively. When a consumer subscribes to a producer on a given topic, a new subscription WS-resource is created to represent that subscription. It is this WS-resource that clients can then later pause, unpause, destroy, etc. However, notably lacking in the definition of this port type are how the subscriptions are created (there is no explicit factory mechanism defined in WSRF), and how those subscriptions are retrieved by the notification producer when it is time to send out notifications. In both cases, this detail is considered implementation specific. However, it is easy to imagine that subscription

WS-resources would be created by notification producers sending messages to separate SubscriptionManager services and notification producers would then query these same services to determine who should receive any particular notification. However, since this linkage is undefined, it is unlikely that a notification producer from one implementation of WSRF would interoperate with a SubscriptionManager from another implementation. This is indicative of a larger problem regarding interoperability in WSRF, which is the lack of standardized mechanisms to create WS-resources.

- **Complexity and atomicity in WS-notification:** WS-notification in particular has a rather large amount of complexity built in. Take for example the process by which, in the limit, the notification broker must go through in order to create a demand based publisher. The broker receives a registration from a publisher and as a result must make a subscription back to the publisher based on the registered topic/topics. This subscription is maintained, as always, by a subscription manager, but now the broker is also responsible for pausing and unpausing it based on the state of the subscriptions that other consumers have to the broker on the given topics. If no subscriptions currently exist to the broker on a given topic, then all subscriptions for demand-based publishers on the same topic must, according to the spec, be paused (telling the producers to not even waste effort generating the message for the broker in the first place). In total, when you consider the interactions between these various services and resources, a demand-based publisher registration interaction can involve as many as six separate Web services and WS-resources. More messages are generated in response to a demand-based publisher scenario then in any other spec, by what we estimate to be an order of magnitude at a minimum. Further, the WSRF specification does not address the topic of atomicity in its state transitions—while this is perfectly acceptable in many of the simpler interactions between the various Grid services, the need for some kind of transactional semantics becomes increasingly clear in the more complicated scenarios hinted at by WS-BaseNotification and WS-BrokeredNotification. In response to a subscription being created or being destroyed in a demand-based publisher scenario, messages must be sent out, which may further cause other messages to be produced—any of which may fail for any reason including the more common one of network failure. Each new failure condition (especially in a distributed system) makes it increasingly difficult for clients and/or services to understand what is happening (much less take corrective action). Lack of any definition about what clients can expect, other than "best effort," makes services simpler to create, but harder to use in complex scenarios. For the simpler request/response scenarios in WSRF, leaving the failure model up to the application is reasonable. For more complex, multi-message interactions, such as are possible in WS-notification, "best effort" seems likely to produce non-interoperable systems.

Conclusion

Some in the Web services community have argued that we are entering the "con-traction" phase of Web services, whereby people realize that too many moving parts potentially compromises the core interoperability story. However, we cannot ignore the fact that complex application logic may require complex infrastructure to support it. In the end, WSRF and WS-Notification should be viewed as building blocks on which applications or other "higher-level" infrastructure can selectively be built. WSRF's importance as a building block comes from its argument that canonical exposure to and manipulation of state by clients is important. Given that most Web services contain state, this argument may be valid, even if it comes with the risk of added complexity. We have implemented WSRF.NET to enable our project and others to evaluate this approach through hands-on experience. While the potential of WSRF remains strong, a number of concerns have been raised. It can be difficult to decouple WSRF and WS-notification from the higher-level Grid functionality that we know we want to build using these specifications. In general, there is a balancing act between creating specifications that provide functionality that can be composed into many different usage patterns and creating specifications that are too vague to be used effectively. While the WSRF specifications may imply a (possibly complex) programming model, we feel that this complexity may not be unwarranted. The technical committees of OASIS for WSRF and WS-notification will undoubtedly address and improve many of our concerns, and more experience with implementations such as WSRF.NET will provide insight into understanding the general usability of WSRF.

It is interesting to note that interest in the remote management of state using Web services remains strong. The WS-transfer, WS-enumeration, and WS-eventing specifications (along with the associated WS-management) define a similar "resource based" abstraction of use in Web services. While these specifications addressed many of the same issues as WSRF/WS-Notification, they provided only simpler, "lower level" interfaces. For example, while WS-notification contained advanced concepts such as notification brokering and hierarchical topic spaces, WS-eventing defined only an event message format and a subscription protocol. The authors of WS-transfer, and so forth, contend that these specifications were not meant to underlie all Web services, but were to be used in appropriate contexts, such as the remote management of hardware resources. As such, the simplest possible interface was the most appropriate as it was the easiest for potential implementers to provide. Advanced, but unused concepts, made the specifications less likely to be adopted. In the end, many in the community saw that some of the more advanced concepts of WSRF and WS-notification could be implemented on top of the WS-transfer/enumeration/eventing stack. In 2006, IBM and Microsoft announced a "reconciliation" of the two sets of specifications (Cline et al., 2006) to promote better adoption within the Web services community. While the specifications to be produced by this reconciliation have yet to be released, there seems little doubt that a single stack for management of state in Web services that is implemented by all major vendors is a positive step for those using stateful Web services for Grid computing.

References

Alexander, J., Box, D., Cabrera, L., Chappell, D., Daniels, G., Geller, A., et al. (2004). *Web services transfer (WS-transfer)*. Retrieved June 24, 2006, from http://msdn.microsoft.com/library/en-us/dnglobspec/html/ws-transfer.pdf

Arora, A., Cohen, J., Davis, J., Golovinsky, E., He, J., Hines, D., et al. (2004). *Web services for management (WS-management)*. Retrieved June 24, 2006, from http://www.intel.com/technology/manage/downloads/ws_management.pdf

Booth, D., Haas, H., McCabe, F., Newcomer, E., Champion, M., Ferris, C., et al. (Eds.). (2004). *Web services architecture*. W3C Web Services Architecture Working Group. Retrieved June 24, 2006, from http://www.w3.org/TR/ws-arch/

Box, D. (2004). A guide to developing and running connected systems with indigo. *MSDN Magazine, 1*.

Box, D., Christensen, E., Curbera, F., Ferguson, D., Frey, J., Hadley, M., et al. (2004). *Web services addressing (WS-addressing)*. Retrieved June 24, 2006 , from http://msdn.microsoft.com/webservices/default.aspx?pull=/library/en-us/dnglobspec/html/ws-addressing.asp

Cline, K., Cohen, J., Davis, D., Ferguson, D., Kreger, H., McCollum, R., et al. (2006). *Toward converging Web service standards for resources, events, and management*. Retrieved June 24, 2006, from http://msdn.microsoft.com/library/default.asp?url=/library/en-us/dnwebsrv/html/convergence.asp

Czajkowski, K., Ferguson, D., Foster, I., Frey, J., Graham, S., Snelling, D., et al. (2004a). *From open Grid services infrastructure to web services resource framework: Refactoring and evolution*. Retrieved June 24, 2006, from http://www-128.ibm.com/developerworks/library/ws-resource/ogsi_to_wsrf_1.0.pdf

Czajkowski., K., Ferguson, D., Foster, I., Frey, J., Graham, S., Sedukhin, I., et al. (2004b). *The WS-resource framework*. Retrieved June 24, 2006 from http://www-106.ibm.com/developerworks/library/ws-resource/ws-wsrf.pdf

Fielding, R. (2000). *Architectural styles and the design of network-based software architectures*. PhD dissertation. University of California at Irvine.

Foster, I., Kesselman, C., Nick, J., & Tuecke, S. (2002). *The physiology of the Grid: An open Grid services architecture for distributed systems integration*. Retrieved June 24, 2006, from http://www.Gridforum.org/ogsi-wg/drafts/ogsa_draft2.9_2002-06-22.pdf

Globus Project. (2006). Retrieved from http://www.globus.org

Graham, S., Hull, D., & Murray, B. (Eds.). (2004). *Web services base notification (WS-base notification), Version 1.3*. Retrieved June 24, 2006, from http://docs.oasis-open.org/wsn/wsn-ws_base_notification-1.3-spec-pr-03.pdf

Grimshaw, A., Ferrari, A., Knabe, F., & Humphrey, M. (1999). Wide-area computing: Resource sharing on a large scale. *IEEE Computer, 32*(5), 29-37.

Hapner, M., Burridge, R., Sharma, R., Fialli, J., & Stout, K. (2002). Java message service, Version 1.1. *Sun Microsystems Inc.*, 14. Retrieved June 24, 2006, from http://java.sun.com/products/jms/docs.html

Humphrey, M., Wasson, G., Morgan, M. & Beekwilder, N. (2004). *An early evaluation of WSRF and WS-notification via WSRF.NET.* Presented at the 2004 Grid Computing Workshop (associated with Supercomputing 2004), Pittsburgh, PA.

Little, M., Webber, J., & Parastatidas, S. (2004). Stateful interactions in web services: A comparison of WS-context and WS-resource framework. *SOA Web Services Journal.* Retrieved June 24, 2006, from http://www.sys-con.com/story/?storyid=44675&DE=1

Microsoft Corporation. (2005). *Web services enhancements, Version 3.0.* Retrieved from http://msdn.microsoft.com/webservices/webservices/building/wse/default.aspx

OASIS Web services resource framework (WSRF) Technical Committee. (2006a). Retrieved from http://www.oasis-open.org/committees/tc_home.php?wg_abbrev=wsrf

OASIS Web services notification (WSN) Technical Committee. (2006b). Retrieved from http://www.oasis-open.org/committees/tc_home.php?wg_abbrev=wsn

Object Management Group. (2005). *CORBA.* Retrieved June 24, 2006, from http://www.corba.com.

Ruslan, B., Box, D., Cabrera, L., Davis, D., Ferguson, D., Ferris, C., et al. (2005). *Web services ReliableMessaging protocol (WS-ReliableMessaging).* Retrieved on June 24, 2006, from http://specs.xmlsoap.org/ws/2005/02/rm/ws-reliablemessaging.pdf

Sun Microsystems. (2005). *Java 2 platform enterprise edition.* Retrieved June 24, 2006, from http://java.sun.com/j2ee/

Tuecke S., Czajkowski, K., Foster, I., Frey, J., Graham, S., Kesselman, C., et al. (2003). *Open Grid services infrastructure (OGSI), Version 1.0* (GFD-R-P.15). Global Grid Forum.

Wasson, G. (2005). *WSRF.NET programmer's reference.* Retrieved June 24, 2006, from http://www.cs.virginia.edu/~gsw2c/ WSRFdotNet/WSRFdotNet_programmers_reference.pdf

Wasson, G., & Humphrey, M. (2005). Exploiting WSRF and WSRF.NET for remote job execution in Grid environments. In *Proceedings of the International Parallel and Distributed Processing Symposium*, Denver, CO.

Wasson, G., Beekwilder, N., Morgan, M., & Humphrey, M. (2004). OGSI.NET: OGSI-compliance on the .NET framework. In *Proceedings of the 2004 IEEE International Symposium on Cluster Computing and the Grid*, Chicago.

WSRF.NET Project. (2005). Retrieved June 24, 2006, from http://www.ws-rf.net

Chapter X

QoS-Aware Web Services Discovery with Federated Support for UDDI

Chen Zhou, Nanyang Technological University, Singapore

Liang-Tien Chia, Nanyang Technological University, Singapore

Bu-Sung Lee, Nanyang Technological University, Singapore

Abstract

Web services' discovery mechanism is one of the most important research areas in Web services because of the dynamic nature of Web services. In practice, UDDI takes an important role in service discovery since it is an online registry standard to facilitate the discovery of business partners and services. However, QoS related information is not naturally supported in UDDI. Service requesters can only choose good performance Web services by manual test and comparison. In addition, discovery among private UDDI registries in a federation is not naturally supported. To address these problems, we propose UDDI extension (UX), an enhancement for UDDI that facilitates requesters to discover services with QoS awareness. In this system the service requester invokes and generates feedback reports, which are received and stored in local domain's UX server for future usage. By sharing these experiences from those requesters in the local domain, the UX server summarizes and predicts the service's performance. A general federated service is designed to manage the service federation. The discovery between different cooperating domains is based on this general federated service, and therefore the links between domains are maintained dynamically. The system handles the federated inquiry, predicates the QoS difference among different domains, and provides a simple view over the whole federation. Meanwhile, the UX server's inquiry interface still conforms to the UDDI specification.

Introduction

With the industry's efforts on promoting the used Web services, a huge number of Web services are being developed and made available on the Web. Organizations now wish to offer electronic services worldwide and this creates several technical problems. First, being able to discover what services are available. Second, being able to determine which services match your specification. Third, being able to control which services are advertised to whom, and when. Fourth, being able to assess previous and current service usage for future selection.

There are three major roles in the Web services architecture: the service provider, the service requester and the service registry. The service provider is the business entity that provides software applications as Web services. The service requester is the entity who has a need that can be fulfilled by an available Web Service. The service registry is a searchable repository of Web services descriptions where service providers publish their Web services and service requesters locate Web services and obtain binding information to invoke the services. UDDI (Bellwood et al., 2002) stands for universal description, discovery and integration. It is a public specification that defines a service registry to publish information regarding the Web services and to make this information available to potential clients.

As more and more services appear on the Web, service requesters are presented with a group of service offers providing similar services. Different service offers may have different qualities of service. This will require sophisticated patterns of negotiation. For example, the trade-offs between quality and cost or invocation of another trade service determining the QoS of various service offers. Current UDDI registries are neither accountable nor responsible for the QOS descriptions in service offers.

Some extension can be made for UDDI to register the service's QoS description. However, even with the QoS descriptions registered on UDDI through extension, the QoS description may still be a bad prediction of the service's real performance.

This is mainly caused by the following reasons. Firstly, the published description could use false information just to attract potential clients. Through the development of trust mechanism and digital signatures, this problem may be solved. Secondly, the false prediction inherits from the architectural aspect of UDDI system. The most distinctive architectures of UDDI registry system contain centralized architecture and semicentralized model (the cloud model). Single public UDDI is a centralized architecture model. To this model, UDDI is a central point which mediates service publishing/discovering in the framework. All services are registered on it and can be accessed by all those potential requesters. Different service requesters have quite different connection conditions and routing paths. This difference leads to the requester's different experiences of service QoS even when the service's server side processing condition is not changed at all. The unique service QoS description in the central UDDI is therefore not a good prediction for requester's reference. To the semi-centralized model (the cloud model), where there's more than one UDDI registries, replication technology will be used to ensure consistent content in different registries. Service provider is required to publish the service descriptions to any one of the cloud nodes. After the replica, service requesters can discover the service from any one of the cloud nodes. Through replication, the service requester can choose the most suitable cloud node and this improves the inquiry speed. However, when the services continue to emerge and the cloud continues to grow, the total amount of service description in each registry increases quickly and will affect the registry's scalability. Furthermore, the replication may still suffer from the incorrect QoS description that occurs in the centralized model. Replication of the QoS description will still remain a problem, as the correct prediction is not possible since the requester's network condition is very likely to be different from the replicated registry.

The solution being proposed in this chapter is called UDDI extension (UX) (Zhou et al., 2003). The main motivation for this work is the need to provide QoS-awareness in UDDI and service discovery between enterprise domains. It assesses previous and current service usage for future service selection. With analysis of the network model, the condition of service requester's connection is recorded by the server to enable better predictions in a future service's request. Instead of the QoS description published by service provider, QoS feedbacks made by a service requesters are used to generate summaries for invoked services. These summaries are then used to predict the services' future performance. The extended inquiry interface in UX is the counterpart of inquiry interface in UDDI and it conforms to the UDDI specification. A general federated service is designed so that server nodes can be administratively federated across network boundaries. Based on this federated service, lookup interface is provided on a UX server that facilitates the discovery between different registries and the exchange of service QoS summaries.

The chapter is organized as follows. The section, "Related Work" introduces the related work in this field. In "Network Model and Design Choices" we present the network model and design choices used in our system. The next section describes the system's components, their communications and the measured QoS metrics. In the following section, general federated service's design is presented and UX's federated discovery is discussed. The next section studies the system's implementation. The final section of this chapter presents our conclusions and directions of future work.

Related Work

The UDDI specification (Bellwood et al., 2002) provides no QoS related inquiry in the discovery interface. Service requesters cannot filter the unqualified service nor can they get and compare between different services without testing them first. To solve this problem, some work has been done to enhance the UDDI registry's inquiry/publish interface to embed the QoS information in the message. For example, UDDIe project (Shaikhali et al., 2003) is targeted mainly towards the QoS-supported interface enhancement for UDDI. UDDIe extends the UDDI registry to support searching on attributes of a service and develops the find method to enable queries for UDDI with numerical and logical (AND/OR) ranges. QoS management support is provided through the definition of QoS attributes in the extended UDDI API. The QoS information is provided on publishing, and the publisher can provide arbitrary QoS attributes with selected lease for a service. If such information can be trusted, the UDDIe provides the lifetime control and QoS-supported discovery for UDDI.

Compared with UDDIe project, our system does not modify the standard UDDI interface and the client- side software can transparently plug on to our system. Although the UDDIe incorporate the arbitrary QoS attributes, the definition of the attributes is by the service provider when publishing the service. On the contrary, our system continuously collects the feedback reports so that the QoS information summarized is closer to the service's real performance. The service provider does not need to worry about the selection and publishing of proper QoS attributes in UDDI. When the service provider and service requester are located in different network domains, our system understands the difference of their connection conditions. The prediction of the service performance is therefore more precise than centralized model.

WS-policy (Box et al. 2002) provides a flexible and extensible grammar for expressing the capabilities, requirements, and general characteristics of entities in an XML Web services-based system. Together, with the WS-policy attachment (Box, Curbera, et al., 2002), policy expressions can be associated with WSDL type definitions and UDDI entities. QoS characteristics assertions may be defined in subsequent specifications and reasoned about in a consistent manner. This provides an alternative solution to the QoS-supported discovery in UDDI registry.

As discussed earlier in a centralized model or a cloud model based on replica, even if the UDDI registry is enhanced with QoS-supported discovery, it cannot provide a precise prediction for the real service performance because the performance is influenced by the service requesters' different connection conditions.

In addition to the centralized model and the cloud model, a decentralized P2P network provides another option for the service discovery. Paolucci et al. (2003) propose a pure P2P service discovery network and show how to perform matching capability between Web services on the Gnutella network. This approach avoids a single point of failure and there is no danger of a bottleneck effect. Ping/pong process is used to discover other server nodes. It is more appropriate in dynamic environments.

Our federation approach sits between the pure P2P mechanism and the static configuration. P2P systems are more appropriate in dynamic environments such as ubiquitous computing. Serious security threats may exist in pure P2P for enterprise domain's usage. Static configuration does not provide good fault tolerance and needs a bit of management work. It is suitable in static environments where information is persistent. For enterprise domains, the cross-domain connections are less dynamic than P2P networks but still need enough mechanisms for easy link managements. The proposed federation service suits this well. It has good load distribution and tolerance for network or node failures. The topology is stable and with knowledge about the global federation, each node can be reached and no service discovery information will be missed during the search.

Zhang (2002) points out that the next generation Web services discovery mechanism should meet following requirements: Using standard interface, simplifying the developer's work, hiding the complexity of UDDI search client and WSIL (Brittenham, 2001) search client, performing result aggregation from one or multiple sources, and acting as an advanced search portal on the application server. According to these requirements, BE4WS (Zhang et al., 2003) provides higher level APIs to take advantage of UDDI4J or other clients, such as the WS-inspection search tool, to define a script-based search request, aggregate search results, and explore multiple UDDI registries concurrently. The aggregation includes, but is not limited to, intersection, union, and script-based logic operation for the resulting responses from multiple sources.

In addition, Web services relationships language (WSRL) (Zhang et al., 2002) describes the relationships about the Web services rather than the requests. UDDI specification lacks the definitions and descriptions of the generic relationships among business entities, business services and operations. In WSRL, Web services relationships are defined at different levels: Business-business relationship (BBR), business-service relationship (BSR), service-service relationship (SSR), business-operation relationship (BOR), service-operation relationship (SOR), operation-operation relationship (OOR). Through the capturing of these relationships, WSRL provides better support for composing and executing dynamic business processes integration. Since it is based on UDDI, QoS related service discovery is still not supported.

WS-QoS (Tian et al., 2004) defines the XML schema for Web services to describe their services' high and low level QoS properties. The assistant framework is designed for the language specification to assist the service selection and publish. High-level QoS requirement can be mapped to the actual QoS-enabled transport layer through its proxy. It uses ontology style XML schema to define custom metrics. Two levels of metrics, the service performance level metrics, and the transport level metrics are defined in their system. However, the connection's QoS condition is not considered in their system yet, hence the discovery among different enterprise domains would lead to imprecise.

Our UX system uses the federated enhancement to provide federated registries' service inquiry and result aggregation. Standard interface is used in system and the service requester's work is simplified. In each enterprise domain, the UX system can be viewed as an advanced UDDI portal on application server. Compared with BE4WS, BE4WS provides one additional abstract layer for the client-side software to hide the complexity of UDDI search client. We keep the availability of current client side software and add one abstract layer for UDDI server to achieve the federated discovery and QoS-awareness. BE4WS does not mention the registries' link management problem. General federated service is presented in our system to achieve the dynamic link management for federation. Our approach does not support the advanced aggregation operations such as intersection and script-based logic operation presented in BE4WS. Private UDDI registries enhanced with WSRL can be used to specify confidential preference information about services. Complicated relationships among services, among business entities, and among service types can be encapsulated to enable dynamic e-business integration. Our approach uses the defined QoS metrics and service requester's customization to get the preference information about services. No explicit relationship information is currently used in our system.

Network Model and Design Choices

In this section, we discuss the underlying network model and some design choices used in our UX architecture.

Network Model

In our system, the network model is abstracted into domains. Each domain has relatively high bandwidth, low latency, and uncongested connections. The properties of connections between different domains are unknown. Different interdomain connections may have quite different qualities. (See Figure 2).

In our system, these domains mainly stand for organizations such as enterprises, universities, and so forth. These organizations federate with each other by contracts. A local UDDI registry works in each domain for a Web service's discovery and it will maintain a registry of the local domain's services.

Design Choices

Our architecture incorporates five important design choices that offer value-added services over standard UDDI:

First, the architecture is aware of the provider service's QoS. The QoS reports of services are sent back and shared to predict the services' performance. We rely on service level measurements such as response time or reliability to help requesters make decisions. Many network level measurement system exists in which they use metrics such as routing metrics, link bandwidths, geographic locality, etc., to predict the relative performance of different hosts. Unfortunately, these metrics often do not correlate with service level performance. Servers' conditions, such as load, popularity, and so forth, may also affect the service's performance.

Second, the measurement results are shared (Stemm et al., 2000). Requesters explicitly share the QoS reports they made by sending them to the local UX server. By

Figure 1. Network model

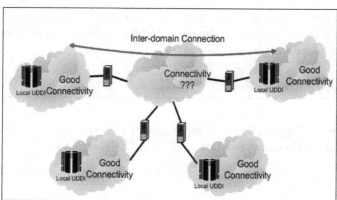

sharing the measurements, the requesters do not need to make manual test invocations. Hence, network resource is saved and server load is reduced. The decision to share measurements is followed directly from the network model. Two requesters in the same domain are likely to observe similar service performance because of similar connection condition. Measurements made in other domains may not be utilized directly because of the unknown interdomain connection properties. The way to process the cross-domain measurements is proposed in the section "Federated Support for UX Servers."

Third, customization is available in the discovery procedure (Davis et al., 2001). Different requesters may have different QoS preferences for discovery. For example, some requesters may prefer good service response time, while others prefer low cost. In order to help the requesters in locating the best fit services, the system allows the requesters to describe their preference in their profiles and then generates the result according to their preference. The requester can setup their profile on the server for customization.

Fourth, the extended inquiry interface conforms to the UDDI specification. The requesters can even use their original discovery software to make queries. In the federated discovery, the interface remains the same because the discovery is performed by the local UX server on behalf of the requester. If the requester wants to use some advanced features such as customization and authorization, client software needs to specify the user's identity in the discovery process for the server to get the user's profile. This feature is already supported in the UDDI4J package.

Lastly, additional policies are recommended to manage behavior of the UDDI registry. For example, *hop_count* is used to control the depth of the query's propagation in the UDDI federation. Some other policies such as cache's *living_time* are also designed to control the behavior of a registry.

UX System

In this section we describe the components of UX system architecture and how they communicate with each other. We also describe how we define the QoS metrics and the customization process in our system.

Components of UX system

Figure 2 shows a diagram of the components of UX system. It is comprised of service requester, UX server, test host, and local UDDI registry.

Figure 2. Components of the UX system

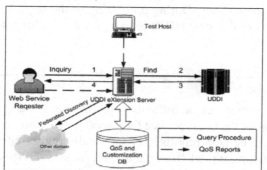

Service Requester

The service requester queries the UX server to find the matching services, chooses one, invokes the service and measures the performance of the service. During the measurement it creates QoS reports to record the performance data and sends them back in batches to the UX server. In the current system, we defined a set of the general QoS metrics that requesters are interested in, which will be described in the section "UX Server." To facilitate automatic QoS reports, a client side QoS reporter is provided. The reporter works as a SOAP intermediator and no code modification is needed from the requester side. The reporter may cause potential security problems. Firstly, to the service requester, the unknown reporter may eavesdrop or modify the SOAP content for certain purpose. This risk can be minimized through open source and checksum verification to the reporter. Secondly, to a UX server, a malicious reporter may send false QoS reports back to UX server to fake the service performance. This may be solved by digital signature technologies and allowing only those trusted reporters to feedback. However, the security problem is not the major concern of this chapter and we will not discuss this anymore. If the measurement does not need requester's participation, it can be moved from client side to one special site in the local domain for easier control. Currently the reporter measures those synchronized request-response Web services and most Web services do belong to this category.

Local UDDI Registry

The local UDDI registry is a standard UDDI registry that records the local domain's services descriptions. Local service providers are required to publish their service descriptions to local UDDI registry, not the external ones. To ensure generic support, the local UDDI is connected to the UX server as a backend registry using SOAP (Box et al., 2000) connections. During processing of the requests, the UX server acts as a client to query the local UDDI registry for local information.

Test Host

In practice, it may sometimes be difficult to predict a service's performance because the system lacks the latest service QoS reports. The test host is designed to generate current service QoS reports only for locally registered services. It tests the service with random or predefined parameters to gain service reports. The test interval is carefully selected so that the test host will not create obvious overhead to the network and its QoS reports only occupy a small portion of the total reports. The system manager has the option to configure the interval manually.

UX Server

The UX server plays an important role in the system. When the UX server receives an inquiry from the requester, it searches the local UDDI for related results. If the number of items in the result is insufficient, the federated discovery is started to find more related items. The discovery of services across domains will be discussed later. After collecting all these results, the UX server filters and merges these results. If the inquiry is service related, the server sorts the service results according to the QoS summaries and then sends the results back to the requester. The UX server also receives the requester's QoS reports, stores them in a database, and processes them to generate the QoS summary, which is used in the sort procedure.

QoS Metrics

QoS covers a whole range of technologies that match the needs of service requesters with those of service providers based on the available resources. The major requirements for supporting QoS in Web services are like performance, reliability, security, and so forth (Mani et al., 2002). Each Web service may have different QoS metrics to evaluate and describe its QoS. In our current system, we aimed at general Web services from an end-user's view. Based on the previous experience, we have constructed the QoS metrics that include system-centric category. Currently the QoS metrics measured in our system contain response time, cost and reliability (Cardoso et al., 2002). The type of QoS metrics is extensible in our system and it is not limited in the feedback interface. To utilize the extended metrics, the processing logic for the new metric should be defined for summarization.

Response time metric is defined as the total time needed by the service requester to invoke the service. We measure the response time from the time the requester initiates the invocation to the time the requester received the last byte of the response. This is a service level measurement and the response time can be divided into server execution time, queuing delay and the network transportation time.

Cost represents the cost associated with the execution of the service. It is necessary to estimate the guarantee that financial plans are followed. The cost in the QoS report is gained by the volunteer requester's input. If no feedback is made on this metric, the QoS report is sent back with this metric labeled unknown. The cost can be broken into major components, which include the service execution cost and network transportation cost.

Reliability corresponds to the likelihood that the service will perform when the user demands it and it is a function of the failure rate. Each service has two distinct terminating states: One indicates that a Web service has failed or aborted; the other indicates that it is successful or committed. By appropriately designed redundancy, one can build highly reliable systems from less reliable components. We use the stable reliability model proposed by (Nelson, 1973), for which the reliability of a Web service is $R(t) = 1 - failure\ rate$. Each QoS report records the terminating state of the service, which will be summarized on UX server to generate the reliability.

The UX server generates a summary of the reports for each service regularly. It calculates the response times, terminating state and cost in each received QoS report to a summary which contains response time, reliability, cost, timestamp and report number. This summary is used to sort the query result. The service's performance may depend on the service's input and the variance of the performance may be obvious. Using only the summarized value is not a perfect reflection of the service's performance. (Cardoso et al., 2002) uses min, max, avg value and the probability distribution function to describe a service's performance information. Currently we utilize only the summarized mean value to describe the service QoS. The establishment of better QoS metrics model is out of this chapter's scope and it is part of our future work.

To the summarization phase, we design and compare three types of functions to generate the summary from report fields:

1. **Average function:** $f = \sum_{i=1}^{n} r_i / n$, where r_i is the ith received QoS report's field value during the interval of two summarizations, and n is the total reports number during the interval.

2. **Low-pass filter function:** $f_i = \alpha * f_{i-1} + (1-\alpha) * r_i$ (Richard, 1994), where α is a smoothing factor, r_i stands for the ith sorted record's field value during the interval of two summarizations, and f_i stands for the calculated field value when processing the ith report. Value f_0 is initialed by the last summary's field value. To apply this function, QoS reports in the interval are first sorted by

timestamp and then processed sequentially on these reports. This method helps the summary to include all the history measurement information. If α is set as 0.8, 80% of each new calculated f_i is from the previous value and 20% is from the report's value.

3.   **Median function:** median value of the related field during the interval of two summarizations is selected.

In the local test, we set up two Web services with the same service function for comparison. The only difference between these two services is their processing speed: One is much faster than the other. The test is conducted on the university's LAN with a node/server pair. During each service invocation, we collected the response time and end state information. The cost is chosen to be zero. More than 400 service invocation data is collected and the experiment lasts for about 10 hours. From the experiment we find that the response time is highly converged at its summarized value, and about 80% of invocations for the faster version of the service are within 20% away from the summarized response time value. This shows that using summarized value to predict the service is reasonable for major invocation instances. To compare with three summarization functions (*average, median,* and *low-pass filter* function), we draw the diagram of the percentage deviation of Web services invocations from the summary of response time using the summarization function respectively (see Figure 3).

The weighted average of the deviation, where the deviation is percentage away from the summarized value to the invocation value and the weight is the corresponding invocations' occupied percentage, shows the mean deviation from the summarized value to the record values. The summarized function has better estimation of the record values if the mean deviation of the function is lower. By comparison of three functions' mean deviations, we find that the *low-pass filter* function f_i has the minimum deviation (see Table 1). Furthermore, if α is chosen as 0.6960, f_i will reach the minimum value of 12.64. Therefore, the *low-pass filter* function f_i is chosen as the summary function in UX server.

Another remote test is made on the Xmethods' listed stock service (http://www.swanandmokashi.com/HomePage/WebServices/StockQuotes.asmx). During each service invocation, we collect the response time and end state information. More

Table 1. Mean deviation of summary functions for fast add

Function Name	Mean Deviation (%)
Average Function	19.03
Median Function	17.38
Low-pass Filter Function with $\alpha = 0.8$	15.10

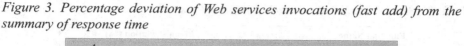

Figure 3. Percentage deviation of Web services invocations (fast add) from the summary of response time

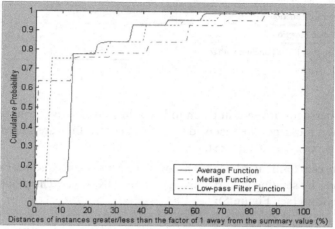

than 900 service invocations' data are collected and the test lasts for 24 hours. From the percentage deviation of Web services invocations from the summary (see Figure 4), we can see the response time is converged to the summarized function. More than 90% of the service invocations are within 10% away from the summarized value. The summarized value in remote test is much larger than the local test. However, the result in remote test converges better than the local test. The service's response time is divided into the server's execution time and the network transportation time. In the LAN, the network transportation time is neglectable so that the server's execution time is the major factor in the response time. Therefore the server's performance in the local LAN's test tends to be more noticeable. In the remote Web service's test, a substantial part of the response time is due to the network transportation time. The absolute network transportation time is also much higher in the public test compared with the local test and with a small server execution time. The variance in the remote test is therefore relatively small and from the test we can see that the perceived response time in remote test converges better. For the comparison of three summary functions, the *low-pass filter* function with $\alpha=0.8$ still gets the best results (see Table 2).

Communication between Components

All communications between the components of our system use SOAP (Box et al., 2000) messages for easy extensibility and adoption. There are mainly two kinds of messages in the system, the QoS report messages and the inquiry messages.

Table 2. Mean deviation of summary functions for stock

Function Name	Mean Deviation (%)
Average Function	11.57
Median Function	4.24
Low-pass Filter Function with $\alpha = 0.8$	4.12

QoS report messages are sent in batch to keep the network overhead reasonable. After the report messages are received by the UX server, they are stored in a local database for processing at a later stage.

The system uses a 'pull' approach to discover the services. Requester can find the related services by sending inquiry messages to the UX server. The processing step is listed as follows (see Figure 5):

1.   Requester sends the UDDI inquiry to the UX server. If the inquiry does not contain an identify information, default QoS weights are used for customization. Otherwise the weights are extracted from user profile database.

2.   UX server first checks its local cache to see if the cache can provide the result. If so, it sends the result back to the requester and ends the process. Otherwise, it sends the query to the local UDDI registry and goes to step 3.

Figure 4. Percentage deviation of web services invocations (stock) from the summary of response time

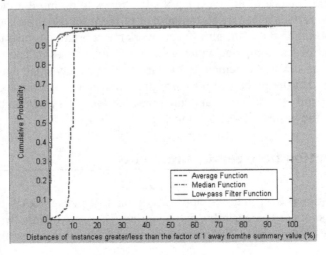

3. Local UDDI registry processes the inquiry and then returns the result.

4. The UX server checks the record number in the result. If the number is less than the requester's intended number, it starts the federated discovery to get additional results and then merges the results (this will be described in the "Federated Support for UX Servers" section). If the inquiry is service related, UX server will sort the result according to QoS summary and requester's preference. Otherwise the UX server returns the result directly. The format of the returned result conforms to UDDI specification.

Customization

Service requesters may have different preference on the service's QoS metrics. By customization of his user-profile (currently we provide a Web interface to help requesters in setting up their profile), the requester can set different weights on different metrics. The requester puts his identify in the inquiry and the server extracts his profile information from the database. If weights information is unavailable, default value is used (e.g., each weight is set to 1).

If the inquiry is service related, the UX server generates the service score list according to the QoS summary and the weights. This contains two steps: Normalization of the QoS summary and score calculation.

In the normalization phase, each metric field is mapped to a value between 0 and 1 and higher normalized value means better score. Therefore, an inverse function $S_x = 1/(x+1)$ is chosen for cost and response time metrics. x is the field value and S_x is the normalized value. Reliability value has already been in the range of 0 to 1 so that its value is kept.

In score calculation phase, the service score is calculated by weighted average function:

$$score = \frac{W_{cost} \times S_{cost} + W_{resptime} \times S_{resptime} + W_{reliability} \times S_{reliability}}{W_{cost} + W_{resptime} + W_{reliability}},$$

where S_{cost}, $S_{resptime}$, and $S_{reliability}$ are normalized summary scores; w_{cost}, $w_{resptime}$ and $w_{reliability}$ stand for the customized weights respectively.

The higher the score is the better the service's quality. The result is sorted according to this score list so that the top item has the highest score. If some metric field's value happens to be unknown, random value is generated so that the service has a chance to be invoked by the requester. When the requester gets the result, it can easily choose among the several top services in the list.

Federated Support for UX Servers

The previous section detailed the components of the architecture and the local interactions between them. In this section, we focus on how UX server interacts with other UX servers across domains in order to support federated service discovery. When the UX server gets the requester's inquiry, it will propagate the inquiry to UX servers in other domains only if the local UDDI registry does not have enough services to form the result set.

Using the federated discovery requires the system to be able to scale and support a potentially huge number of requesters and services while adapting the underlying domains' changes (e.g., due to network partitions and node failure). This requires a proper link management and query propagation model.

In addition to the underlying model, a lookup interface between UX servers is extended to support the federated discovery. A general interface of a UX server is presented in Figure 5. The interfaces contain the UX server's extended inquiry interface, lookup interface, the original UDDI publish interface and the Admin interface. The extended inquiry interface provides the QoS-aware Web services discovery over the original UDDI and local domain's service requesters query through the local UX server. Lookup interface is designed to support federated discovery between UX servers. The original UDDI publish interface is kept for service provider to publish their business services. Extended admin interface manages the domain links and policies.

The input to the lookup interface is a string of XML (as shown in Figure 6) that describes the federated query information for other domain's UX servers' process. It contains mainly query ID, hop number, original sender, last sender and query content. The response from other domain's UX server is also a string of XML that

Figure 5. System's interface

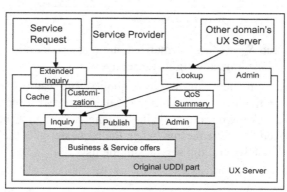

describes the query result and related QoS summary if the query is service related. It contains mainly query ID, sender, query response and QoS summary.

Link Management and Query Propagation

In the network, different domains' links can be manually or statically established amongst individual UX server nodes. Examples of static establishment include the CORBA Trading Service, ODP Trader (ITU, 1994), DNS systems (M. P., 1987) and LDAP directory services (Wahl et al., 1997). However, works has been done in which domain links are managed dynamically. CSG (Belaid, et al., 1998) models B2B peering contracts and the policies would define the associations between how companies can use each other registries. Links are established according to these contracts and policies and they can then be managed dynamically.

CSG Model (Balad et al., 1998)

The aim of the cooperating server graph model (CSG) is to optimize and dynamically manage links between cooperating servers over a wide area network. Based on CSG model, we extend it into the Web services arena. A general federated service has been designed and cooperated into our UDDI extension system as the message propagation layer.

Figure 6. Federated server's propagation interface

```
public class DederatedmEssageHeadData {
  public String version; // the CSG version.
  public String messageType; // the message type  "UXLookup",
"VersionUpdate", "SendbackSinceLowerVersion"
  public String queryID;
  public String originalSender, // correspond to the node Identifier
  public String lastSender;
  public PropagationCondition pCondition;
}
  public void multicast)GraphNode bypassNode, ArrayList theNodes, String head,
String content);
  public void alternativeBehavior(GraphNode failedNode, GraphNode preFailedNode,
String head, String content);
}
```

CSG approach uses a minimum-weight spanning tree to optimize links between UX servers automatically. The shortest path trees are not chosen to avoid generation of star trees. The weight is defined by a distance function to represent the communication cost between the couple of nodes (e.g., the inquiry latency, the hop number, etc.). Prim (1957) algorithm is used to calculate the minimum-weight tree. In our general federated service design, each node in CSG is called a federated server (FS).

The CSG model and propagation tree have to adapt dynamically to the change of cooperating servers and the underlying network topology. In order to be more efficient for the graph's management and reduce the control overhead, different events are treated accordingly. The dynamic administration of CSG takes three levels of events into account:

1.   **Alternative behavior in case of failure:** Once a federated server (FS) detects a failure of its neighbor nodes (i.e., when it cannot propagate information to one of its neighbors in the tree), the FS uses the alternative behavior in case of failure. It propagates the information, on behalf of the failed neighbor (the communication failure may come from a failed FS or a network failure), to the neighbors of the failed neighbor in the tree. This behavior maintains the continuity of the service and it is feasible because of the global knowledge of the propagation tree.

2.   **Local reconfigurations:** The local reconfigurations level is used to take into account FS's long time failure, FS's long time failure recovery, as well as FS's addition and removal. Long time failure can be decided according to predefined failure time threshold. Instead of the propagation of a new CSG version, the local reconfiguration updates the local propagation tree and enables the CSG's minor change at a lower cost. A local reconfiguration is possible if and only if each node, after the reconfiguration, knows its own neighbors and the neighbors of its neighbors in the effective propagation tree. A node cannot participate in two local reconfigurations simultaneously. As a result the reconfiguration progress is made atomic. After accepting a local reconfiguration, a node buffers incoming requests so as to retransmit them at the end of the reconfiguration process.

3.   **Global change of the CSG version:** A version change federated server, chosen dynamically in the federation, triggers the version change of the CSG. Each FS sends its local long time reconfigurations to the version change server, which includes the long time failures, long time distance changes, addition and removal of the nodes. Then the version change server triggers a new CSG version when the degradation rate of the propagation tree (the sum of the weights of the degraded tree divides that of the minimum spanning tree which is still in use) goes past a given threshold. The new version is then propagated to all the domains' FSs, via the propagation tree. Two nodes (sender and receiver)

have to agree on a version before they can communicate through CSG. If the receiver has an older version, the request is buffered on the receiver until its version is updated. On the other hand, if the sender has an older version, it will send the request back to the source node, which in turn will reinitiate the propagation after updating its CSG version.

This model can tolerate a great number of failures. All the CSG updates are made dynamically, and the number of CSG version changes is greatly reduced by dividing the failures into different levels of events.

Federated Service Design

The federated service takes the Web services layer approach instead of network layer approach to achieve the extensibility and easy adoption. There are two basic communication semantics in the federation service: The local tree modifications and the propagation of messages. When the local tree modification happens, the local tree modification has to be made coherently on a group of neighbor servers one and two steps away from the center coordinator of the modification. This modification should guarantee that either all these neighbor server nodes make the modification or none of them does. A service node cannot participate in two local tree modifications simultaneously. In short, the behavior of modification is kept consistent and atomic.

Different from the local tree modification, the query propagation does not need to guarantee the atomicity or the message's ordering. Each federated server in the propagation's chain becomes a coordinator when it receives the information to propagate. It has to forward the information to all its neighbors in the propagation tree, except for the one from which information was forwarded. If one neighbor does not acknowledge, the propagation should still go on and the coordinator triggers the alternative behavior in case of the neighbor's failure.

According to the two different communication semantics, we divide the federated service design into two service groups: The LocalChangeGroup and the PropagationGroup. The LocalChangeGroup provides the atomic and consistent invocation for the local tree modification. The PropagationGroup offers the propagation invocation for the normal messages. The message order and the atomic of this invocation are not ensured.

The local reconfiguration procedure is showed in Figure 7. To ensure the atomic modification semantic, the LocalChangeGroup is told to multicast the save method to the neighbors of the UX server and the neighbors of its neighbor. A boolean result is returned to indicate whether the LocalChangeService is ready to process the modification. If all neighboring LocalChangeServices are ready, the commit method is invoked on all the neighboring LocalChangeServices which in turn invoke their add/remove method to modify the local graph. Otherwise, the abort method is invoked and the multicast method returns to indicate the failure of the local reconfiguration. The interface definition is shown in Figure 8. All the successful local reconfiguration information is sent to ChangingVersionFederatedServer, which controls the CSG version. It triggers a new CSG version if the degradation rate of the propagation tree (the sum of weights of the degraded tree divides by that of the minimum spanning tree which is still in use) goes past a given threshold.

The federated service can be applied to a wide range of Web services. For example, better efficiency can be supported through federating similar services together and serving the service requesters from nearer and faster servers; robustness can be increased through reconfiguration of the federation and skipping of those failure nodes; performance can be enhanced if each service finishes different portion of the target and works together for the final result. In our UDDI eXtension system, we build our special UXFederatedServer class through the generalization of FederatedServer, add "UXLookup" message type for federation propagation and define special handling logic for "UXLookup" message by providing a federatedLookup method. Additional propagation condition can also be extended in federatedLookup method to control the propagation logic. This design achieves the separation of the CSG model and UDDI lookup logic. The FederatedServer manages the message propagation and failure control, while the UXFederatedServer deals with the special UDDI lookup logic for service discovery. Therefore, complexity reduction and code reuse is achieved.

Figure 7. Federated service's local tree modification

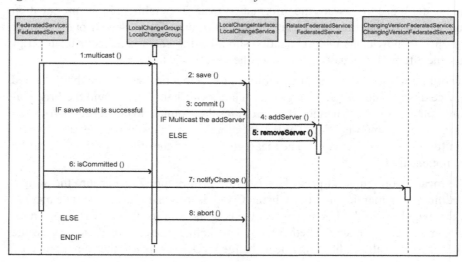

Figure 8. Federated server's local tree change interface

```
public class LocalChangeAdminMessageData {
    public String adminType; // addServer or removeServer
    public String nodeIdentity;
    public EdgeDetail[] edgesDetail;
}
public class LocalChangeGroup{
    public synchronized boolean multicast(String messageContent);
    public boolean isCommitted(String messageID);
    ...
}
public class LocalChangeService
{
    public synchronized boolean save(String messageID, String messageContent);
    public void commit(String messageID);
    public void abort(String messageID);
}
```

Query Propagation

When the original UX server finds its local UDDI registry does not have enough results, it begins to propagate queries (Czwerwinski, 1999). To reduce unnecessary delays in response, the propagated servers respond to the original UX server directly. Currently the propagation condition contains hop_count and intended_number. See Section 0 for their detailed descripton. The hop_count is decreased by one when the inquiry is delivered one step further along the CSG. If the hop_count reaches 0, the inquiry is not delivered further. Otherwise the system uses federatedLookup interface in UXFederatedServer to propagate the query along the CSG links. intended_number is used by the original UX server to check whether the local UDDI registry returns enough results. Each UX server is responsible for its local registered services so that they are included in the response. If the query is service related, the related services' QoS summaries are also included. When the original UX server receives the results from an external UX server, it accumulates the result number and checks it with the intended_number. The result collection ends when the result number reaches the intended_number or the timeout set according to the hop_number is reached. After the collection, it merges these results into a single result set for the service requester. If the query is service related, the result set is sorted according to the QoS summaries. The received QoS summaries are first mapped and then utilized in the sort phase. The sort procedure is similar to the local discovery mode. See the "QoS Similarity Domains" section for details of the received QoS mapping processing.

Because of the CSG model's global knowledge of the propagation tree, the cyclic dependencies can be avoided. However, the ordering of the propagated message is not guaranteed. To choose among the different returned results and then merge them according to the original query we use query identity to distinguish different results. In order for this to work, the UX server must remember the query identities of all recent federated query operations that it has performed. When a federated query is received, the UX server checks this history and then processes the results.

QoS Similarity Domains

The similarity of QoS between two domains is a measure of the differences between the same service's performances by requesters in different domains. There may be several possible ways to determine whether some other domain is QoS-similar. First, it may be manually defined by the system administrator. Second, it may be learned dynamically. The periodical test for sample public benchmark services in each domain or the analysis of the QoS summaries' differences between domains are possible ways for dynamic learning.

We take the dynamic learning approach to decide the QoS similarity by analyzing the QoS summaries. Notice that the local domain's feedback QoS reports contain two parts. The first part records the QoS of services that is registered in local domain while the second part records the QoS of services that is registered in other domain. In federated discovery, the first part is exported by the UX server while the second part is not exported because the service is not in the local domain. This part is used to measure two domains' QoS similarity. When some other domain's service QoS summary is returned in federated discovery, this service's QoS summary information in the second part of local domain's QoS summaries is located and the difference between these two summaries is judged. If the average relative difference between these domains is below a predefined threshold (e.g., 20%), these two domains are deemed as QoS similar domains. The QoS summary returned from such domains is used directly. Otherwise, two domains are not QoS similarity domains and the differences are recorded. The QoS similarity measurement is taken on regular basis to update the similarity information so that the server's performance is not influenced significantly.

If two domains are not QoS similarity domains, according to the network model, the dissimilation of service performance between two domains is mainly caused by the network connection between two domains. Therefore the correct prediction of another domain's service summary can be achieved through the translation on received summaries according to the recorded differences. To achieve better efficiency, we divide the QoS metrics into two parts: First part is the stable metrics whose change is neglectable from different domains' views (stable metrics). Second part is the changeable metrics that may change greatly from different domain's view (changeable metrics). In our selected metrics, we choose the cost and reliability as the stable metrics, while the response time as the changeable metrics. To correct these changeable metrics between domains, a simple linear function is used to change the metric response time's value (i.e., to add the average difference directly to the received QoS summary as the predicted summary). The server then uses this predicted summary to sort the result.

Discovery Policies

hop_count policy is used to control the depth of the query's propagation. When query is propagated one step further, the value of *hop_count* is decreased by one and when the *hop_count* reaches zero, the query is not propagated any more. The *hop_count* can be set statically or described in the user's profile. It makes a tradeoff between response time and total result number.

intended_number policy describes how many result items the requester intends to get. When it is specified in the inquiry, the UX server will start the federated discovery unless enough inquiry result has been found. If it is not specified in the inquiry message, local-only discovery is assumed. The *intended_number* is extracted from the UDDI inquiry's max row attribute and it is not changed during propagation.

To expedite the discovery procedure and improve the system's scalability, especially for federated discovery, each UX server stores a least-recently-used (LRU) result cache. Each cached item contains the inquiry, result, and the service summary if the inquiry is service related. Cache on the UX server only serves the local domain's requesters. Cache's *living_time* policy is set to define the cache entry's maximum living time.

System Implementation

We have implemented a prototype of the UX system. The system uses Apache Axis (Axis Development Team, 2002), UDDI4J and WSIF (Apache Software Foundation, 2003) as the basic components. The IBM UDDI registry software is used as the local registry. The UX server is mainly implemented on the Axis platform. Because the service and tModel list is returned in ID forms, a mapping between the ID and the service's location is generated by the test host and stored in the database for UX server's usage.

On the requester side, a test tool designed as a SOAP intermediator is used to facilitate the service QoS measurement and feedback. The service's access point is extracted and stored by parsing the envelope of the SOAP message. After the response message is returned from the service provider, the service's response time and the end status are decided. The cost of the service invocation is provided by requesters or left blank as unspecified. If a service invocation reaches timeout, its end status is deemed as failure and the response time is set to be unspecified.

When the service requester sends the inquiries to the UX server, the UX server extracts the intended number from the inquiry message, gets the requester's identity and preference from user profile database (default customization options will be assumed if the requester's identity is not specified or no customization information for the user is available), and then checks the local UDDI registry first. If the inquiry is service related (currently we support the find_service function's inquiry in our system. Other inquiry functions such as find_business, get_bindingDetail, get_serviceDetail, etc., will not be modified in our system), QoS summary information is retrieve from the QoS database. Then the results will be sorted according to these summarizations. If the number of returned results from local UDDI registry, compared with the intended_number, is sufficient then the results are sent back to the service requester immediately. Otherwise, the federated service discovery procedure is triggered. PropagationGroup handles the message multicast and other domain's UX server will return the results directly back to the original UX server. The cache can fasten the procedure and improve the performance. Figure 9 shows the UML sequence diagram for service discovery in UX server.

The UML class diagram of the FederatedServer is available in Figure 10. The FederatedServer uses a composite design pattern to compose the LocalChangeGroup and the PropagationGroup. It is itself a generalization of GraphNode for graph so that each FederatedServer can be easily combined into the federation graph. The FederatedServer controls the addition and removal of service nodes, encapsulates the

Figure 9. Sequence diagram of service discovery in UX system

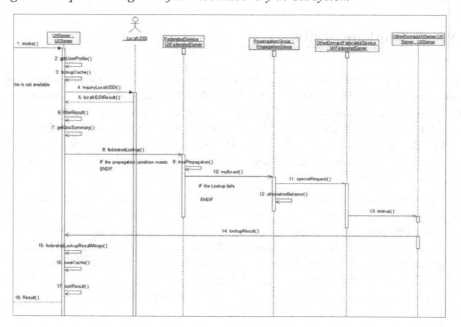

propagation interface and accepts the requester messages from special services.

Take a stock service inquiry as an example: Service requester "Steve" has already setup his customization profile on the UX Server to specify that his preferences on response time, reliability, and cost as 2, 1, 1 respectively. He uses UDDI4J as the inquiry tool and specifies his user name and password in the configuration file. When he sends find_service inquiry to the UX server with name = "stock" and intended_number = 10, the UX server checks the cache and finds that there's no such inquiry recently. Then UX server looks for the local UDDI registry and gets six services in the returned result. According to the serviceInfos, the QoS summary for these six services is extracted. Because the result number is less than the intended_number, federated discovery is initiated. No hop_number is specified in the customization profile so that the original UX server sets the hop_number as the maximum hop_number 5 in the current CSG. The original UX server sets the timeout as 5*10 seconds (each hop waits for 10 seconds which is set by the administrator) and begins the collection of returned results. The first neighboring UX server gets the federated lookup inquiry, reduces the hop_number by 1, propagates the lookup inquiry, queries its local UDDI registry and returns five serviceInfos together with the QoS summarizations. The original UX server received this service list and finds that the total discovered services of 11 is already larger than the intended_number so the original UX server stops the collection. Additional returned results from other UX servers are not collected to improve the inquiry speed. The original UX server starts the mapping and merging of the QoS summaries. Merged results and QoS

Figure 10. FederatedServer's class diagram

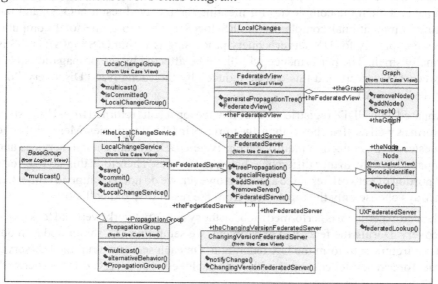

Figure 11. UX federation experiment setup

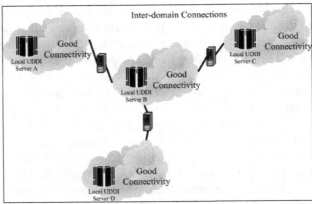

summaries are stored in the cache and then sorted according to Steve's preference. Finally the services result list is returned back to Steve.

To the CSG model's management, if the size of the CSG is N, then the size of the adjacent matrix is N^2, and the size of propagation edges is N-1. On the Changing-VersionFederatedServer, prim algorithm's computation complexity is $O(N^2)$ and the space complexity is $O(N^2)$ to store the adjacent Matrix. On each UX server, only propagation edges are stored and the space complexity is $O(N)$. The neighbor of each UX server is pre-computed so that the computational complexity is constant. To each UX server's inquiry processing, if the all returned results' number for one inquiry is S, then the complexity for merging the received result is $O(S)$, and the sorting computational complexity is $O(S \log(S))$. Therefore, the total computational complexity for UX server's query processing is within $O(S \log(S))$ and S is normally small. The performance will likely be affected by the propagation delay between UX servers and this can be reduced by the cache (see "Discovery Possibilites" section).

Compared with UDDI registries, we see that the top results returned from UX system perform as well as, if not better than, the top ones in UDDI registries. Meanwhile, the requester does not need to inquiry each private UDDI to gain enough services and compare the performance differences between services. Therefore, this saves efforts and portion of network resource as well. However, we do not recommend requesters to always choose only the top service from the result to avoid collision.

Federated experiment is performed to check the system's network overhead for service discovery. During the federated experiment, we setup four UX server nodes in our test environment to form the UX federation. On each server we run the UX server in the Tomcat servlet container with Axis deployed. These server nodes' network

Figure 12. The network overhead of UX federation experiment

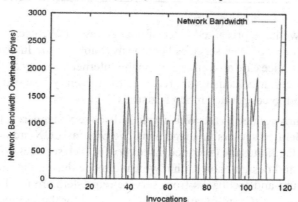

topology is shown in Figure 11. Nodes A, C, and D join the federation through node B. Node D receives the inquiry in its domain. If the local inquiry does not provide enough services for the requester, the federation discovery is triggered by node D. By this experiment, we try to check out the percentage of federation inquiries among the total inquires received by node D, and the network overhead for these nodes caused by the federated discovery. Since the network has good connections within the local domain, we are more interested in the network overhead among cross domain connections. The cache mechanism is disabled in this experiment to gain a precise result.

During the experiment, the inquiries in node D's domain are randomly generated with two alphabet letters. It issues a series of inquires, by which we record the network usage across the domain links. The hop number is set to be 2 so that all nodes in the federation can receive the inquiry. When the federated discovery is performed, the inquiry is delivered to node B, C, and D through the propagation tree. The experiment shows that the percentage of federated discovery in all of the inquiries is about 43%. Figure 12 shows the network overhead of each cross domain network link for the inquiry. The X axis is the index of the invocation, and the Y axis is the average bandwidth overhead on each cross domain connection caused by this federation query. The zero points in the figure means that the federation discovery is not executed in this inquiry. From the figure we can see that the average network overhead for each inquiry is about 1.5 KB on each cross domain network link. This overhead is less than a normal Web page's size, which is affordable for the normal discovery in most industries. The cache mechanism can be turned on to avoid the duplicated invocations across enterprise domains. Since the requesters in enterprise domain are often interested in some common services, the network's overhead can be reduced even more by the cache mechanism.

Conclusion and Future Work

In this chapter we have presented a set of challenges for Web services discovery when a large amount of Web services become available on the Internet. A number of similar Web services are also emerging on the Internet and they are competing to offer better services. Mechanisms are required to efficiently discover and compare such services and to cooperate among registries.

Our work is tightly related to the Web services discovery standards, QoS's prediction and the federated servers' management. We present a UX architecture that is QoS-aware and facilitates the federated discovery for Web services. We describe the network model and design choices that we have made during the implementation of our architecture and feedbacks from service requesters are used to predict the service's performance. Customization is also provided for the service requesters to describe their preferences for discovery.

A general federated service is designed according to the CSG model. It maintains the links among federated servers and deals with the message propagation. It can tolerate a great amount of node failures so that the global version change is reduced considerably. Based on the CSG model, UX server supports federated discovery across domains. The method to process different domain's difference based on QoS summaries as well as some additional policies are incorporated to support the system.

Compared with the original UDDI system, our system is aware of the basic service performance information with relatively small overhead from the feedback. The federated discovery helps the system to perform the discovery in the wider areas and estimate the QoS difference between domains dynamically. The replication consistency in a normal UDDI is a problem that is absent in our system as federated discovery is possible for UX servers. However, some drawbacks exist within UX system. The inquiry speed is slowed down during federated discovery because of the inquiry propagation. This is partially alleviated by implementing the cache at each UX server. The service requester's feedback is a potential security hole and needs certain security mechanism to overcome this.

The UX architecture presented in this chapter may be extended in the following ways. First, is to incorporate the semantic service descriptions in the registry so that the service capabilities are available in the matching procedure and precise matching can be supported. The current keyword matching cannot provide precise and flexible matching result. Second, is to design several template QoS metric classes for different kinds of Web services. These classes will provide better granularity for brokers to predict the service's performance. Measurement code reuse can be achieved according to the metric classes. The metrics can also provide more detailed information such as the variance, distribution, etc.

References

Apache Software Foundation. (2003). *WSIF: Web services invocation framework, Version 2.0*. Retrieved from http://ws.apache.org/wsif/

Axis Development Team. (2002). *Apache Axis, Version 1.0*. Retrieved http://ws.apache.org/axis/

Belaid, D., Provenzano, N., & Taconet, C. (1998). Dynamic management of CORBA trader federation. In *Proceedings of the 4th USENIX Conference on Object-Orented Technologies and Systems (COOTS)*.

Bellwood, T., et al. (2002). *UDDI API specification, Version 2*. Retrieved from http://uddi.org/pubs/ProgrammersAPI-V2.04-Published-20020719.htm

Box, D., et al. (2000). *Simple object access protocol (SOAP), Version 1.1*. Retrieved from http://www.w3.org/TR/SOAP/

Box, D., et al. (2002). *Web services policy framework (WS-policy), Version 1*. Retrieved from http://www.verisign.com/wss/WS-Policy.pdf

Box, D., Curbera, F., et al. (2002). *Web services policy attachment (WS-PolicyAttachment)* (Version 1). Retrieved from http://www.verisign.com/wss/WS-PolicyAttachment.pdf

Brittenham, P. (2001). *Web services inspection language specification (WSIL)*. Retrieved from http://www.ibm.com/developerworks/webservices/library/ws-wsilspec.html

Cardoso, J., Sheth, A., & Kochut, K. (2002). *Implementing QoS management for workflow systems*. Retrieved from http://lsdis.cs.uga.edu/lib/download/CSK02-QoS-implementation-TR.pdf

Christensen, E., Curbera, F., Meredith, G., & Weerawarana, S.(2001). *Web services description language (WSDL), Version 1.1*. Retrieved from http://www.w3.org/TR/wsdl

Czerwinski, S. E., Zhao, B. Y., Hodes, T. D., Joseph, A. D., & Katz, R. H. (1999). An architecture for a secure service discovery service. In *Proceedings of Mobicom '99*.

Davis, J. S., Bisdikian, C., Jerome, W. F., & D. M. Sow. (2001). *Emerging research opportunities in service discovery*. Presented at the New York Metro-Area Networking Workshop.

ITU. (1994). *ODP trading function* (ITU/ISO Committee draft standard, ISO 13235/ITU.TS Rec.9tr).

Mani, A., & Nagarajan, A.(2002). *Understanding quality of service for Web services*. Retrieved from http://www-106.ibm.com/developerworks/library/ws-quality.html

M. P. (1987). *Domain names: Implementation and specification* (STD 13, RFC 1035).

Tian M., Gramm, A., Ritter, H., and Schiller, J. (2004). Efficient selection and monitoring of QoS-aware Web services with the WS-QoS framework. In *Proceedings of the International Conference on Web Intelligence (WI '04)*.

Nelson, E. C. (1973). *A statistical basis for software reliability assessment* (TRW systems report).

Paolucci, M., Sycara, K., Nishimura, T., & Srinivasan, N. (2003). Using DAML-S for p2p discovery. In *Proceedings of the International Conference on Web Services (ICWS '03)*.

Prim, R. C. (1957). Shortest connection networks and some generalizations. *Bell Syst. Techno. J., 36.*

Richard S. W. (1994). *TCP/IP Illustrated.* Addison Wesley Longman, Inc.

Stemm, M., Katz, R., & Seshan S.(2000). A network measurement architecture for adaptive applications. In *Proceedings of INFOCOM 2000* (pp. 285-294).

Shaikhali, A., Rana, O. F., Al-Ali, R. J., & Walker, D. W. (2003). UDDIe: An extended registry for Web services. In *Proceedings of the Symposium on Applications and the Internet Workshops (SAINT '03 Workshops)*.

Xu, D., Nahrstedt, K., & Wichadakul, D. (2001). *QoS-aware discovery of wide-area distributed services.* Presented at CCGrid 2001.

Wahl, M., Howes, T., & Kille, S. (1997). *LDAPv3 protocol* (RFC 2251). Retrieved from http://www.ietf.org/rfc/rfc2251.txt

Zhang, L.-J., Chao, T., Chang, H., & Chung, J.-Y. (2003). XML-based advanced UDDI search mechanism for B2B integration. *Electronic Commerce Research Journal, 3,* 25-42.

Zhang, L.-J. (2002). Next generation Web services discovery. *Web Services Journal.*

Zhang, L.-J., Chang, H., & Chao, T. (2002, June). Web services relationships binding for dynamic e-business integration. In *Proceedings of the International Conference on Internet Computing (IC '02)* (pp. 561-567).

Zhou, C., Chia, L. T., Silverajan, B., & Lee, B. S. (2003). UX: An architecture providing QoS-aware and federated support for UDDI. In *Proceedings of the International Conference on Web Services (ICWS '03)*.

Chapter XI

Proactively Composing Web Services as Tasks by Semantic Web Agents

Vadim Ermolayev, Zaporozhye National University, Ukraine

Natalya Keberle, Zaporozhye National University, Ukraine

Oleksandr Kononenko, Nokia Research Center, Finland

Vagan Terziyan, University of Jyväskylä, Finland

Abstract

This chapter presents the framework for agent-enabled dynamic composition of Semantic Web services. The approach and the framework have been developed in several research and development projects by ISRG and IOG. The core of the methodology is the new understanding of a Semantic Web service as a capability of an intelligent software agent supplied with the proper ontological description. It is demonstrated how diverse Web services may be composed and mediated by dynamic coalitions of software agents collaboratively performing tasks for service requestors. Middle agent layer is introduced to conduct the transformation of a

Web service request to the corresponding task, agent-enabled cooperative task decomposition and performance. Discussed are the formal means to arrange agents' negotiation, to represent the semantic structure of task-activity-service hierarchy and to assess fellow-agents' capabilities and credibility factors. It is argued that the presented technique is applicable to various application domains. Presented is the ongoing work on designing and implementing agent-based layered architecture for intelligent rational information and document retrieval. Finally, the discussion of the OntoServ.Net framework for the development of P2P mobile service infrastructures for industrial asset management provides the extension of the Web service composition approach.

Introduction

Semantic Web services are the emerging technology promising to become one of the future key enablers of the Semantic Web. There are strong prerequisites that, being self-described and self-contained modular active components, Web services will appear to be the key elements in assembling intelligent software infrastructures in the near future.

There is the emerging consensus that the ultimate challenge is to make Semantic Web services automatically tradable and usable by artificial agents in their rational, proactive interoperation on the next generation of the Web. It may be solved by creating frameworks, standards, and software for automatic Web service discovery, execution, composition, interoperation and monitoring (McIlraith et al., 2002). The personal opinion of the authors is that the list should be extended by the means-making services to the subject of automated negotiation and trade. It is also important for future service enabled Semantic Web infrastructures to cope with business rules,[1] the notions and mechanisms of reputation and trust with respect to services and service providing agents, dynamic character, flexibility, re-configurability of partial plans (Ermolayev & Plaksin, 2002), workflows, and modeled business processes.

Current industry landscape provides only initial and very partial solutions to the ultimate problem. Existing de-facto standards for Web service description (WSDL), publication, registration and discovery (UDDI), binding, invocation, and communication (SOAP) provide merely syntactical capabilities and do not fully cope with service semantics. Known industrial implementations, such as HP E-speak (Karp, 2003), are based on these standards and do not completely solve the challenge of semantic interoperability among Web services. It should be mentioned that major industrial players realize the necessity of further targeted joint research and development in the field (Layman, 2003).

More recent research and standardization activities of the DARPA DAML community resulted in offering semantic service markup language DAML-S (Ankolekar et al., 2002) based on RDF platform. This initiative has later resulted in the development of OWL-S—the successor of DAML-S based on the World Wide Web Consortium's Web ontology language (OWL). The constellation of XML based languages/ontologies for business process description is also expanding: WSFL, ebXML, BPML, RuleML, BPEL4WS.

This chapter is the reworked and extended version of (Ermolayev et al., 2004). It is intended to highlight what should still be done on the top of recent research findings in order to make Web services automatically tradable and usable by Semantic Web agents in their rational, proactive interoperation on the next generation of the Web. Conceptual frames for this development are under intensive discussion and some proposals have already appeared for example WSMF (Fensel & Bussler, 2002). Recent research activities of the Semantic Web community in Europe and the Americas in several projects clearly demonstrate that the problem of dynamic composition (or orchestration) of Semantic Web services is one of the mainstream tasks. The approaches to solve this problem differ. However, the common trend is to use a goal-directed technique as it is done in distributed problem solving and dynamic distributed planning. For example, DIP project[2] proposes a mediation approach for goal-directed Semantic Web service orchestration using goal mediators, DIP interface description ontology based on WSMO (Roman et al., 2005). The tendency one can smell in the air is the search for a synergetic technology enhancing Semantic Web services with the ability to demonstrate a kind of a goal-directed (i.e., proactive) behavior. A natural locus of such a capability is known as an intelligent software agent.

The chapter offers a new understanding of a service as an intelligent agent capability implemented as a self-contained software component. From the other hand, provided that agents negotiate and trade, exchanging services in the process of their cooperative activities in open organizations, a service may be considered (as, say, in E-speak) a kind of a generalized resource. This approach evidently implies the appearance of a rational service providing agent demanding certain incentives and aiming to increase its utility. If, for example, a service requested from a travel agency is 'BookRoundtrip('Kiev,' 'Erfurt' 22/09/2003, 25/09/2003, ...)', the price paid by the requestor will comprise the prices of consumable (OWL-S, 2003) resources (air fare, hotel room, etc.) plus the incentive paid to the service holder for 'BookRoundtrip' service component usage. This remark seems to be rational as far as we pay either the salary to the office manager or a fee to a travel agent, who make arrangements for us in a human-business environment. Moreover, it is not in the eye of the service requestor, but the agent performing the 'BookRoundtrip' service who will realize according to the service markup or the partial local plan (PLP) in our terminology (Ermolayev et al., 2001; Ermolayev et al., 2005) that the requested process (OWL-S, 2003) or the task in our terminology (Ermolayev et al., 2001; Ermolayev et al.,

2005) is composite and will require cooperation with at least air companies' service providing agents and hotel booking service providing agents. These independent actors will evidently also intend to increase their own utilities by requesting fees for their services.

The chapter first provides the overview of the basic notions, approaches and architectural solutions with respect to agent paradigm, the World Wide Web (WWW) and the Semantic Web, Semantic Web services. Detailed discussion of the popular travel planning scenario helps to claim that full-scale Web service exploitation needs solutions beyond the facilities of today's semantic service markup. The chapter focuses on one of the major open problems—dynamic composition of a desired complex service by a coalition of rational cooperative freelance software agents.

Next, it is argued that it is a reasonable architectural solution to introduce an agent middle layer, for example (Sycara et al., 1999) between services and service consumers. Negotiation on Web service allocation based on the authors' approaches (Ermolayev & Plaksin, 2002) is proposed as the mechanism for dynamic composite service formation. OWL-S (OWL-S, 2003), our *task* and *negotiation ontologies* (Ermolayev et al., 2001; Ermolayev et al., 2005; Ermolayev & Keberle, 2006) are used for service dynamic composition and to facilitate inter-agent-operability.

Further on it is described how the approach to dynamic agent-based service composition is applied to intelligent rational information retrieval from distributed autonomous resources. Finally, the OntoServ.Net (Kaykova et al., 2004; Terziyan, 2005; Terziyan & Kononenko, 2003) framework and the aspects of service mobility and service adaptation are discussed. The architectural principles for service composition in a peer-to-peer service network are also outlined.

What is an Agent?

Agent paradigm in software engineering is one of the powerful means to narrow the semantic gap between the conceptualizations we use to analyze and to model the phenomena of the real world and the resulting distributed software system. If compared to the objects in OOSE, which may be interpreted as the analogy of inanimate entities in the real world, agents generally represent sentient animate objects, those able to cognize, typically human beings. Intelligent software agents are therefore used when the software needs to possess some "human" features like the ability to perceive the environment and reactivity, apparent proactive behavior in succeeding at a goal on behalf of the human owner, ability to learn from their experience, and social behavior. One of the inherent intelligent features of agents is the ability to form social structures—teams, communities, coalitions, and organizations. A *rational agent* as the member of a social structure needs to balance its *individual rationality* and *benevolence* in facilitating to the growth of the group utility. Agents often use *negotiation* mechanisms adopted from human encounters for that. An agent also needs to obey its social commitments and the conventions that regulate group behavior within the social structure. A team or an organization of agents that cooperate in a physically and, possibly, geographically distributed network form a software system called a *multiagent system* (MAS). An agent and a MAS are the main conceptual patterns of agent-oriented software engineering (AOSE). From the engineering perspective at the lower level of abstraction the essential features of agents in a MAS are their ability to communicate with each other and to coordinate their activities. Coordination means achieving coherence in the group activities and thus providing that the solution of a problem or the accomplishment of a task is obtained with less effort, fewer resources consumed, and better quality. Communication stands for the ability to exchange the pieces of information within an encounter in a uniform way and using shared terminology. Communication among agents in open systems, which are typical in the majority of real world cases in e-business, enterprise application integration, and so forth, is a challenging interoperability task. The solutions are approached by standardizing the languages for communication (for example FIPA ACL), and developing formal machine-processable representations of the common terminology in the form of ontologies. Ontologies, formalized in ontology description languages (for example OWL) provide: a conceptualization—a formal model of real world phenomena in a domain; a vocabulary—a set of terms or symbols identifying concepts; and an axiomatization—the rules and the constraints on concepts and their properties that capture the characteristic aspects of a domain.

Agent paradigm and AOSE gain more and more popularity as one of the key enablers of the emerging Semantic Web—the new generation of the Web. The abstract architecture of the Semantic Web is outlined in W3C[3] WWW Technical Architecture Group (TAG) architecture specification.

More details may be borrowed from, for example, Jennings (2000) and Ermolayev and Plaksin (2002).

W3C WWW Architecture

WWW architecture provides the abstract specification of the architecture of the Web. It figures out the conceptual model, the properties and the semantics of WWW constituents, and defines the underlying principles and the basic constraints of Web-based system development. WWW architecture specification fixes the design choices approved by W3C and approves the good practices of using Web technology that guide future growth, consistent and successful evolution of the Web.

The primary task of W3C TAG is to develop and maintain the consensual specification of the basic principles of the Web technology in order to facilitate and coordinate cross-technology architecture developments inside and outside W3C. TAG claims *identification*, *interaction*, and *representation* as the key aspects of Web architecture and derives its abstract specification from these concepts.

Identification on the Web is based on the semantics and the use of the uniform resource identifiers (URIs) which are global identifiers and are central to the architecture of the Web.

Interaction is defined by TAG as the communication of resources that involves URIs, messages, and data among agents over WWW. TAG provides the basic concepts for messages, Web agents, interaction styles, and the use of metadata and the protocols for agents. TAG also defines the architectural constraints and the assumptions for agent interaction and the patterns for human user interaction on the WWW.

Representation of data on the Web is grounded on the defined concepts of media types, data formats, encoding, namespaces, general hypertext infrastructure and the use of XML as the core language. It is worth mentioning in the context of the representation aspect that the *representation of metadata* on the Web is not explicitly defined by the Web architecture specification yet and is likely to be based on the Semantic Web principles for the next generation of the Web.

The *separation* of content, presentation, and interaction is yet one more important principle of the WWW architecture. It concerns the development of the standards for highly interoperable distributed systems in open and dynamic environments, where information is created, accessed, and processed at the high level of autonomy with respect to the capabilities and the heterogeneity of the Web agents involved.

W3C Web Service Architecture
and the Semantic Web

Web service architecture specifies generic concepts and defines the framework for the creation of Web services. Web services are modular software components accessible over a WWW. A Web service is supplied with the description specifying its interface in a machine-processable way to provide for the interoperability in open distributed software systems. These descriptions contain the specifications of the message formats, data types, transport, and serialization protocols.

The following de-facto industrial standards outline today's technological frames for Web service development and publication: Web service description language (WSDL); universal description, discovery and integration (UDDI); simple object access protocol (SOAP) for Web service binding and invocation; and XML and

HTTP for serialization. However, ongoing research activities push forward the state-of-the-art by developing an extensible ontology-based framework for Semantic Web services.

W3C Semantic Web initiative aims primarily to provide a comprehensible framework for identifying, representing and processing the semantics of WWW resources. The ultimate vision of the Semantic Web is the worldwide distributed device for computation, inhabited with artificial service providing agents. It is therefore extremely important to have Web service semantics formally and explicitly represented in a machine-processable way. Such semantic representations in the form of ontologies are essential for automated service discovery, invocation, orchestration, and trade and evidently extend today's technological frames. Semantic Web resources and services will have semantic annotations—small ontologies providing both a meta-description of the resource and the vocabulary of the relevant concepts. Semantic Web initiative spends substantial effort on ontology language (RDFS, DAML, OWL) development and standardization.

OWL-S and Semantic Web Services

The concept of Semantic Web services (SWS) is the synergy of Web service technologies with the Semantic Web framework. It assumes that the Semantic Web infrastructure is the top layer of the conventional WWW. This semantic layer contains Web service ontologies, notations and standards for service description, facilities for service discovery, orchestration and integration. SWS will be widely used in the future Web, where intelligent agents will discover Web service providers, reason about their capabilities by analyzing their semantic descriptions and dynamically compose services on demand in cooperation with the service providing agents having appropriate capabilities.

One of the pioneering targeted SWS initiatives is the development of OWL-S (OWL-based Web service ontology). OWL-S is the extension of OWL ontology language. It specifies the core set of concepts for describing the granularity, the properties, the capabilities and the grounding of a Web service. If compared to current industry standards, OWL-S provides a higher degree of flexibility and expressiveness in describing service semantics, allows to model extensible service hierarchies and type systems, and provides the means for specifying the constraints and the rules for Web services.

Travel Planning Scenario

Let us consider the mentioned travel planning scenario having in mind that our intentions have become true and Web services are available at the desired level of semantic interoperation. The authors have played the following exercise assuming themselves as "intelligent software agents" participating in cooperative execution of a conference trip planning task (Figure 1). Each agent possessed their beliefs about the environment, and capabilities in performing one or another activity related to the overall high-level goal achievement—'BookRoundtrip("Kiev, Ukraine", "Erfurt, Germany", 22/09/2003, 25/09/2003, "ICWS'03-Europe", ...)'. Agents' capabilities were: their knowledge of relevant Web sites providing human-oriented services, and their ability to operate these services via Web interfaces. Agent roles were:

- AUTHOR (A): An agent representing one of the research paper authors intending to attend ICWS'03-Europe and requesting 'BookRoundtrip' service

- TRAVEL AGENT (T): An agent actually providing 'BookRoundtrip' service by generating and conducting corresponding task execution

- FARE AGENT (F): Agents providing various airfare information and booking services

- ICWS INFO (I): An agent providing information services on ICWS '03-Europe local arrangements, infrastructure, accommodation, and so forth at Erfurt

Figure 1. "BookRoundtrip" task execution and service composition

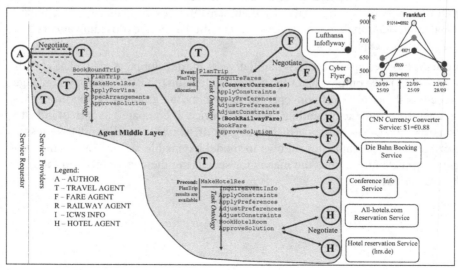

- HOTEL AGENT (H): Agents providing hotel room reservation services
- BUSINESS PARTNER (P): An agent representing A's business partner in Austria with whom A intends to meet in Germany at the time of the conference to discuss a joint proposal

As usual in travel planning A is capable of just invoking a T with 'BookRoundtrip' task, to formulate his or her constraints, preferences and needs for special arrangements, and to approve the solutions proposed by the chosen T. According to 'BookRoundtrip' description in terms of task ontology (Ermolayev et al., 2001) known both to A and T (but with different granularity), service inputs are[4]:

Starting_Point=   "Kiev,   Ukraine"
Destination="Erfurt,   Germany"
Beg_Date   =22/09/2003
End_Date=25/09/2003
Event="ICWS'03-Europe"
Preferences=("low fare," "fast connections," "4-star hotel," "continental breakfast,"
" conference   discounts")
Constraints =(Budget = €1500, Payment=(VISA, USD), Hotel >= 3-star, Room-per-night
<=€110, Hotel_Location="in Max 20 min walk from the Conference venue")
Special_Arrangements=((Event="business dinner",Agent = ("Prof. Heinrich C. Mayr," http://
www.ifi.uni-klu.ac.at/IWAS/HM/Staff/Heinrich.Mayr/),   Date=(23/09/2003-
24/09/2003), Location=(Erfurt, Munich))

The process starts with the arrangement (Ermolayev & Plaksin, 2002). A undertakes to hire one of the Ts as the contractor for the job. This arrangement is performed in frame of the extended iterative contract net negotiation. The flow of round trip booking, which T performs for A, is presented in Figure 1. At first, T accepts the task

Figure 2. Fare desirability function and service prospositions

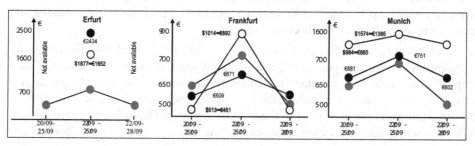

from A, using the agents' communication interface. This interface is based upon ACL (FIPA, 2003) for FIPA[5]-compliant agents (e-Appendix A-1[6]). T then uses its beliefs on how to 'BookRoundtrip'(e-Appendix A-2), formalized according to the task ontology (e-Appendix A-6), to derive that the accepted task is complex and involves at least 'PlanTrip', 'MakeHotelRes', 'ApplyForVisa', 'SpecArrangements' and 'ApproveSolution' activities. The 'PlanTrip' activity is chosen as the first one to be performed (PLP of task ontology (Ermolayev et al., 2001)) and appears to be also a complex task: 'InquireFares', 'ApplyConstraints', …, 'BookFare', 'ApproveSolution.' Before outsourcing fare inquiry to F, T 'notices' that a slight change in the starting or ending date of the trip may result in a substantial decrease in the airfare expenses because of the Sunday rule discounts[7] commonly offered by air companies. In our example this means to T that the dates 20/09-25/09 and 22/09-28/09 should be also rationally considered for the trip. T negotiates these input changes with A, asking A to provide desirability values for these dates (Figure 2—gray dots) indicating max price A is ready to pay for the fare within the specified dates. Requirements, which T specifies for 'InquireFares' service, are thus slightly changed by introducing the list of date pairs for which the service should be performed. Contract Net negotiation is then initiated by T having Fs as participants.

F's propositions[8] resulting from the 'InquireFares' service execution are also outlined in Figure 2. These results imply the necessity to use one more service, which was not initially planned by T's PLP for the task. As far as the offers are provided in different currencies, T needs to change the task and to request the service for currency conversion[9] (+('Convert Currencies,' e-Appendix A-3), Figure 1). Conversion results are presented in Figure 2. It is now easy for T to derive that the acceptable proposition is still for the dates 22/09-25/09, but with the destination at Frankfurt (not at Erfurt) which were not the initial 'BookRoundtrip' task inputs received from A. However, this result complies with A's preferences as far as there are nonstop flights available from Kiev to Frankfurt (but not to Erfurt and Munich). This implies the necessity for T to 'AdjustPreferences' by inquiring A's service. The mechanism may be similar to inputs negotiation discussed previously and the outcomes may cause the invocation of some new activities. For example, change to a train at Frankfurt-Main Airport inquires the 'BookRailwayFare' service from Die Bahn[10] agent. The discussion of these emerging task branches is omitted, as far as it is conceptually similar to that already given before. It is however important to notice that the activities that were not initially planned often emerge and appear to be critical to the overall goal achievement not only in the discussed scenario.

It is not informative to discuss subsequent activities of T. Hotel booking and visa application services are performed merely in the same manner and the agents use similar mechanisms of task decomposition and negotiation for that. A special arrangements list is also considered as the list of trip planning tasks. However, it should be mentioned that the execution of these activities should be properly coordinated: For instance, hotel reservation requires that the fare has been already booked as the precondition (check-in and check-out dates, money left) and German consular service may require that the fare and the hotel room have been booked before issuing the visa.

Other important aspects not previously mentioned are the ones of credibility, trust, and meaning negotiation among agents participating in cooperative task performance and service composition. Recall special arrangements input for the illustration. T will negotiate with P on various aspects while arranging the business dinner. The dilemma for P in this case is if to trust T (as the contractor of A, which is the trusted one because of the long record of partnership) and allow him or her to make the arrangements for P, or to reason that A may not be experienced in arranging business dinners in Germany and to decide to better rely on their credible partners from Germany. In the latter case, P will inform T that it will better arrange the event on its own. This, in turn, may affect the necessity of the approval from A.

Cooperative Dynamic Service Composition

Let's enumerate the features needed to rationally provide composite flexible services for the automation of the scenarios like that of travel planning in e-business settings. Intelligent service provider needs to be capable of:

- Understanding the semantics of the activity it is supposed to perform, reasoning on if the activity is atomic or complex, decomposing tasks according to their knowledge and experience.

- Adjusting activity inputs, requestor preferences, and constraints in order to proactively reach the higher-level goal.

- Negotiating with the requestor and the other service providers in a rational way on optimal service execution or allocation in order to increase its own utility or to obtain the common meaning of the service inputs, outputs, preconditions and after-effects.

- Monitoring and assessing the credibility and the trustworthiness of the other service providers to minimize risks.

- Coordinating service performance flow according to the inputs and preconditions.

It seems obvious that a service providing distributed open software systems possessing these capabilities may be most naturally designed and assembled of intelligent software agents. Software agent platforms and agent-based software systems are already used for service brokerage (McIlraith et al., 2002), matchmaking (Sycara et al., 1999), and coordination (Papadopoulos, 2001). The remainder of this section will present the formal approach to dynamic task decomposition and performance by dynamically formed teams or coalitions of rational software agents (Ermolayev et al., 2001; Ermolayev & Plaksin, 2002).

Middle Agents for Service Composition

The conceptual idea of service mediation is not new and has been argued by many authors. Strong mediation has been for instance claimed as one of the basic principles of WSMF (Fensel & Bussler, 2002). However, the framework for intelligent dynamic service composition adaptable to the changes in the environment affected by the service execution flow has not been worked out before.

The proposal of the mediation framework for agent-enabled service provision targeted to dynamic service composition is presented in Figure 3. Control flows are labeled with legends in italic; data flows are marked by bold legends. The principles on which the proposal is centered are:

- Agent-based middle layer is required for scalable, intelligent, dynamic service composition.

Figure 3. Agent-based service provision mediation framework

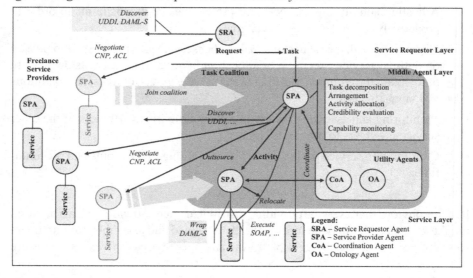

- Composite services are interpreted as tasks comprising activities of varying granularity by the agent middle layer.

- Service mediator is formed dynamically as the coalition of service providing agents (SPAs) participating in the task execution.

- SPAs join task coalitions only for the time their service is required for the respective task.

- SPAs are economically rational (Nwana, 1996), autonomous and independent in making their decisions—the only fact one SPA believes about the behavior of another SPA is: it is at worst individual rational (Sandholm, 1996).

- SPAs are capable of: Incoming task decomposition according to their local knowledge (task ontology, PLP); making arrangements for activity outsourcing to other SPAs based on extended iterative contract net negotiation; activity outsourcing to the chosen contractor SPA; adjusting their beliefs on other SPAs' capabilities and evaluating SPAs' credibility through monitoring cooperative activities.

- Services are self-contained modular loosely coupled program components wrapped by SPAs; an SPA may allow another SPA to use its service by providing service context relocation.

- Specialization of an SPA is defined by the set of services it wraps.

If the framework is examined from the point of implementability with existing service markup solutions the state of affairs may look like given in Figure 3. Yet, unsolved or partially unsolved problems of service mediation are:

- Lack of common semantic ground and commonly accepted mechanism for activity allocation, activity parameters adjustment and meaning negotiation—negotiation ontologies family.

Research findings attacking this problem are published in Ermolayev et al. (2005b) and Ermolayev and Keberle (2006).

- Insufficient representation of task/activity/service dynamic structure and granularity—task/process ontologies family.

These ontologies have been further developed in PSI project (Ermolayev et al., 2006b).

- Lack of common specifications/criteria for capability monitoring, credibility and trustworthiness assessment.

The proposed architectural layering is likely to remain valid for the request-task-activity-service ontology hierarchy: a service request is interpreted as the task at the requestor layer; these tasks are decomposed into activities at the middle layer; and activity descriptions wrap service markups. The remainder of the section provides some outlines to approach the solutions of the open issues.

Request-Task-Activity-Service Hierarchy

The semantic hierarchy for a request-task-activity-service reflects the principles of the proposed architectural layering. A request belongs to the sphere of service requestor layer and is specified in terms of *task ontology* (Ermolayev et al., 2001; Ermolayev et al., 2006b). The function of the SPA chosen as the contractor for the specified request is to determine if the incoming task is the atomic activity according to its local specifications. In case the task is complex and should be decomposed into atomic activities at the local level of granularity, the next round of activities allocation negotiations is initiated. Only the activities that the given SPA is not capable to perform on its own are negotiated with other SPAs, while the ones corresponding to the initiator's capabilities are scheduled for self-performance. Only an activity for which it is true that: (a) it is atomic and (b) the SPA is able to perform it on its own, is in the relationship with the corresponding service or service loop. Atomic activity execution is performed by the SPA through invoking its capability model (Ermolayev & Plaksin, 2002): Activity context is translated into OWL-S markup

Figure 4. Semantic layering

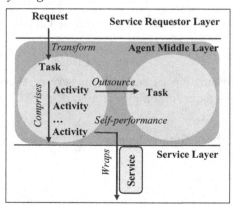

corresponding to the service profile; the service is then invoked via the interface specified by its binding (or grounding in terms of OWL-S) description. A service invocation loop may actually result in one or several service runs depending on the wrapping activity inputs. For example 'InquireFares' service will be performed three times as far as three different date intervals are to be processed (Figure 2). Semantic facet of request-task-activity-service layering is presented in Figure 4. Specifications for 'InquireFares' activity and service are given in e-Appendix A-5.

Capability and Credibility Assessment

An SRA and SPAs are to be able to determine which of the SPAs are capable to perform the task to be allocated. Possible mechanism to define the perspective contractors is capability matchmaking (for example based on LARKS (Sycara et al., 2002)), or service discovery technique based on UDDI, or another service matching facilities, for example semantic matching based on OWL-S profiles (Paolucci et al., 2002), or WSMO SWS descriptions (Roman et al., 2005). However, in case there is some capability beliefs record maintained autonomously by an SPA in the course of cooperative task execution, the use of this knowledge may substantially facilitate lowering computation costs by eliminating unnecessary directory/matching service usage. Evidently, if A believes that B, C and D are capable of performing desired activity because they did it before, it will rather proceed to contracting negotiation with B, C and D directly instead of trying to find some other SPAs[11] with matching capabilities.

A model and a mechanism of agents' capability assessment based on SPA beliefs representation in the form of Fellows' capability expectations matrix (FCEM) has been elaborated in frame of the reported research (Ermolayev & Plaksin, 2002). SPAs accumulate and adjust their local beliefs on the capabilities of their collaborators from the experience of cooperative performance. New portions of this knowledge appear each time an activity is being outsourced to an SPA. Subjective beliefs of the SRA on the probabilities of its fellows' capabilities to perform the given activity are thus updated. FCEM for capability beliefs representation is maintained in the following form:

$$
\mathbf{C} =
\begin{array}{c}
 \\
SPA_1 \\
 \\
\ldots \\
 \\
SPA_n
\end{array}
\begin{array}{ccccc}
a^1 & \ldots & a^j & \ldots & a^m \\
\left[\begin{array}{ccccc}
c_1^1 & & c_1^j & & c_1^k \\
& & \ldots & & \\
\ldots & c_i^j = (q_i^j, p_i^j) & \ldots & \\
& & \ldots & & \\
c_n^1 & & c_n^j & & c_n^m
\end{array}\right]
\end{array}
\qquad (1)
$$

where dimensions m and n change reflecting the appearance of new incoming activities and newly discovered or perishing SPAs.

Capability estimations c^j_i change each time an agent negotiates with its fellows on outsourcing an activity. Element q^j_i in tuple c^j_i stands for the quantity of recorded negotiations with fellow agent SPA$_i$ concerning activity a^j. Element p^j_i stands for the capability expectation. The rule for c^j_i updates is as follows:

1. $$p^j_i \leftarrow p^j_i + \frac{r}{q^j_i}$$
2. $$q^j_i \leftarrow q^j_i + 1 \tag{2}$$

where r is equal to: 0—if the fellow rejected the activity, 0.5—if the fellow replied that it can accept the activity and 1—if the activity was finally allocated to the fellow.

One more aspect influencing a task requestor's decision to allocate an activity to one or another negotiation participant is its assessment of the participant's credibility. A self-interested SPA, due to the appearance of the new highly attractive activity offers in the competitive environment or due to the peculiarity of its behavior, may lower previously declared capacity (Ermolayev et al., 2001; Ermolayev & Plaksin, 2002) it is spending for the bulk of the activities under execution. This will lead to the increase of the performance duration, which may therefore seriously decrease the requestor's desirability of these results and, thus, lower the credibility value for the SPA selling its fellows short.

Let, for example, a service outsourced to an SPA be 'DeliverAirTickets'. The result of the service is: The tickets are at the gate counter. The agreed delivery time is 30 minutes before the check-in, though the deadline advertised by the SRA before is the time when the check-in starts. The SRA will evidently consider the SPA that delivered the tickets before or right in the agreed time as credible. However, if the SPA delivers the tickets in five minutes before the check-in, the SRA may rightfully feel aggrieved, though it still has the chance to check in for the flight. The credibility of the SPA in the eye of the SRA will therefore be lowered. Further on, if the tickets appear at the counter after the check-in has been opened already, the SRA may rightfully consider that the contract terms were seriously violated by the SPA. Its credibility should be therefore drastically lowered. Finally imagine an SRA still waiting for its tickets at the counter when the plane is already taking off. In the latter case the SRA may even want to require a penalty in addition to lowering SPA's credibility to zero. To summarize, it is natural to measure the changes of an SRA's beliefs on the SPA's credibilities by the losses of the desirability of the service results based on the stricken contract deal (refer to Figure 5).

The mechanism of accounting fellows' credibility values is similar to that of adjusting the beliefs on changing fellows' capabilities (1-2). Credibility assessment values

Figure 6. Extended iterated FIPA contract Net protocol

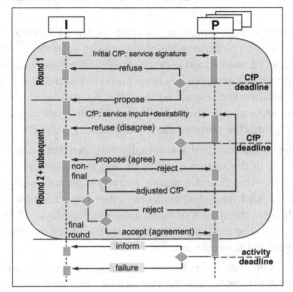

change over time as the requestor agent adjusts its subjective beliefs by comparing the desirability values (Figure 5) derived from:

- **1st:** Activity duration the executive committed to within the activity allocation arrangement negotiation
- **2nd:** Actual results delivery time; corresponding credibility matrix elements are then recomputed due to the following:

$$Cr_{i,j} := Cr_{i,j} \times \begin{cases} 1, t_r \le t_a \\ p_a(t_a / t_r), t_a < t_r \le d_a \\ 0, t_r > d_a \end{cases} \tag{3}$$

where: t_a is the time the parties have agreed to accomplish the activity a, t_r is the actual time of a results delivery, d_a is the deadline and p_a is the weight coefficient characterizing the current priority of a for the activity requestor agent.

Credibility threshold values associated with respective activities and stored in agents' PLPs are used by task requesting agents to assess possible risks and alter their strategies.

Negotiation on Activity Allocation

As it was aforementioned, negotiation on activity allocation takes place each time an agent realizes, according to its knowledge of the activity or because of the overload, that the activity should be outsourced to one of the fellow SPAs. An extension of the *FIPA Iterated Contract Net protocol* has been proposed as the interaction protocol for this kind of negotiation (see Figure 6). An SRA is considered an initiator (**I**) in this encounter. The SPAs about which **I** believes that they are capable to perform the activity (FCEM) form the party of the invited participants (**P**).

The first round of the interaction, which is actually the extension of the FIPA protocol, aims to find out if any of the known capable **P**s may agree to perform the activity. The negotiation set for this round contains activity signature only (for example 'DeliverAirTickets'). An **I** may start exploring other opportunities of outsourcing the activity if all **P**s from the sphere of its awareness (Ermolayev & Plaksin, 2002) refuse in the first round. For example **I** may require the list of matching SPAs from the matchmaker agent (MA, see Figure 8).

Negotiation on the second and the subsequent rounds is about the terms of the possible contract. An **I** advertises the activity inputs and the discrete results desirability function as the incentive over time. **I** than chooses the best **P**s proposal weighted by the respective credibility values in case several **P**s proposals result in the agreement. Subsequent rounds are used to adjust the activity inputs or the desirability function in the case if no one of the **P**s has agreed on the previous round (for example, dates or destination point in Figure 2).

Ps' refusals and propositions are shown in Figure 7. These feedbacks are formulated in a constructive way allowing **I** to adjust its CfP in the subsequent round. A feedback contains two incentive-time points defining the segment on which a possible agreement may be stricken. Evidently, the area of agreement for the current round could be formally defined as the union of all those parts of the feedback segments that are on and below the **I**'s desirability function polyline. All other points of **P**s' feedbacks indicate their disagreement with the offer in the current negotiation round.

Figure 7. Negotiation: Agreement and disagreement

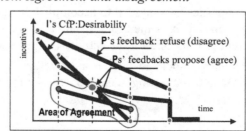

Figure 8. RACING reference architecture

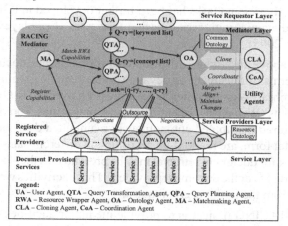

An **I** considers the negotiation round as final if it can accept one of the **Ps'** agreement and strike the contract deal. The chosen **P** becomes the contractor and commits itself to the task coalition for the time necessary to perform the outsourced activity. Task coalitions are considered to be a kind of social structure. Coalition members are bounded with coalition commitments and convention regulating their ratios of self-interest and benevolence (Ermolayev et al., 2001).

Negotiation ontology (Ermolayev et al., 2001) is used as the namespace and the formal semantic frame for the contents of the messages agents communicate with while negotiating on activity allocation. Further development of the Negotiation ontology in PSI project[12] resulted in generic negotiation ontology (Ermolayev & Keberle, 2006).

Racing[13] Functionalities, Agents, and Services

A reader might fairly argue that travel planning is not the task that really requires sophisticated agent-enabled automation technique: negotiations, coalitions, service wrapping and composition—at least from the customer's side. Travel planning is not that time consuming to make its performance impossible without automation. Moreover, a human will sometimes be better in arranging loosely formalized things that require intuition and context-dependent understanding with the complexity beyond the capacity of, say, first order logic based languages. However, the presented technique is applicable not only in case you plan your conference trip (Ermolayev et al., 2001; Ermolayev & Tolok, 2002). The similar approach of dynamic cascading composition of activities and tasks has been further developed in PSI for modeling a simulation of dynamic engineering design processes (Ermolayev et al., 2005; Gorodetski et al., 2005)

Let us project the above discussion to distributed information and document retrieval domain. In the terms of document retrieval a service request is commonly formulated as a search phrase—a first order logic expression over the list of keywords or phrases. Documents (Web pages, scientific papers, magazines, books) are stored at disparately structured distributed autonomously maintained databases or text collections in a digital form, are marked-up according to different standards and *often cost money*. A task for document retrieval may be presented as the set of interrelated activities distributed over the document providers. These activities wrap the (partial) queries derived from the initial user's request.

The goal of the RACING project is to provide mediation facilities for user query processing by the means of semantic decomposition of the initial query, rational distribution of the partial queries among independent, autonomous, rational document retrieval service providers wrapping respective document resources, and the fusion of the obtained results (Figure 8). User agents acting on behalf of the human users or real organizations (for example libraries) and service providing agents are considered as business representatives or business models in frame of the project. RACING mediation may thus be classified as B2B mediation. It is evident that such a kind of intelligent activities really needs sophisticated automation to be scalable and gracefully downgradable.

User query processing, resource wrappers registration by the capability matchmaker and common ontology maintenance are the basic functionalities of the RACING mediator (Figure 8). Though only query processing may be considered as a real business process involving third-party service providers for money, the other two ones are also performed as tasks and require various types of negotiation and semantic interoperation.

For example, the outline for the user query processing scenario is as follows. The process starts at UA with the formulation of the query in terms of the key phrases familiar to the given user. UAs are cloned by CLA utility agent each time a new user comes to the mediator and perish when the user leaves. User profiles (mappings of their most frequently used key words or phrases to the Mediator Common Ontology (MCO) concepts) are incrementally collected, stored at OA (Ermolayev et al., 2003) in the form of the reference ontology and used by QTAs. The UA actually generates and conducts the task of query processing and acts as the proxy between the user and the mediator. Query processing task generated by the UA contains 'CloneQTA', 'TransformQry', 'CloneQPA', 'ExecuteQry' activities. Cloning activities are outsourced to CLA, which clones QTA and QPA for query processing. 'TransformQry' activity is outsourced to QTA, which performs the transformation of the query in terms of keywords to semantically matching query in terms of the concepts of the MCO. The last activity is outsourced to QPA, which generates the following set of activities for 'ExecuteQry' task: 'DecomposeQry,' 'PerformQryset.' Query decomposition is performed by QPA in order to extract the parts of the incoming query that may require different capabilities from document service providers. This extraction is guided by topic classification of the Common Ontology. The resulting set of partial queries is performed by QPA as the following activity sequence: 'MatchRWA,' 'PerformQry.' Matching activity is allocated to MA for a certain incentive over accomplishment time. MA returns[14] the list of RWAs capable to perform document providing services relevant to the partial query. 'PerformQry' activity allocation is negotiated with pre-selected RWAs in terms of service 'overheads' over time and document price and the contractor is chosen for query performance. Contractor RWA receives the partial query in terms of MCO. It therefore needs to transform the query into the terms of its resource ontology. This transformation activity is outsourced to OA, which actually holds the necessary mappings. RWA than invokes document service that it wraps with the transformed query and provides documents relevant to the query to QPA.

RACING mediator has been partially implemented as a mock-up application. RACING framework for intelligent ontology-enabled distributed information retrieval has been further on elaborated in UnIT-Net[15] project (Ermolayev et al., 2004b). UnIT-Net research prototype has been implemented as the distributed system with the centralized mediator using semantically reinforced Web services as intelligent Information Resource providers (Keberle et al., 2004).

Service Composition in P2P Service Networks

One of the essential prerequisites for the implementation of a RACING-like service composition platform is the provision of the proper underlying infrastructure. It becomes even more important in the cases when the environment requires more sophisticated capabilities than those provided by the conventional WWW. This section presents the OntoServ.Net framework (Terziyan, 2005; Terziyan & Kononenko, 2003) for the intelligent composition of Web services on the Semantic Web enabled industrial environment. OntoServ.Net is the agent-enabled framework for the management of industrial devices in the peer-to-peer network of maintenance Web services. In OntoServ.Net the principles of the Semantic Web are used for the development of interoperable Web services and ontology-based information management. Peer-to-peer technology provides the means to organize the communication infrastructure, and agent technology enables the implementation of the problem-oriented behavior of network components (Terziyan, 2003).

OntoServ.Net is a fully decentralized environment that is a peer-to-peer network comprising service platforms located at maintenance sites and service providing centers. P2P structure of OntoServ.Net reflects existing approaches towards the creation of business-partnership environments where companies can share resources (in particular, Web services) that were previously used only internally. The enlargement of such resource sharing environments heads towards a global P2P network with highly independent nodes. Though a semi-structured architecture will likely be used (with large service centers within newly created communities), peer-to-peer interactions reflect the reality of today's businesses.

The maintenance of complex industrial machinery, for example a paper mill, requires the control hundreds of factors and involves many services to monitor various sensor data, analyze general condition parameters, performance, etc. Hardware configurations vary from one machine to another, and thus, require an individual approach to the organization of the maintenance process and servicing.

The set of condition monitoring and maintaining services in OntoServ.Net is dynamically composed depending on the current needs of a machine. It changes when a fault state processing is required, or some service is substituted by the other one in order to provide more efficiency or to follow degradation processes along the machine's lifetime. OntoServ.Net service network improves performance and maintenance quality by providing the most appropriate services available on the network.

Recently, the synergetic approaches to the design of service infrastructures combining the features adopted from the Semantic Web, Web services and P2P computing are under intensive research. Latest results prove good potential of such combinations for the cooperative use of distributed heterogeneous information sources and services (see, e.g., Sivashanmugan et al., 2002; Terziyan, 2003). Service discovery and composition of Semantic Web services in a decentralized network present new challenges for the research community and demand thorough study.

In addition to a P2P structure of the service network OntoServ.Net presents new aspects related to the service composition problem, which were not thoroughly studied before: service mobility, individual rationality of SPAs and their intended readiness to cooperatively work in a P2P environment.

Service Mobility

The specificity of the maintenance activities performed by services in OntoServ. Net requires that these services are mobile. The reasons are: a need for guaranteed service availability, a need for minimization of the communication traffic over the network during long-term servicing due to costs and/or technical restrictions, strict constraints for service response time, security and privacy issues, etc. Service mobility may naturally be implemented if the services are provided by mobile agents able to migrate between agent platforms. Mobile services persist on the local service platforms on the site and terminate after servicing. Actually, service instances arrive to a local platform and are withdrawn later. However, some data may be returned to the original SPA to update its knowledge base regarding the performed diagnostics and efficiency of actions taken. This knowledge is used later on for the improvement of the service quality (Terziyan, 2005).

Services Provided by Rational Agents

OntoServ.Net services are wrapped by SPAs. SPAs, in addition to providing their services on SRAs' requests, reason about which activities to perform in a given case. OntoServ.Net has no division for service requestor and service provider layers, since both services and agents are conceptually the same. Resource wrapping agents (RWAs) represent industrial machines or their parts and provide Web services to grant access to or operation on the respective devices. RWAs also act as SRAs. For example, they acquire advanced diagnostic services from another SPA to monitor basic parameters of the machine.

Resource wrapping agent shell (OntoShell, a framework for resource and service adaptation to the Semantic Web-enabled environment (Terziyan, 2003)) can be applied to a wide range of resource types, including humans, knowledge bases, and industrial devices. OntoShell allows wrapping services implemented within the framework of W3C Web service architecture or, in principle, any other software development technology that provides external application programming interfaces.

Service Composition Strategy in OntoServ.Net

Service composition in OntoServ. Net is performed by platform-manager agents that act as mediators between service agents scattered over the network and local RWAs. A platform manager controls services' mobility and supports the P2P discovery mechanism of the OntoServ.Net environment, which is based on the matchmaking of a service request to dynamic service profiles (Kaykova et al., 2004; Khriyenko et al., 2004). A profile presents not only the service interface and the semantics, but also comprises the generalized description of SPA's successfulness in some states of the previously serviced SRAs. A dynamic profile is therefore required for credibility assessment. Since services are assumed to implement various learning techniques, their quality highly depends on the previous invocations, the samples for self-learning collected by SPAs, and initial training sets. If a service is complex and requires the invocation of other services, the performance is conducted by a local platform manager. The platform manager agent performs service discovery either locally or network-wide and provides inter-platform communication facilities.

To round up, OntoServ.Net framework provides the means for the development of agent-enabled P2P Web service infrastructures in the networks of complex industrial machinery. The framework is applied to the development of the business models and the implementation of the secure service platforms that support new type of mobile services. It is based on the synergy of P2P and the Semantic Web, which ensures the successful deployment of industry-strong solutions based on agent technology.

Further Development of OntoServ.Net Framework

Since the previous publication in (Ermolayev et al., 2004) many elements of the conceptual framework described above have been implemented by the IOG in SmartResource Project[16] (Kaykova et al., 2005a; Kaykova et al., 2005b; Terziyan., 2005). The main focus of these development activities is to contribute to fast adoption of Semantic Web and related technologies in industry. It includes research and development aimed to design a global understanding environment (GUN) as next generation of Web-based platforms by making heterogeneous industrial resources (files, documents, services, devices, business processes, systems, organizations, human experts, etc.) web-accessible, proactive and cooperative in a sense that they will be able to automatically plan their own behavior, monitor and correct their own state, communicate and negotiate among themselves depending on their role in a business process, utilize remote experts, Web services, software agents and various Web applications. Three fundamentals of GUN platform are interoperability, automation, and integration. Interoperability in GUN requires utilization of Semantic Web standards, RDF-based metadata and ontologies, and semantic adapters of the resources. Automation in GUN requires proactivity of resources based on the use of agent technologies. Integration in GUN requires ontology-based business process modeling and integration, and multi-agent technologies for coordination of business processes over resources. GUN is a concept which is used to name a Web-based resource "welfare" environment which provides a global system for automated "care" of (industrial) Web resources with the help of heterogeneous, proactive, intelligent, and interoperable Web services. The main players in GUN are the following resources: service consumers (or components of service consumers), service providers (or components of service providers), decision-makers (or components of decision makers). All these resources can be artificial (tangible or intangible) or natural (human or other). It is supposed that "service consumers" will be able: (a) to proactively monitor their own state over time and changing context; (b) to discover appropriate "decision makers" and order the remote diagnostics of their own condition to these "decision makers." The "decision makers" will then decide in the automatic manner which maintenance ("treatment") services are applicable to that condition; (c) to discover appropriate "service providers" and order the required maintenance to them.

Industrial resources (for example devices, experts, software components, etc.) can be linked to the Semantic Web-based environment via adapters (or interfaces), which include (if necessary) the sensors with digital output, data structuring (for example XML) and semantic adapter components (XML to Semantic Web). Agents are assumed to be assigned to each resource and are able to monitor semantically rich data coming from the adapter about the states of the resource, decide if a deeper diagnostics of the state is needed, discover other agents in the environment which represent "decision makers," and exchange information (agent-to-agent communication with semantically enriched content language) to get diagnoses and decide if a maintenance is needed. It is assumed that "decision making" Web services will be implemented based on various machine learning algorithms and will be able to learn based on the samples of data taken from various "service consumers" and labeled by experts. The implementation of agent technologies in GUN framework allows for the mobility of service components between various platforms, decentralized service discovery, FIPA communication protocols utilization, and MAS-like integration/composition of services (Terziyan, 2006).

Concluding Remarks

The chapter presented the framework for agent-enabled dynamic Web service composition. The core of the methodology is the new understanding of a Web service as an agent capability having proper ontological description. It is demonstrated by the travel planning example how diverse Web services may be composed and mediated by dynamic coalitions of software agents collaboratively performing tasks for service requestors. It is also claimed that such a mediation facility may substantially enhance today's solutions available in Web service provision. This vision is grounded on the results obtained in agent-enabled business process modeling and management. Some parts of the presented framework have been implemented in several research and development projects run by ISRG and IOG.

It is stated that though the concept of service mediation is not totally new there is still some work to be done before it becomes a real engineering technology. For example, the framework for intelligent dynamic service composition and decomposition according to the changes in the environment affected by the service execution flow has not been explicitly worked out before. The framework introduces the agent middle layer to conduct the transformation of a service request to the corresponding task and for further cooperative task decomposition and performance. Outlined are the formal means to arrange agents' negotiation on activity allocation, to represent the semantic structure of the request-task-activity-service hierarchy and to assess fellow-agents' capabilities and credibility factors. Further on, it is argued that the presented formal technique is applicable not only to the tasks like travel planning. Presented is the reference architecture of the rational multi-agent mediator for intelligent information and document retrieval of the RACING project. Presented aspects of service composition and mobile-agent service representation in a peer-to-peer network of service integration platforms extend RACING principles of service composition by the aspects of mobility. The experience of applying OntoServ. Net framework to the development of P2P service infrastructures provides also the evidence of the applicability of the agent-enabled Web service composition framework to real-world industrial applications

Though thorough standardization and harmonization work should be performed before the presented approach becomes an engine for Web service provision, the authors are certain that agent-enabled rational Web service composition and mediation may provide a substantial contribution, bringing closer the day when the brave new world of machine-processable automated Web services comes true.

References

Ankolekar, A., Urstein, M., Hobbs, J. R., Lassila, O., Martin, D., McDermott, D., et al. (2002, June 9-12). DAML-S: Web service description for the Semantic Web. In *Proceedings of the 1st International Semantic Web Conference (ISWC 2002)*, Sardinia, Italy.

OWL-S. (2003). *The DAML services coalition. DAML-S: Semantic markup for Web services*. Retrieved from http://www.daml.org/services/owl-s/1.0/

Ermolayev, V., Jentzsch, E., Karsayev, O., Keberle, N., Matzke, W.-E., & Samoylov, V. (2005, October 24-28). Modeling dynamic engineering design processes in PSI. In J. Akoka, S. W. Liddle, I.-Y. Song, M. Bertolotto, I. Comyn-Wattiau, S. S.-S. Cherfi et al. (Eds.), Perspectives in Conceptual Modelling, ER 2005 Workshops. In *Proceedings of the 7th International Bi-Conference Workshop on Agent-Oriented Information Systems* (LNCS 3370, pp. 119-130). Klagenfurt, Austria. Springer.

Ermolayev, V., Jentzsch, E., Keberle, N., Samoylov, V., & Sohnius, R. (2006b, April). *The family of PSI ontologies reference specification*, Version 1.5 (Tech. Rep. No. 47). Cadence Design Systems, GmbH.

Ermolayev, V., Keberle, N. (2006, May 30-31). A generic ontology of rational negotiation. In D. Karagiannis & H. C. Mayr (Eds.), *Proceedings of the 5th International Information Systems Technology and Its Applications Conference (ISTA 2006)*, (LNI 84, pp. 51-66). Klagenfurt, Austria.

Ermolayev, V., Keberle, N., Kononenko, O., Plaksin, S., & Terziyan, V. (2004). Towards a framework for agent-enabled semantic Web service composition. *International Journal of Web Services Research, 1*(3), 63-87.

Ermolayev, V., Keberle, N., Matzke, W.-E., & Vladimirov, V. (2005b, November 6-10). A strategy for automated meaning negotiation in distributed information retrieval. In Y. Gil et al. (Eds.), *Proceedings of the 4th International Semantic Web Conference (ISWC 2005)*, (pp. 201-215). Galway, Ireland.

Ermolayev. V., Keberle, N., Shapar, V., Vladimirov, V. (2004b, June 15-17). Ontology-driven sub-query extraction for distributed autonomous information resources in UnIT-Net IEDI. In A. Doroshenko, T. Halpin, S. W. Liddle, & H. C. Mayr (Eds.), *Proceedings of the 3rd International Information Systems Technology and Its Applications Conference (ISTA 2004)*, (LNI 48, pp. 137-150). Salt Lake City, UT.

Ermolayev, V., Keberle, N., & Tolok, V. (2001, November 27-30). OIL ontologies for collaborative task performance in coalitions of self-interested actors. In H. Arisawa, Y. Kambayashi, V. Kumar, H. C. Mayr, & I. Hunt (Eds.), *Proceedings of the Conceptual Modeling for New Information Systems Technologies ER 2001 Workshops, HUMACS, DASWIS, ECOMO, and DAMA*. Yokohama, Japan.

Ermolayev, V., Keberle, N., Plaksin, S., & Vladimirov, V. (2003). Capturing semantics from search phrases: Incremental user personification and ontology-driven query transformation. In M. Godlevsky, S. Liddle, & H. Mayr (Eds.), *Proceedings of the 2nd International Information Systems Technology and Its Applications Conference (ISTA 2003)* (LNI 30, pp. 9-20).

Ermolayev, V. A., & Plaksin, S. L. (2002). Cooperation layers in agent-enabled business process management. *Problems of Programming, 1-2*, 354-368.

Ermolayev, V. A., & Tolok, V. A. (2002). Modelling distant learning activities by agent task coalitions. In Q. Jin, J. Li, J. Cheng, C. Yu ,& S. Noguchi (Eds.), *Enabling society with information technology*. Tokyo: Springer-Verlag.

Fensel, D., & Bussler, C., (2002). *The Web service modeling framework (WSMF)*. White paper. Retrieved June 3, 2002, from http://www.cs.vu.nl/~dieter/ wese/ wsmf.paper.pdf

FIPA. (2003). FIPA Communicative Act library specification (Doc. No. XC00037H). Retrieved June 14, 2003, from http://www.fipa.org/specs/fipa00 037/ XC00037H.pdf

Jennings, N. R. (2000). On agent-based software. In K. P. Sycara, M. Klusch, S. Widoff, & J. Lu. (Eds.), Dynamic service matchmaking among agents in open information environments. *SIGMOD Record, 28*(1), 47-53.

Karp, A. (2003). E-speak explained (External Tech. Rep. No. HPL-2000-101 20000807). Retrieved June 3, 2003, from http://www.hpl.hp.com/techreports /2000/HPL-2000-101.pdf

Kaykova, O., Khriyenko, O., Kovtun, D., Naumenko, A., Terziyan, V., & Zharko, A. (2005a). General adaption framework: Enabling interoperability for industrial Web resources. *International Journal on Semantic Web and Information, 1*(3), 31-63.

Kaykova, O., Khriyenko, O., Terziyan, V., & Zharko, A. (2005b, August 25-27). RGBDF: Resource goal and behaviour description framework. In M. Bramer & V. Terziyan (Eds.), *Proceedings of the 1ˢᵗ International IFIP/WG12.5 Working Conference, Industrial Applications of Semantic Web (IASW 2005)*, (pp. 83-99). Jyvaskyla, Finland. Springer.

Kaykova O., Kononenko O., Terziyan V., & Zharko A. (2004, February 17-19) Community formation scenarios in peer-to-peer Web service environments. In *Proceedings of the IASTED International Conference on Databases and Applications (DBA 2004)*, (pp. 62-67). Innsbruck, Austria.

Keberle N., Ermolayev V., Shapar V., & Vladimirov V. (2004). Semantically reinforced Web services for wrapping autonomous information resources. *Bulletin of V. Karazin Kharkiv National University, 629*(3), 56-69.

Khriyenko, O., Kononenko, O., & Terziyan, V. (2004). OntoEnvironment: An integration infrastructure for distributed heterogeneous resources. *Presented at the IASTED International Conference on Parallel and Distributed Computing and Networks*.

Layman, A. (2001, April 11-12). Web services framework. In *Proceedings of W3C Workshop on Web Services 2001*, San Jose, CA. Retrieved June 3, 2003, from http://www.w3.org/2001/03/ wsws-program/

McIlraith, S.A., Son, T.C., & Zeng, H. (2002). Semantic Web services. IEEE Intelligent Systems, *Special Issue on the Semantic Web, 16*, 46-53.

Nwana, H. S. (1996). Software agents: An overview. *Knowledge Engineering Review, 3*(11), 205-244.

Paolucci, M., Kawamura, T., Payne, T., & Sycara, K. (2002, June 9-12). Semantic matching of Web services capabilities. In *Proceedings of the 1ˢᵗ International Semantic Web Conference (ISWC 2002)*, Sardinia, Italy.

Papadopoulos, G. A. (2001). Models and technologies for the coordination of Internet agents: A survey. In A. Omicini, F. Zambonelli, M. Klusch, & R. Tolksdorf (Eds.), *Coordination for Internet agents: Models, technologies, and applications*. New York: Springer-Verlag.

Roman, D., Keller, U., Lausen, H., de Bruijn, J., Lara, R., Stollberg, et al. (2005). Web service modeling ontology. *Applied Ontology, 1*(1), 77-106

Sandholm, T. (1996). *Negotiation among self-interested computationally limited agents*. PhD thesis, University of Massachusetts, Amherst, MA.

Siebes, R. (2002, October 30). *Peer-to-peer solutions in the Semantic Web context: An overview (EU-IST Project IST-2001-34103 SWAP)*. Vrije Universiteit Amsterdam.

Simple object access protocol (SOAP), Version 1.1 (W3C note). (2000). Retrieved June 3, 2003, from http://www.w3.org/TR/2000/NOTE-SOAP-20000508/

Sivashanmugan, K., Verma, K., Mulye, R., & Zhong, Z. (2002). *SpeedR: Semantic peer-to-peer environment for diverse Web service registries (Final Project, CSCI 8350)*. Enterprise Integration.

Sycara, K., Widoff, S., Klusch, M., & Lu, J. (2002). LARKS: Dynamic matchmaking among heterogeneous software agents in cyberspace. *Autonomous Agents and Multi-Agent Systems, 5*, 173-203.

Terziyan, V. (2003). Semantic Web services for smart devices in a "global understanding environment." In R. Meersman & Z. Tari (eds.), *On the Move to Meaningful Internet Systems 2003: OTM 2003 Workshop*s (LNCS 2889, pp. 279-291).

Terziyan, V. (2005). Semantic Web services for smart devices based on mobile agents. *International Journal of Intelligent Information Technologies, 1*(2), 43-55.

Terziyan V. (2006). Challenges of the "global understanding environment" based on agent mobility. In V. Sugumaran (Ed.), *Advanced topics in intelligent information technologies* (Vol. 1, pp. 121-152), Hershey, PA: Idea Group Publishing.

Terziyan, V., & Kononenko, O. (2003). Semantic Web enabled web services: State-of-art and industrial challenges. In M. Jeckle & L.-J. Zhang (Eds.), *Web Services—ICWS-Europe 2003* (LNCS 2853, pp. 183-197). Springer-Verlag.

UDDI. (n.d.). *UDDI. Technical white paper*. Retrieved from http://uddi.org/

Thaden, U., Siberski, W., & Nejdl, W. (2003). *A Semantic Web based peer-to-peer service registry network*. Techical report.

W3C. (2001, March). *Web services description language (WSDL)*, Version 1.1 (W3C note 15). Retrieved from http://www.w3.org/TR/2001/NOTE-wsdl-20010315/

Endnotes

[1]   International Workshop on Rule Markup Languages for Business Rules on the Semantic Web, 14 June 2002, Sardinia (Italy) http://tmitwww.tm.tue. nl/staff/gwagner/RuleML-BR-SW.html. Diffuse: Guide to Web Services http://www.diffuse.org/Web Services.html

[2]   DIP- Data, Information, and Process Integration with Semantic Web Services, http://dip.semanticweb.org/

[3]   World Wide Web Consortium, http://www.w3.org/

[4]   Service inputs are given semi-formally in order to avoid unnecessary details and save space.

[5]   Foundation for Intelligent Physical Agents, http://www.fipa.org/

[6]   e-Appendixes A-1 – A-7 may be downloaded from http://ermolayev.com/services/app.htm

[7]   "One of the most common low fare restrictions is the requirement for your stay to incorporate at least one Sunday. For example for a round-trip New York to Miami a passenger flying Tuesday to Thursday might pay £328, but a passenger whose stay includes a Sunday would pay much less - £188." – http://www.flightcatchers.com/helpmenu/Howtofindcheapestfare.htm

[8]   Lufthansa Infoflyway Booking Service http://lufthansa.com/ and Cyber Flyer Booking Service http://cyberflyer.galileo.com/ were used in the described exercise to obtain the offers from F's.

[9]   CNN Currency Converter: http://qs.money.cnn.com/tq/currconv/

[10]   http://www.bahn.de/

[11]   Applying to a capability registry may still appear to be necessary in case B, C and D fail to provide constructive proposals.

[12]   Performance Simulation Initiative (PSI) is the research and development project of Cadence Design Systems, Gmbh.

[13]   RACING: Rational Agent Coalitions for Intelligent Mediation of Information Retrieval on the Net. http://www.zsu.zp.ua/racing/ Project funded by the Ukrainian Ministry of Education and Science under the grant No 0102Y005339.

[14]   As QPAs in RACING have limited life time, RWAs' credibility and capability assessment is performed by MA for registered resource wrappers. QPAs supply MA with necessary data obtained from cooperation with RWAs.

[15]   UnIT-Net - IT in University Management Network, http://www.unit-net.org.ua/

[16]   SmartResource project, http://www.cs.jyu.fi/ai/OntoGroup/SmartResource_details.htm

Chapter XII

Web Services Identification:
Methodology and CASE Tools

Hemant Jain, University of Wisconsin-Milwaukee, USA

Huimin Zhao, University of Wisconsin-Milwaukee, USA

Nageswara R. Chinta, Tata Consultancy Services, India

Abstract

Web services technology has been envisioned as an important trend in application development and integration. It allows pre-built applications/application components wrapped as Web services to interact with each other through standardized interfaces and to from larger application systems. This chapter describes a formal approach to Web services identification, which is a critical step in designing and developing effective Web services. The approach takes an analysis level object model, representing a business domain, as input and generates potential Web service designs, in which the classes in the object model are grouped into appropriate Web services based on static and dynamic relationships between classes. An initial hierarchical grouping of classes is derived using a maximum spanning tree algorithm or a hierarchical clustering algorithm. A set of managerial goals for evaluating alternative designs is derived based on business strategy of Web service fabricator. Since the managerial goals are conflicting, a multiobjective genetic algorithm has been designed to search for alternative nondominated solutions, from which a preferred solution can be selected. The approach has been implemented in a Web services identification tool and used for designing Web services in an auto insurance claims domain.

Introduction

Web services are envisioned as the next technological wave. Leading software vendors, including Microsoft (Miller, 2003), Sun (Williams, 2003), and IBM (Kreger, 2003), are investing extensively in the development of protocols and products that facilitate the development, deployment, discovery, and composition of Web services. At the same time, a set of Web services technologies is being standardized and supported by the industry (Kreger, 2003).

Web services are expected to greatly enhance Web application interaction and integration and can facilitate assembly of larger business applications from reusable components wrapped as Web services. Based upon emerging standards, such as HTTP, XML, SOAP, WSDL, UDDI, and WPEL4WS, Web services allow loosely coupled Web based application systems to be quickly built by assembling application components wrapped and published as Web services. In these applications, the individual components that provide focused business functionalities can communicate with each other through standardized interfaces (i.e., XML messaging) to form larger application systems that carry out more complex business processes. Offering a language-neutral, environment-neutral computing model, Web services technology is promoting application interaction and integration through the Internet, both within and across enterprises (Gottschalk et al., 2002).

The development and integration of Web services resemble Component Based Software Development (CBSD), where pre-built parts, known as business components, are assembled into larger-scale applications (Herzum & Sims, 2000; Kim & Chang, 2004; Vitharana et al., 2003a, 2003b, 2004). A Web service is essentially a business component that implements an autonomous business concept or business process. Development of Web services typically requires following steps: Domain analysis and modeling, Web services identification, Web service design and implementation, testing, acceptance, and deployment and publication. A critical step among these is Web services identification, where related object classes are grouped into Web services.

The problem of identifying appropriate Web services has not been addressed in the literature. No formal methodology and tools that allow the designer to generate and evaluate alternative designs based on a set of managerial design goals exist. This chapter describes a formal approach to Web services identification.

The chapter is organized as follows. First, the Web services identification problem is discussed and approaches being used in identifying reusable assets and in designing business components are briefly reviewed. A formal approach to Web services identification is then presented. An implementation of the approach in a CASE tool and its application to identifying Web services for auto insurance claim system are then described. Finally, conclusions and future research directions are given.

Web Services Identification Problem

Web services need to be developed such that they can be reused within the same domain and may possibly be reused across domains. The challenge is to identify Web services that can be developed in a cost-effective manner, are suitable for reuse, easy to assemble into larger applications, easy to maintain, and provide capability to customize end applications by proper selection and assembly of Web services.

Identifying reusable artifacts is recognized as one of the difficult tasks in classical software reuse (Apte & Sankar, 1990). Design issues related to traditional reusable software artifacts, such as code, have been discussed in the literature (Mili et al., 1995). However, these approaches are targeted at reusing low-level code and are not applicable for identifying and designing Web services which can be effectively used to assemble applications. Additionally, several methodologies for component development have been proposed. Many of these approaches use top down decomposition and focus on the component interfaces as the key design abstraction (Brown, 2000). Even though component interface is an important abstraction, it does not consider component fabricator's objectives, such as lower development cost, high level of reuse, and ease of maintenance. In the context of using classes to identify appropriate components, Pfister and Szyperski (1998) observe the difficulty of extracting components from a large collection of classes. In fact, Szyperski (1998) states that the *"modeling of component-based systems is still a largely unresolved problem."* In further discussing challenges to identifying components, Levi and Arsanjani (2002, p. 45) claim that *"design engineers often have difficulty determining the initial set of key abstractions that constitute the key elements of a domain in a repeatable and nonarbitrary fashion."* Vitharana et al. (2003, 2004) propose a strategy based approach for designing reusable business components. We adopt parts of this approach for identifying Web services.

Web services differ from traditional software artifacts in various ways and business components in some ways. Thus, the Web services design process must account for these differences. For instance, traditional reusable artifacts, such as code segments and classes, are mostly fine-grained and portray a low-level technical-oriented representation of the application domain. Web services on the other hand are more coarse-grained and are intended to provide a high-level business-oriented representation of the domain. The fine-grained technical-oriented nature of traditional reusable artifacts prevents managers from working with them effectively. On the other hand, the coarse-grained business-oriented nature of Web services allows managers to identify the Web services that satisfy their business needs and subsequently assemble the Web services into full-scale business application systems. Additionally, Web services generally are hosted, thus making the implementation environment of Web services distributed. The effective operation of this resulting distributed application requires that the Web services are loosely coupled and messaging between the services is minimized.

Some other characteristics of Web services include: (1) a Web service is a self-contained executable program that provides a specific service; (2) has a standardized interface, which is used to communicate with other Web services; and (3) is published on the Internet and could be used in a context that is unanticipated by its initial designers.

Next section describes a formal approach to Web services identification, which assists Web service designers in organizing classes into Web services.

A Formal Approach for Identifying Web Services

We propose a formal approach to Web services identification, which is recognized as a crucial step in the overall Web service development process. The approach uses an analysis level domain model as input. We assume that application domain has been modeled using an object-oriented approach. Thus, the domain model (in the UML notation) consists of class diagrams representing significant object classes and structural relationships among the classes, use cases, and sequence/interaction diagrams representing dynamic relationships among the classes. The static (class diagram) and dynamic (use case and sequence diagram) relationship information from the domain model is used to derive an aggregate measure of the class relationships. The dynamic relationships also consider the relative importance of the use cases to the end-user. A hierarchical clustering algorithm and a maximum spanning tree algorithm have been developed to help organize classes into a hierarchical structure, which helps Web service designers to identify initial grouping of classes into Web services. Heuristics (Jain et al., 2001) and multiobjective genetic algorithm-based approach (Coello Coello et al., 2002) can be used to further refine the initial design. The approach is described in detail in the following sub-sections.

Evaluating Class Relationship Strength

The process of Web services identification begins by grouping related classes of an analysis level model of the application domain. In evaluating the strength of relationships between classes, static and dynamic relationships are considered. Static relationships (Rosenberg & Scott, 1999) are computed based on class diagrams; dynamic relationships are computed based on use cases and sequence diagrams.

Static relationships represent the way various classes are related to each other. The use of static relationships in the Web services identification process ensures that only related classes are grouped together. Relationship types (e.g., inheritance, association, and dependency) can be weighted according to their relative importance.

Dynamic relationships represent the way various classes interact through messaging to support various business processes. Use cases and the corresponding sequence diagrams are used as a basis for computing dynamic relationships between classes. Use cases are assigned relative weights based on their importance to the user in the application domain. The importance can be based on the criticality of the business process supported by the use case, frequency, or any other considerations.

The total relationship strength between a pair of classes is computed as follows (Jain et al., 2001). First, the strength of the static relationship (S_{ij}) between classes i and j is defined as:

$$S_{ij} = \sum_{t=1}^{T} (WT_t \bullet N_{ijt})$$

where,

T = Number of relationship types.

WT_t = Weight assigned to relationship type t.

N_{ijt} = Number of type t relationships between class i and class j.

The strength of the dynamic relationship (D_{ij}) between class i and class j is defined as:

$$D_{ij} = \sum_{u=1}^{U} (WU_u \bullet M_{iju}),$$

where

U = Number of use cases.

WU_u = Weight assigned to use case u.

M_{iju} = Number of messages between class i and class j in use case u.

S_{ij} and D_{ij} are scaled into the range of [0, 1]. The total strength (TS_{ij}) of the relationship between the two classes is then computed as:

$$TS_{ij} = RI_S \bullet S_{ij} + RI_D \bullet D_{ij}.$$

Where $RI_S + RI_D = 1.0$. R_S and R_D are weights assigned to S_{ij} and D_{ij} based on their relative importance.

Organizing Classes into Initial Set of Web Services

Taking the characteristics of Web services into consideration, Web service design should strive for tight cohesion within a Web service and loose coupling between Web services (Chang et al., 2005; Jang et al., 2003; Lee et al., 2001). Cohesion refers to the strength of relationships between elements (classes) in a Web service, while coupling refers to the extent to which classes in one Web service relate to classes in other Web services (Vitharana, 2003). The ideal scenario is one in which the cohesion within a Web service is maximized and the coupling between Web services is minimized.

Finding a Web service design that maximizes intra-service cohesion and minimizes inter-service coupling can be formalized as a graph partitioning problem (Schloegel et al., 2000). The classes and the strength of relationship between classes can be represented as a graph $G=(V, E)$, where V is a set of vertices and E is a set of edges. Each vertex corresponds to a class. The weight of an edge e_{ij}, denoted $w(e_{ij})$, equals TS_{ij}, the total strength of the relationship between two classes (vertices) i and j. The objective is to partition V into k disjoint subsets (i.e., Web services) V_1, V_2, ..., V_k, such that the total edge-cut caused by the partitioning (i.e., inter-service coupling) is minimized. Additional partitioning constraints, such as the maximum and minimum numbers of classes allowed in each Web service, may be added to the problem formulation.

There are several difficulties in directly solving the graph-partitioning problem for Web services identification. First, the graph partitioning problem in general is NP-complete. Heuristic methods are needed to generate good, but possibly not optimal, partitions efficiently. Second, there is no natural choice for the number of Web services, k. It is desired that a series of designs under different k's be provided to the Web service designer for further evaluation.

We apply a "greedy" approach to deal with these difficulties. We first find a maximum spanning tree of the graph (Cormen et al., 1990). Efficient polynomial-time algorithms, such as Kruskal's (Krustal, 1956) and Prim's (Prim, 1957), exist for finding a maximum (or minimum) spanning tree out of a graph. Maximum spanning tree provides a reasonably good (but possibly not optimal) way for grouping the vertices in a graph according to their connections. We then generate a hierarchical structure of the classes based on the maximum spanning tree. The tree is broken into sub-trees on a series of threshold values against *TS*. On each threshold, the classes in a sub-tree are suggested to be included in a Web service. The smaller the threshold, the fewer classes in a Web service, and the more Web services recommended. This method provides the Web service designer a series of potential designs with different levels of inter-service coupling and is particularly attractive when a hierarchical Web service design is needed, where classes are organized into Web services, and smaller Web services are successively integrated into bigger ones.

Figure 1. Web services identification process

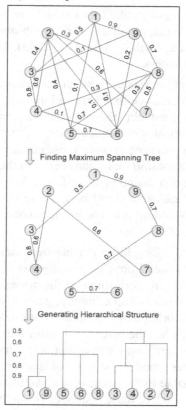

Figure 1 illustrates the Web services identification process using a simple example. There are nine classes in this example. Classes are represented as vertices in a graph. The total strength of relationships between two classes is represented as the weight of the edge between the two classes. A maximum spanning tree of the graph is found and then converted into a hierarchical structure. Two, four, seven, eight, and nine Web services can be formed, respectively, on different inter-service coupling levels. The designer uses this structure to select an initial solution based on the preferred size of Web service and number of Web services desired for the domain. The selected initial solution is used in the next phase to further refine it based on either a set of heuristics or a multiobjective genetic algorithm.

Another alternative to the maximum spanning tree approach is a hierarchical clustering algorithm, described in detail in Jain (2001). These two methods often produce very similar results. When the results are different, the user may compare the results and select an initial solution, which is subsequently refined.

Refining Initial Set of Web Services

The initial set of Web services identified above can be refined by using a set of heuristics described in detail in (Jain et al., 2001) or a multiobjective genetic algorithm based approach described in detail in (Jain et al., 2003). These methods are briefly described here for completeness.

Placing all the classes that are related through 'inheritance' or 'generalization' in a single Web service can enhance the initial solution by increasing the cohesion within the Web service and reducing the inter-service coupling (Riel, 1996) which are desirable characteristics of Web service design. If there is inheritance between classes, then it is more appropriate to place those classes in the same Web service because of the strong relationship (cohesion) between them. If the classes related through inheritance were distributed across different services, then it would result in an increase in dependency (coupling) between services. In this approach, we replicate a super class by adding it to the services containing one or more of its sub-classes.

In addition, a set of hill climbing heuristics has been developed for further refining the initial solution obtained from the spanning tree algorithm or the clustering algorithm. These heuristics are performed by the system when the designer opts for them. These heuristics mimic hill climbing, gradually moving towards the local optimum in the neighborhood of the initial solution. While hill climbing is an efficient search heuristic, it has the potential shortcoming of being trapped to local optima. A more powerful, but also more computationally involved, genetic algorithm approach will be described in the next sub-section. Amongst the heuristics, the various options available to the designer are: Add heuristics, move heuristics, and exchange heuristics. Each of these heuristics is briefly described here.

- **Add heuristics:** In this type of heuristics, redundant assignment of classes to multiple services is used to arrive at a more desirable solution. At each iteration, a class is added to a service and the solution is evaluated in terms of the managerial goals (described in the next section) associated with it. Since the evaluation model contains multiple conflicting objectives a set of nondominated solutions are generated and presented to the designer. The process is similar to the one used in Jain (1987). Figure 2 depicts an iteration of add heuristics.

- **Move heuristics:** In this type of heuristics, a class from a service is moved to another service, during an iteration. The managerial goal values are computed after every iteration. As in the case of add heuristics, only the nondominated solutions are displayed. Figure 3 depicts an iteration of move heuristics. During the iteration, Class A is moved from service 1 to service 2. Unlike add heuristics, classes are not redundantly assigned to services.

- **Exchange heuristics:** This heuristic operates by making even exchanges of classes between services. During an iteration of exchange heuristics, a class from a service is exchanged with a class from another service. Figure 4 depicts the exchange of Classes A and X between services 1 and 2, respectively.

In addition to the hill climbing heuristics, the system also allows the user to manually edit a solution. If the designer feels that a particular class is more appropriate in another service, he or she can move the class to that service. This manual editing function is designed to provide opportunity for fine tuning the service by the designer.

Figure 2. Add heuristics

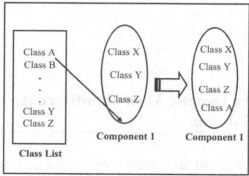

Figure 3. Move heuristics

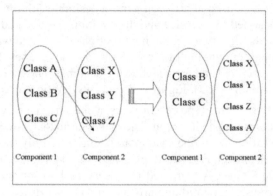

Figure 4. Exchange heuristics

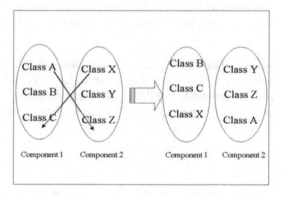

A Multiobjective Genetic Algorithm Based Approach to Evaluation of Solution

Vitharana et al. (2003, 2004) identified five managerial goals (cost effectiveness, ease of assembly, customizability, reusability, and maintainability) and five technical features (coupling, cohesion, number of components, size of component, and complexity) that are closely related to the managerial goals in the context of component based system development. They identified the relationship coefficients between the technical features and managerial goals from a survey. We adopt this model for evaluating the Web services identification solutions.

Since the multiple managerial goals may conflict with each other, there may not exist one solution, which is optimal with respect to all managerial goals. If the Web service fabricator can weight the relative importance of the managerial goals properly based on its business strategy, a consolidated objective (i.e., weighted sum of the managerial goals) can be optimized. However, it is usually very hard for decision makers to make the tradeoffs among the managerial goals and assign the weights exactly. We, therefore, formulate Web services identification as a multiobjective optimization problem and seek a set of alternative solutions, which are superior to other possible solutions when all objectives are considered but may be inferior to other solutions in a few objectives. Such solutions are known as Pareto-optimal solutions or nondominated solutions (Srinivas & Deb, 1994). Decision makers can compare the alternative nondominated solutions and select appropriate ones. The formulation of the multiobjective optimization problem is described in detail in (Jain et al., 2003). The approach is briefly described here for completeness.

Multiobjective Optimization

In general, a multiobjective optimization problem that needs to minimize (or maximize) a set of n objective functions and is subject to a set of m constraints can be mathematically denoted as:

Min $\quad Obj_i(\mathbf{x}) \quad i=1, 2, ..., n$

S.t. $\quad f_j(\mathbf{x}) \leq 0 \quad j=1, 2, ..., m$

A solution to the problem is an instantiation of the vector of variables, $\mathbf{x}$, that satisfies the constraints. A solution $\mathbf{x}^p$ is said to dominate another solution $\mathbf{x}^q$, if and only if

$$\forall i = 1, 2, ..., n, \, Obj_i(\mathbf{x}^P) \leq Obj_i(\mathbf{x}^q) \quad \wedge$$
$$\exists i = 1, 2, ..., n, \, Obj_i(\mathbf{x}^P) < Obj_i(\mathbf{x}^q).$$

A solution that is not dominated by any other solution is called a Pareto-optimal solution or nondominated solution. Typically, there are many nondominated solutions, which form the so-called nondominated front (or Pareto-optimal front) in the solution space.

An optimization algorithm may attempt to find one, many, or even all of the points on the nondominated front. Classical methods consolidate the multiple objective functions into a single objective function in some manner and reduce the problem to a single-objective optimization problem (Srinivas & Deb, 1994). For example, the method of objective weighting calculates a consolidated objective function:

$$Z(\mathbf{x}) = \sum_{i=1}^{n} w_i Obj_i(\mathbf{x}),$$

where the weights w_i's are assigned by the decision maker based on his/her perception of the relative importance of the objectives. This method usually generates only a single solution and is sensitive to the weighting scheme. The decision maker may need to try different weighting schemes and solve the reduced problem many times to find a preferred solution. Genetic algorithms can approach multiple nondominated solutions simultaneously (Coello Coello et al., 2002; Srinivas & Deb, 1994; Zitzler et al., 1999) and allow the decision maker to compare the suggested alternative solutions and to select a preferred one.

Genetic Algorithms

Genetic algorithms belong to a class of evolutionary algorithms (Bäck, 1996). They can be viewed as search procedures that mimic the mechanics of natural selection and genetics (Goldberg, 2002). They have been widely applied to solve computationally hard optimization problems.

Figure 5 shows a generic procedure of genetic algorithms. In a genetic algorithm designed to solve a particular optimization problem, each solution to the problem is encoded as an artificial chromosome (or individual). A chromosome consists of a sequence of genes, which are often encoded as binary bits. An initial population of chromosomes can be created randomly or by using prior knowledge of possibly good solutions. The population then evolves from generation (i.e., iteration) to generation.

Three mechanisms—that is, selection, crossover, and mutation—together ensure that the population evolves towards better individuals as time goes on. Selection allocates more offspring to individuals with better "fitness" (i.e., objective function) values, following the survival of the fittest principle. Crossover mates a portion of the selected individuals to form new, possibly better offspring. Some genes of the chromosomes are occasionally mutated to explore new possibilities not present in the current population and to prevent the evolution from being trapped on local optima. Basic parameters that can be tuned include the population size, the probability of crossover (or crossover rate), and the probability of mutation (or mutation rate). The evolution goes on forever, unless a terminating control (e.g., a maximum number of generations, a specified time period, or an external interruption) is used.

Figure 5. A generic procedure of genetic algorithms

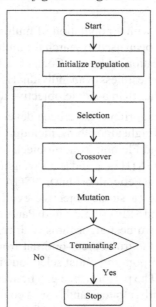

Many methods for selection, crossover, and mutation have been developed. Some examples of selection methods include proportional selection, ranking, tournament selection, and elitist selection (Goldberg, 2002). In proportional selection, each individual is given a probability of selection that is proportional to its fitness value. In ranking, the selection probability of an individual is assigned based on its rank instead of its absolute fitness value. In tournament selection, the best individual in a randomly selected tournament consisting of some number of individuals is elected to survive to the next generation. In elitist selection, the best several individuals are guaranteed to survive, so the best individual in a population will never degenerate. Basic crossover methods include one-point crossover, multiple-point crossover, and uniform crossover (Goldberg, 2002). In one-point crossover, one crossover point in the chromosomes is chosen at random and the genes to the right of that point are exchanged between two individuals. Multiple-point crossover is a generalization of one-point crossover; multiple crossover points are chosen at random and every other segment between two crossover points is exchanged between two individuals. In uniform crossover, each gene is decided at random whether or not to be exchanged. Although more complex mutation methods are available, the simplest mutation method is often used, in which each gene is decided at random with a specified probability whether or not to be mutated. Some other selection, crossover, and mutation methods are described by Bäck (1996) and Goldberg (2002) and are not discussed in this chapter.

Since genetic algorithms deal with a population of multiple solutions instead of a single solution, they have also been used to search for multiple nondominated solutions to multiobjective optimization problems (Coello Coello et al., 2002;Srinivas & Deb, 1994). In such situations, the fitness of an individual is evaluated by considering all objectives collectively, rather than a single objective alone.

Many multiobjective genetic algorithms have been developed. An empirical study (Zitzler et al., 1999) compared eight algorithms, including RAND (a random search algorithm), FFGA (Fonseca and Fleming's multiobjective EA), NPGA (the niched Pareto genetic algorithm), HLGA (Hajela and Lin's weighted-sum based approach), VEGA (the vector evaluated genetic algorithm), NSGA (the nondominated sorting genetic algorithm), SOEA (a single-objective evolutionary algorithm using weighted-sum aggregation), and SPEA (the strength Pareto evolutionary algorithm). The results indicate that the two best algorithms with respect to the distance between the achieved front and the true Pareto-optimal front are SPEA and NSGA. The study also found that incorporating elitist selection significantly improves the performance of an algorithm. The performance gap between SPEA and NSGA was largely attributed to SPEA's elitist strategy and NSGA could match the performance of SPEA by borrowing the elitist strategy from SPEA.

A Genetic Algorithm for Web Services Identification

We have designed an algorithm named MOGA-WSI (multiobjective genetic algorithm for Web services identification) to solve the multiobjective optimization problem of Web services identification. The building blocks of MOGA-WSI are described in detail in Jain et al. (2003).

Encoding of Solutions: A solution to the Web services identification problem consists of an assignment of $N \times M$ binary variables $x_{ij}(i=1,2,...N; j=1,2,...M)$, where N is the number of classes and M is the number of Web services; $x_{ij}=1$, if class i is included in Web service j, or 0 otherwise. The chromosome that corresponds to a solution is encoded as a string of $N \times M$ bits, each of which represents one variable. The size of the entire solution space is on the order of $2^{N \times M}$. MOGA-WSI starts with the initial solution selected from the spanning tree or clustering approach and evolves towards better ones. If MOGA-WSI is run multiple times, each new run can also use the results from previous runs as starting solutions. Copying the available starting solutions and randomly changing some of the genes of the individuals generate the initial population. The 1s and 0s of the individuals are in different proportions in the Web services identification problem. The ratio of 1s to 0s is roughly $\frac{1}{M-1}$.

The changing probability of 0s and that of 1s are therefore kept in the same ratio. Constraints (e.g., every class must be included in at least one Web service) are checked. Invalid solutions are repaired immediately.

- **Selection:** A combination of elitist selection and proportional selection is used in MOGA-WSI. Several best individuals (i.e., the "elitists") are selected to survive from the current generation to the next. The rest of the new population will be selected from the old population, with each individual given a probability of survival that is proportional to its fitness value. MOGA-WSI supports two optimization strategies, that is, objective weighting and not-dominated sorting. In objective weighting, the fitness value is derived by linearly scaling a consolidated objective, which is a weighted sum of the managerial goals, and the Web services identification problem reduces to a single-objective optimization problem. In nondominated sorting, all managerial goals are considered collectively. If objective weighting is used, a specified number of best solutions are treated as elitists and are guaranteed to survive to the next generation. If nondominated sorting is used, the nondominated solutions in the current generation up to a specified percentage of the entire population are treated as elitists. The nondominated sorting procedure of NSGA (Srinivas & Deb, 1994), a general-purpose multiobjective genetic algorithm, is used in MOGA-WSI. This procedure assigns each individual a dummy fitness value based on the individual's degree of nondomination. The nondominated individuals in the current population are identified to form the first nondominated front and are assigned a large fitness value. These individuals in the same front are then shared with their dummy fitness values; the fitness value of an individual is divided by a quantity proportional to the number of individuals close to it. The rest of the population is then processed in the same way to identify the second nondominated front. Individuals in the second nondominated front are assigned a new dummy fitness value that is smaller than the minimum shared dummy fitness of the previous front. This process is repeated until the entire population is assigned dummy fitness values.

- **Crossover:** Crossover selects two parent individuals with a given probability of crossover and recombines them to form two child individuals. The current version of MOGA-WSI uses the one-point crossover mechanism, which chooses one crossover position within the sequence of genes of an individual at random and exchanges the genes to the right of that position between two parent individuals.

- **Mutation:** Mutation occasionally changes single genes of individuals (the mutation probability is usually kept small). Similar to the modification method in generating initial solutions, since the ratio of 1s to 0s is roughly $\frac{1}{M-1}$, the mutation probability of 0s and that of 1s are kept in the same ratio.

- **Fuzzy preferences:** MOGA-WSI also allows the user to specify partial preferences on the five managerial goals (Coello Coello, 2000; Cvetkovic´ & Parmee, 2002). Typically, such preferences are specified as pair-wise tradeoffs. For example, the user may consider cost effectiveness to be between five and 10 times more important than ease of assembly. However, there are several difficulties for the user in specifying such precise pair-wise tradeoffs. First, there are too many ranges to be specified. For five managerial goals, 10 pairs need to be specified. Second, multiple pair-wise tradeoffs may result in conflicts. For example, the user might specify that cost effectiveness is more important than ease of assembly, ease of assembly is more important than customizability, and customizability is more important than cost effectiveness. Third, it may be difficult for the user to precisely pinpoint the particular numbers, although they may have a rough idea about which managerial goals are more important. Considering the aforementioned difficulties, we use a fuzzy mechanism to help the user easily specify preferences on the managerial goals. The user can choose the level of importance for each managerial goal from five levels: not important, less important, average, important, and very important. Pair-wise tradeoff ranges are then automatically derived based on the chosen importance levels on individual goals. Specifying preferences on the managerial goals reduces the set of nondominated solutions and allows the user to focus on a particular region of the Pareto front that is deemed relevant. Otherwise, all nondominated solutions will be presented to the user for consideration.

Visualization

Since many nondominated solutions may be found and presented to the user simultaneously, it may still be a daunting task for the user to evaluate the solutions and make the final selection. Visualization can help the user visually compare the strengths and weaknesses of alternative solutions. The system provides several methods, including star charts and parallel coordinates, for visualizing the five managerial goals of alternative solutions.

Implementation and Application of the Approach

A research team at the University of Wisconsin–Milwaukee (UWM) has implemented the proposed approach in a Web services identification tool. The research program is a joint collaboration between Tata Consultancy Services (TCS), Asia's largest software consultancy firm, and UWM.

The tool has been used in designing Web services in an auto insurance claims domain. A team of domain experts from TCS developed an object model, which comprised of use case diagrams, sequence diagrams, and class diagrams. Figure 6 shows a portion of a use case diagram. There were eight use cases in this model.

For each of the use cases a corresponding sequence diagram was designed. The sequence diagrams show the interaction between classes through messaging. Figure 7 displays a portion of one of the sequence diagrams.

A class diagram, depicting the relationships between classes and the cardinality of the relationships, was also designed. In addition to associations between classes, the class diagrams also incorporated 'generalization/inheritance' relationships between

Figure 6. A partial use case diagram

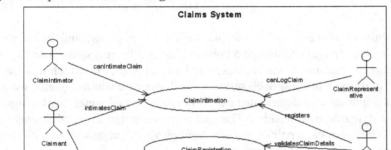

Figure 7. A partial sequence diagram

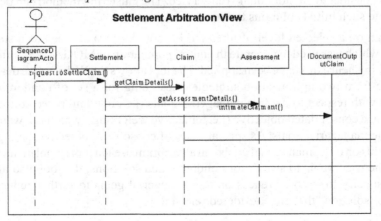

Figure 8. A partial class diagram

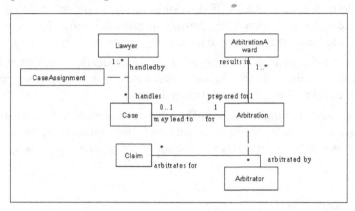

parent and child classes and UML concepts, such as 'aggregation' and 'association classes.' The class diagram contained 52 object classes. Figure 8 shows a portion of the class diagram. The model was then exported into an XML file, which was fed as input to the tool for identifying Web services. Each use case was assigned a weight based on its importance as determined by TCS experts. Equal weight was assigned to static and dynamic relationships. The tool then computed the total strength of relationships between each pair of classes. A graph was then generated with these total weights as edges and classes as nodes.

A maximum spanning tree was then found and converted into a hierarchical structure (Figure 9), which suggested a series of Web service designs. On the lowest inter-service coupling level, all classes are included in a single Web service; on the next several levels, 9, 10, 14, 15, 16, 27, 29, 45, 47, and 50 components are recommended, respectively; on the highest inter-service coupling level, each of the 52 classes is considered an individual Web service. The clustering method can be used to generate such initial solutions too.

The design on a selected level of inter-service coupling was chosen as a starting solution, which was used to generate the initial population of MOGA-WSI, after the hill-climbing heuristics have been applied. The tool allows the Web service designer to choose from two optimization strategies: searching for a set of nondominated solutions with respect to the five managerial goals (i.e., nondominated sorting) or optimizing a consolidated objective (i.e., objective weighting), which is a weighted sum of the managerial goals. As special cases of consolidate objectives, assigning zero weights on other managerial goals can also optimize each individual managerial goal. If the user wants to search for nondominated solutions, the tool also allows them to specify fuzzy preferences on the managerial goals to further reduce the number of solutions that are considered relevant.

Figure 9. A spanning tree result

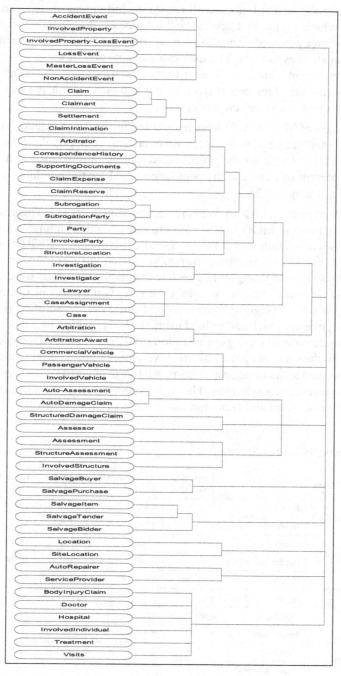

The current best solutions are reported periodically (in a specified display interval). These include the best solutions with respect to individual managerial goals and the elitists, which are the first several best solutions if the objective weighting optimization strategy is used or nondominated solutions if the nondominated sorting optimization strategy is used. The user can evaluate any of these solutions at any time. The execution can go on forever unless the user stops it. The user can also temporarily stop the algorithm at any moment and then resume the execution with the same or a new optimization strategy.

The parameters of MOGA-WSI have been tuned for fast convergence. A suggested setting is: mutation rate of $0s = 0.02$, crossover rate $= 0.8$, population size $= 1000$, number of elitists (used for the objective weighting optimization strategy) $= 10$, maximum percent of elitists in the population (used for the nondominated sorting optimization strategy) $= 25$.

Some results of running MOGA-WSI are summarized in Table 1. These results were generated by running MOGA-WSI for between 17 and 19 hours on a Dell Opti-plex/GX260 workstation with a Pentium 4 CPU running at 2.27GHz and 512 MB RAM. The algorithm was run using the nondominated sorting optimization strategy, using the objective weighting strategy while the managerial goals were given equal weights, and using the objective weighting strategy while only one managerial goal was given a nonzero weight. All runs started from a starting solution suggested by the spanning tree approach and refined using the hill climbing heuristics. In the run using the nondominated sorting optimization strategy, 277 alternative solutions were suggested. In the runs using the objective weighting optimization strategy, the ten elitists converged to the same best solution. All five managerial goals were improved to different degrees in all the runs. The TCS experts felt that the suggested designs are logically consistent and contain most of the good designs.

Table 1. Some MOGA-WSI results

Managerial Goal		Starting Solution	Nondominated Sorting	Equal Weights	Optimizing Single Goals
Development Cost	Best Value	12.38	8.99	10.18	8.48
	Improvement (%)		27.38	17.78	31.50
Ease of Assembly	Best Value	55.51	67.96	60.00	83.42
	Improvement (%)		22.43	8.09	50.28
Customizability	Best Value	53.25	55.27	54.53	55.28
	Improvement (%)		3.79	2.40	3.81
Reusability	Best Value	49.13	51.60	50.60	51.65
	Improvement (%)		5.03	2.99	5.13
Maintainability	Best Value	88.06	89.26	88.90	89.49
	Improvement (%)		1.36	0.95	1.62

The results show that both optimization strategies have their advantages. If the designer has a clearly defined weighting of the managerial goals, the algorithm usually converges faster in the specified optimization direction. For example, in essentially the same time period, optimizing a single managerial goal improved the managerial goal more than the nondominated sorting strategy did. Otherwise, the nondominated optimization strategy can provide the designer with a lot of alternative solutions spreading out on the nondominated front to help the designer choose an appropriate design. If the designer has partial preferences on some of the managerial goals, this information can help to reduce the number of alternative solutions that need to be considered.

The tool can further be used in a lot of flexible ways by combining the two strategies to search for alternative solutions. For example, the designer may start from an initial solution suggested by the spanning tree approach and refined using the hill-climbing heuristics, optimize individual managerial goals independently, and then use the elitists with respect to individual managerial goals as initial solutions to search for a set of nondominated solutions. This is expected to greatly speed up the convergence

Figure 10. A start chart example

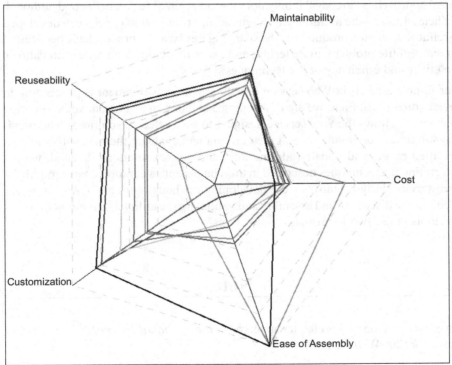

of the nondominated sorting strategy and increase the spread of solutions on the nondominated front. The designer can also search for nondominated solutions first and then use selected solutions as initial solutions to further evolve in a particular direction. This helps the designer prioritize the managerial goals by evaluating alternative preliminary solutions. The designer may even pre-specify a sequence of runs, each starting from the elitists of the previous run, in a batch file.

To help the designer visually compare the alternative solutions, the tool includes several visualization methods, such as star charts and parallel coordinates. Figure 10 shows an example of start charts.

Conclusion and Future Work

As Web services identification has not been adequately studied in the literature yet, this chapter proposes a formal approach to this critical step in Web service development. Such an approach is likely to ease the development of Web services and enhance their subsequent assembly.

We are aware of several limitations of the current approach. First, the spanning tree based approach is "greedy." It may not yield an optimal solution. Second, although the heuristics and the multiobjective genetic algorithm, which have been developed to refine the solution produced by the spanning tree based approach, have been tested on one real life problem, more testing and experimentation are required to validate the utility and efficiency of the techniques.

Our future research in Web service based software development is proceeding in several directions. First, we are developing a solution management and evaluation tool, which allows the Web service designer to save selected solutions, load previous solutions, sort solutions on given criteria and evaluate the best solutions in a specified range, and update (add, modify, and delete) solutions. Second, we are integrating the techniques described in this chapter into a comprehensive toolkit for Web service design. Third, we are developing methodologies and CASE tools for Web service discovery and assembly and validating the utility of our methodologies and tools in real-world business applications.

Note

An earlier version of this chapter appeared in *International Journal of Web Services Research* (2004), *1*(1), 1-20.

References

Apte, U., & Sankar, C. S. (1990). Reusability-based strategy for development of information systems: Implementation experience of a bank. *MIS Quarterly, 14*(4), 421-433.

Bäck, T. (1996). *Evolutionary algorithms in theory and practice.* Oxford, NY: Oxford University Press.

Brown, A. W. (2000). *Large-scale component-based development.* Upper Saddle River, NJ: Prentice-Hall.

Chang, S. H., Han, M. J., & Kim, S. D. (2005). A tool to automate component clustering and identification. In *Proceedings of the 8th International Conference on Fundamental Approaches to Software Engineering (FASE 2005)* (pp. 141-144).

Coello Coello, C. A. (2000). Handling preferences in evolutionary multiobjective optimization: A survey. In *Proceedings of the 2000 Congress on Evolutionary Computation (CEC 2000)*, Piscataway, NJ (pp. 30-37).

Coello Coello, C. A., Van Veldhuizen, D. A., & Lamont, G. B. (2002). *Evolutionary algorithms for solving multi-objective problems.* NY: Kluwer.

Cormen, T. H., Leiserson, C. E., & Rivest, R. L. (1990). *Introduction to algorithms, chapter 24: minimum spanning tree* (pp. 498-513). MIT Press & McGraw-Hill Book Company.

Cvetkovic´ D., & Parmee, I. C. (2002). Preferences and their application in evolutionary multiobjective optimization. *IEEE Transactions on Evolutionary Computation, 6*(1), 42-57.

Goldberg, D. E. (2002). *The design of innovation: Lessons from and for competent genetic algorithms.* Kluwer Academic Publishers.

Gottschalk, K., Graham, S., Kreger, H., & Snell, J. (2002). Introduction to Web services architecture. *IBM Systems Journal, 41*(2), 170-177.

Herzum, P., & Sims, O. (2000). *Business component factory: A comprehensive overview of component-based development for the enterprise.* John Wiley & Sons.

Jain, H. (1987). A comprehensive model for the design of distributed computer systems. *IEEE Transactions on Software Engineering, SE-13*(10), 1092-1104.

Jain, H., Chalimeda, N., Ivaturi, N., & Reddy, B. (2001). Business component identification—a formal approach. In *Proceedings of 5th International Enterprise Distributed Object Computing Conference.*

Jain, H., Zhao, H., & Chinta, N. R. (2003). Web service identification—a multi-objective genetic algorithm based approach. In *Proceedings of the Second Workshop on E-Business (WeB 2003)* (pp. 351-361).

Jain, H., Zhao, H., & Chinta, N. R. (2004). A spanning tree based approach to identifying Web services. *International Journal of Web Services Research, 1*(1), 1-20.

Jang, Y. J., Kim, E. Y., & Lee, K. W. (2003). Object-oriented component identification method using the affinity analysis technique. In *Object-oriented information systems* (LNCS 2817, pp. 317-321).

Kim, S. & Chang, S. (2004). A systematic method to identify software components. In *Proceedings of the 11ᵗʰ Asia-Pacific Software Engineering Conference (APSEC '04)*.

Kreger, H. (2003). Fulfilling the Web services promise. *Communications of the ACM, 46*(6), 29-34.

Kruskal, J. B. (1956). On the shortest spanning subtree of a graph and the traveling salesman problem. In *Proceedings of the American Mathematical Society* (Vol. 7, pp. 48-50).

Lee, J. K., Jung, S. J., Kim, S. D., Jang, W. H., & Ham, D. H. (2001). Component identification method with coupling and cohesion. In *Proceedings of the 8ᵗʰ Asia-Pacific Software Engineering Conference*. Macau: IEEE Computer Society Press.

Levi, K., & Arsanjani, A. (2002). A goal-driven approach to enterprise component identification and specification. *Communications of the ACM, 45*(10), 45-52.

Mili, H., Mili, F., & Mili, A. (1995). Reusing software: Issues and research directions. *IEEE Transactions on Software Engineering, 21*(6), 528-561.

Miller, G. (2003). The Web services debase: .Net vs. J2EE. *Communications of the ACM, 46*(6), 64-67.

Pfister, C., & Szyperski, C. (1998). Why objects are not enough. In T. Jell (Ed.), *Component-based software engineering (CUC '96)*. Cambridge, UK: Cambridge University Press.

Prim, R. C. (1957). Shortest connection networks and some generalizations. *Bell Systems Technical Journal, 36,* 1389-1401.

Riel, A. (1996). *Object-Oriented Design Heuristics.* Addison-Wesley Publishing Company, Inc.

Rosenberg, D., & Scott, K. (1999). *Use case driven object modeling with UML: A practical approach.* Addison Wesley Longman, Inc.

Schloegel, K., Karypis, G., & Kumar, V. (2000). Graph partitioning for high performance scientific simulations. In J. Dongarra et al. (Eds.), *CRPC parallel computing handbook*. Morgan Kaufmann.

Srinivas, N. & Deb, K. (1994). Multiobjective optimization using nondominated sorting in genetic algorithms. *Evolutionary Computation, 2*(3), 221-248.

Szyperski, C. (1998). *Component software: Beyond object-oriented programming*. NY: ACM Press.

Tata Consultancy Services. (1999). *ADEX modeling framework, Version 1.7.*

Vitharana, P., Zahedi, F., M., & Jain, H. (2003a). Design, retrieval, and assembly in component-based software development. *Communications of the ACM, 45*(11), 97-102.

Vitharana, P., Zahedi, F. M., & Jain, H. (2003b). Knowledge based repository scheme for storing and retrieving business components: A theoretical design and an empirical analysis. *IEEE Transactions on Software Engineering, 29*(7), 649-664.

Vitharana, P., Jain, H., & Zahedi, F. M. (2004). Strategy-based design of reusable business components. *IEEE Transactions on Systems, Man, and Cybernetic: Part C, 34*(4), 460-474.

Williams, J. (2003). The Web services debase: J2EE vs. .Net. *Communications of the ACM, 46*(6), 59-63.

Szyperski, C. (1998). *Component Software: Beyond Object-Oriented Programming*. NY: ACM Press.

Zitzler, E., Deb, K., & Thiele, L. (1999). Comparison of multiobjective evolutionary algorithms: Empirical results. In *Proceedings of the 1999 Genetic and Evolutionary Computation Conference* (pp. 121-122).

About the Authors

Liang-Jie Zhang is a research staff member at the IBM T. J. Watson Research Center (USA). He is part of the e-business solutions and autonomic computing research team with a focus on collaborative business process integration and management innovations. He has filed more than 30 patent applications in the areas of e-commerce, Web services, Grid computing, rich media, data management, and information appliances, and he has published more than 60 technical papers in journals, book chapters and conference proceedings. Dr. Zhang is an IEEE senior member and the vice chair of communications for IEEE Task Force on e-commerce. Currently, he was the general chair of the 2004 IEEE International Conference on Web Services (ICWS 2004) and the general co-chair of the 2004 IEEE Conference on E-Commerce Technology (CEC 2004). He is the editor-in-chief of the *International Journal of Web Services Research (JWSR)*. Dr. Liang-Jie received a BS in electrical engineering at Xidian University (1990), an MS in electrical engineering at Xi'an Jiaotong University (1992), and a PhD in computer engineering at Tsinghua University (1996).

***

Elisa Bertino is a professor at the department of Computer Sciences, Purdue University (USA), and research director of CERIAS. Her main research interests include: security, privacy, database systems, object-oriented technology, and multimedia systems. In those areas, Professor Bertino has published more than 200 papers in all major refereed journals, and in proceedings of international conferences and symposia. She is a co-author of the books "Object-Oriented Database Systems: Concepts and Architectures," (1993, Addison-Wesley International Publ.), "Indexing Techniques for Advanced Database Systems," (1997, Kluwer Academic Publishers), and "Intelligent Database Systems," (2001, Addison-Wesley International Publ.). She is a co-editor-in-chief of the *Very Large Database Systems (VLDB) Journal* and a member of the advisory board of the IEEE Transactions on Knowledge and Data Engineering. She serves also on the editorial boards of several scientific journals, including *IEEE Internet Computing, ACM Transactions on Information and System Security, Acta Informatica,* the *Parallel and Distributed Database Journal,* the *Journal of Computer Security, Data & Knowledge Engineering,* the *International Journal of Cooperative Information Systems,* and *Science of Computer Programming.* She has been consultant to several Italian companies on data management systems and applications and has given several courses to industries. She is involved in several projects sponsored by the EU. Professor Bertino is a fellow member of IEEE and a member of ACM and has been been named a Golden Core member for her service to the IEEE Computer Society. She has served as program committee members of several international conferences, such as ACM SIGMOD, VLDB, ACM OOPSLA, as program co-chair of the 1998 IEEE International Conference on Data Engineering (ICDE), as program chair of 2000 European Conference on Object-Oriented Programming (ECOOP 2000), and as program chair of the 7th ACM Symposium of Access Control Models and Technologies (SACMAT 2002). She will be serving as program chair of the 2004 EDBT Conference.

Carsten Buschmann received his master's degree in computer science from the Technical University of Braunschweig (Germany) (2002). He is currently working towards his doctoral degree at the University Lübeck (Germany) in the area of wireless sensor networks. Within the SWARMS project his task is to explore middleware support for application development for distributed pervasive computing.

Wentong Cai is an associate professor with the school of computer engineering at Nanyang Technological University (NTU) (Singapore), and the head of the computer science division. He received his BS in computer science from Nankai University (P. R. China) and a PhD, also in computer science, from University of Exeter (UK). He was a post-doctoral research fellow at Queen's University (Canada) before joining NTU (February 1993). Dr. Cai has been actively involved in the research in parallel and distributed computing for more than 10 years and has published more than

100 research papers in this area. His current research interests include: parallel and distributed simulation, cluster and Grid computing. He is a member of IEEE.

Marcelo Campo (http://www.exa.unicen.edu.ar/~mcampo) received a PhD degree in computer science from the Universidade Federal do Rio Grande do Sul (Porto Alegre, Brazil) (1997). Currently, he is an associate professor at the computer science department and head of the ISISTAN Research Institute of UNICEN. He is also a research fellow of the CONICET. He has published over 60 papers in conferences and journals about software engineering topics. His research interests include: intelligent aided software engineering, software architectures and frameworks, agent technology, and software visualization.

Barbara Carminati is an assistant professor of computer science at the University of Insubria (Varese, Italy). Dr. Carminati received a MS degree in computer sciences (2000), and a PhD in computer science from the University of Milano (2004). Her main research interests include: database and Web security, XML security, WS security, Web semantic security, secure information dissemination and publishing. Dr. Carminati has served as program committee member of several international conferences and workshops (SACMAT, COOPIS, PST, MSW), and as reviewer for various international journals and conferences among (IEEE TKDE, ACM TOIT). She is on the editorial board of the *Computer Standards & Interfaces* journal.

Hsing "Kenny" Cheng is an associate professor of information technology and the American Economic Institutions faculty fellow at the Department of Decision and Information Sciences of Warrington College of Business Administration at the University of Florida (USA). Prior to joining UF, he served on the faculty at the College of William and Mary (1992-1998). He received his PhD in computers and information systems from William E. Simon Graduate School of Business Administration, University of Rochester (1992). Dr. Cheng's research interests involve electronic commerce, economics of information systems, and information technology in supply chain management. His recent research focuses on modeling the impact of Internet technology on software development and marketing, and issues surrounding the application services supply chain and Web services. His work has appeared in *Computers and Operations Research, Decision Support Systems, European Journal of Operational Research, IEICE Transactions, Journal of Business Ethics, Information Technology & Management, International Journal of Electronic Commerce, Journal of Information Systems and E-Business Management, Journal of Management Information Systems*, and *Socio-Economic Planning Sciences*. Dr. Cheng has co-edited several special issues in various information systems journals. He has served on the program committee of many information systems conferences and workshops, and is a program co-chair for the Workshop on E-Business 2003.

Nageswara R. Chinta is a researcher with the R&D group of Tata Consultancy Services (Hyderabad, Andhra Pradesh, India). He received his MTech in computer science and technology from Andhra University (India) (1999). His areas of expertise are real time systems, data structures, object-oriented analysis and design, GUI modeling, client/server applications, and networking. His research interests include: mobile computing, system development using reusable components, and Web services.

Kevin Curran (BSc [Hons], DPhil, SMIEEE, MBCS CITP, MACM, MAIAA, MIEE, ILTM) is a lecturer in computer science at the University of Ulster (UK). His achievements include: winning and managing European framework projects, UK government council funded projects, and many technology transfer schemes. He has published over 200 research papers to date in the field of distributed computing, especially emerging trends within wireless ad-hoc networks, dynamic protocol stacks and middleware. He is a member of the editorial committee of the *Journal of Universal Computer Science (JUCS)*. He is also a member of numerous international conference organising committees.

Vadim Ermolayev (http://google.com/search?q=Ermolayev) is an associate professor at the Department of Information Technologies of Zaporozhye National University (Ukraine) and the lead for the intelligent systems research group. His research interests include: intelligent information integration, agent-enabled e-business and e-learning, ontologies, Semantic Web services, evolution and adaptability in intelligent software systems, and dynamic business process management and performance. He received his PhD in mathematical modeling and computer science from Zaporozhye State University.

Marta Fernández-Alarcón (Madrid, Spain) has an advanced studies degree in computer science from the Pontifical University of Salamanca in Madrid (Spain) (2005), computer engineer from the faculty of computer science of the Pontifical University of Salamanca in Madrid (2001). She has been professor in the languages and computer systems department at the Pontifical University of Salamanca in Madrid (2001-present). Her research interests include: Web engineering, object-oriented technologies, and virtual machines.

Elena Ferrari is a full professor of computer science at the University of Insurbia (Como, Italy). She was an assistant professor at the Department of Computer Science of the University of Milano (Italy) (1998-January 2001). She received the MS degree in computer science from the University of Milano (Italy) (1992), and she received a PhD in computer science from the same university (1998). Dr. Ferrari was a visiting researcher (summer, 1996) at the Department of Computer Science of George Mason University (Fairfax, VA). She has been a visiting researcher at Rutgers University in Neward, NJ (summers of 1997, 1998). Her research activities are related to various aspects of data management systems, including Web security, access control and privacy, multimedia databases, and temporal databases. On these topics she has published more than a 100 scientific publications in international journals and conference proceedings. She gave several invited lectures and tutorials in Italian and foreign universities, as well as on international conferences and workshops. Dr. Ferrari has served as program chair of the 4th ACM Symposium on Access Control Models and Technologies (SACMAT '04), Software Demonstration Chair of the 9th International Conference on Extending Database Technology (EDBT '04), co-chair of the first COMPSAC '02 Workshop on Web Security and Semantic Web, the first ECOOP Workshop on XML and Object Technology (XOT 2000), and the first ECOOP Workshop on Object-Oriented Databases. She has also served as program committee member of several international conferences and workshops. Dr. Ferrari is on the editorial board of the *Very Large Database Systems (VLDB) Journal* and the *International Journal of Information Technology (IJIT)*. She is a member of the ACM and senior member of IEEE.

Stefan Fischer is professor of computer sciences at the University Lübeck (Germany). He worked at the European Center for Network Research (ENC) of IBM (Heidelberg) at the University of Heidelberg where he received his doctoral degree (1996), at the University of Montreal, the International University at Bruchsal, and the Technical University of Braunschweig before. His current research activities are focused on applications and supporting software for state of the art distributed systems.

Brendan Gallagher (BS, MS) is a graduate in computer science of the University of Ulster (UK). He is presently working in the Northern Ireland telecommunications industry and his research interests include: distributed systems, low level protocols, and Internet technologies.

Terence Hung is currently the manager of the software and computing program at the Institute of High Performance Computing (Singapore) where he is responsible for R&D and manpower development in the areas of large-scale collaborative computing, computational intelligence and visualization. Dr. Hung has more than 10 years of experience in IT/HPC technology R&D and has consulted on supercomputing and performance optimization. Currently, Dr. Hung champions R&D in Grid computing to tackle needs in computational science and engineering problems. He plays an active role in various national initiatives. Dr. Hung has been invited to sit on various R&D committees (e.g., Adaptive Enterprise @ Singapore, a collaboration between Hewlett Packard and Infocomm Development Authority of Singapore). He was also appointed by the National Grid Steering Committee to lead the Physical Science Virtual Grid Community efforts. Terence graduated from the University of Illinios at Urbana-Champaign with a PhD in electrical engineering.

Marty Humphrey is an assistant professor in the Department of Computer Science at the University of Virginia (USA). He received a BS and MS in electrical and computer engineering (1986 and 1988, respectively) from Clarkson University (Potsdam, NY), and a PhD in computer science from the University of Massachusetts (1996). Dr. Humphrey joined the University of Virginia as a research assistant professor (1998). His areas of research include: many aspects of Grid computing (including security, programming models, performance), Grid testing, and Grid usability.

Hemant Jain is a Wisconsin Distinguished and Tata Consultancy Services professor of management information system in the Sheldon B. Lubar School of Business at the University of Wisconsin - Milwaukee (USA). Professor Jain received his PhD in information system from Lehigh University (1981), a MTech in industrial engineering from I.I.T. Kharagpur (India), and BS in mechanical engineering from University of Indore (India). Dr. Jain's interests are in the area of electronic commerce, system development using reusable components, distributed and co-operative computing systems, architecture design, database management and data warehousing, data mining and visualization. He has published large number of articles in leading journals like *Information Systems Research*, *MIS Quarterly*, *IEEE Transactions on Software Engineering*, *Journal of MIS*, *Navel Research Quarterly*, *Decision Sciences*, *Decision Support Systems*, and *Information & Management*. Professor Jain is on the editorial board of the following journals: *Information Systems Research*, *Information Technology & Management*, *International Journal of Information Technology and Decision Making*, *Information Management*, and is book review editor for the *Journal of Information Technology Cases & Applications*

Wei Jie is currently a senior research engineer in the Institute of High Performance Computing (Singapore). He received his BS and MS in computer science from Beijing University of Aeronautics and Astronautics (China) (1993 and 1996, respectively). He was awarded a PhD in computer science from Nanyang Technological University (Singapore) (2002). Dr. Jie has been involved in the area of parallel and distributed computing for eight years, and he has about 30 papers published in international journals and conferences. His current research interests include: Grid computing, cluster computing, Web services, parallel algorithms, and languages.

Natalya Keberle (http:// google.com/search?q=Keberle) is an assistant professor at the Department of Information Technologies of Zaporozhye National University (Ukraine) and the member of the intelligent systems research group. Her research interests include: ontological models and methods for presenting evolving semantics in intelligent information systems.

Oleksandr Kononenko (Oleksandr.Kononenko@nokia.com) is a research engineer at Helsinki Nokia Research Center and an associate member of the industrial ontologies group at the Department of Mathematical Information Technology of the University of Jyväskylä (Finland). His research is concentrated around the topics of software architectures for existing and evolving Web technologies.

Bu-Sung Lee received his BS (Hons) and PhD in the electrical and electronics department, Loughborough University of Technology (UK) (1982 and 1987, respectively). Dr. Lee is currently an associate professor at the Nanyang Technological University (Singapore). He is the technology area director of the Asia Pacific Advance Network (APAN) and an associate with Singapore Research & Education Networks (SingAREN). He has been an active member of several national standards organizations such as the National Infrastructure Initiative (Singapore One) Network Working Group, the Singapore ATM Testbed, and the Bio-Medical Grid (BMG) Task Force. His research interests are in network management, broadband networks, distributed networks, and network optimization.

Cristian Mateos is a PhD candidate at the ISISTAN Research Institute, UNICEN (Tandil, Argentina), working under the supervision of Marcelo Campo and Alejandro Zunino. He holds a MS degree in computer science from UNICEN. He has developed part of the runtime support for reactive mobility by failure in MoviLog. He is investigating the relationships between Web services and mobile agents using reactive mobility by failure.

Javier Parra-Fuente (Madrid, Spain) has a PhD in computer science from the Pontifical University of Salamanca (Madrid) (2005), computer engineer from the faculty of computer science of the Carlos III University (1999), computer scientist from the Technical School of Computer Science of the Pontifical University of Salamanca in Madrid specialty Systems (1997) and specialty management (1996). He has been professor in the languages and computer systems department at the Pontifical University of Salamanca in Madrid (1999-present). He coordinates the master's in platforms and Web applications. His research interests include: Web engineering, computational reflection, object-oriented technologies, and virtual machines.

Salvador Sánchez-Alonso (Madrid, Spain) obtained a university degree in computer science from the Pontifical University of Salamanca (1997), and a PhD in computing from the Polytechnic University of Madrid (2005). Dr. Sanchez-Alonso worked as an assistant professor at that University (1997-2000; 2002-2005). He also worked as a software engineer at a software solutions company (2000-2001). Dr. Sanchez-Alonso is a lecturer of the computer science department of the University of Alcala (2005-present). His current research interests include: learning object reusability, metadata, software and Web engineering, and object-oriented technologies.

Vagan Terziyan (http:// google.com/search?q=Terziyan) is an associate professor and a senior researcher at the department of mathematical information technology of the University of Jyväskylä (Finland). He is also the chair of the department of artificial intelligence and information systems at the Kharkiv National University of Radioelectronics. His research interests and competences comprise distributed AI, multi-agent systems, Semantic Web and Web services, peer-to-peer computing, knowledge management and machine learning. He received an engineering degree from Kharkiv National University of Radioelectronics.

Liang-Tien Chia gained a first degree in electronic engineering and a PhD from Loughborough University of Technology (1990 and 1994, respectively). He is currently an associate professor in the division of computer communications, school of computer engineering at Nanyang Technological University (Singapore). Dr. Chia also holds the position of director of the Centre for Multimedia and Network Technology in NTU. Current research interests are in multimedia storage and retrieval, multimedia processing, error concealment techniques, video communication, bandwidth management, and wireless Internet.

Stephen Turner joined the Nanyang Technological University (Singapore) (1999) and is currently an associate professor in the school of computer engineering and director of the Parallel and Distributed Computing Centre. Previously, he was a senior lecturer in computer science at Exeter University (UK). He received his MA in mathematics and computer science from Cambridge University (UK), and his MS and PhD in computer science from Manchester University (UK). His current research interests include: parallel and distributed simulation, distributed virtual environments, Grid computing, parallel algorithms and languages, and multi-agent systems. He is steering committee chair of the Principles of Advanced and Distributed Simulation (PADS) Conference and advisory committee member and general chair of the Distributed Simulation and Real Time Applications (DS-RT) Symposium. He is a member of IEEE (IEEE Computer Society), SCS (Society for Modeling and Simulation) and BCS (British Computer Society).

Harry Wang is currently a PhD candidate at the MIS Department, Eller College of Management, University of Arizona (USA), and will be an assistant professor in MIS at the University of Delaware (starting in the fall of 2006). He holds a bachelor's degree in MIS from Tianjin University (China). His research interests involve workflow technologies and applications, access control in e-commerce, and Web services. He has published several research articles in these areas in journal and conferences including: *International Journal of Web Services Research*, *Workshop on Information Technology and Systems*, *International Conference on Web Services*, and *Americas Conference on Information Systems*.

Glenn Wasson is a senior research scientist in the Computer Science Department at the University of Virginia, where he co-directed the Grid computing group. His research focuses on large-scale distributed and Grid computing systems mainly using Web services and .NET technologies. Developing tools and techniques for constructing such systems is of particular interest. Dr. Wasson received his PhD and MS degrees from the University of Virginia (1999 and 1995, respectively). He received a BS in electrical engineering from Tufts University (1993).

Christian Werner finished his studies at the Humboldt-University (Berlin, Germany) with a diploma (equivalent to a master's degree) in computer science (July, 2002). He is now a PhD student at the Institute of Telematics at the University Lübeck (Germany). His main research interests include: Web services for educational purposes, techniques for transporting SOAP messages efficiently, and Web service applications in the field of Grid computing.

Tianyi Zang is currently engaged in research and development in Grid computing at the Institute of High Performance Computing (IHPC) (Singapore). He received his MS in computer science and engineering (1996), and PhD in computer science and engineering (1999) from Harbin Institute of Technology (China). Then, as a senior engineer, he went to the IT department of China Construction Bank and took part in research and development in large-scale financial applications and network. He joined IHPC as post-doctoral research fellow (April 2002), and his current research interest is service-oriented Grid computing.

Chen Zhou received his BS degree in computer science and technology from Shanghai Jiao Tong University (China) (2002). After that he has been working towards a PhD degree in the school of computer engineering, Nanyang Technological University (Singapore). His current research interests include: Web services discovery, semantic Web, service QoS, and middleware distributed systems.

Leon Zhao is professor and Honeywell fellow of MIS, Eller College of Management at the University of Arizona (USA). He received his PhD from the Haas School of Business, UC Berkeley and taught previously at College of William and Mary, and Hong Kong University of Science and Technology. He holds a PhD in business administration from Haas School of Business, UC Berkeley; MS in engineering from the University of California, Davis; and a bachelor's degree from Beijing Institute of Agricultural Mechanization. Dr. Zhao has published more than 80 articles in major academic conferences and journals including: *Management Science, Information Systems Research, INFORMS Journal on Computing, Journal of Management Information Systems, Communications of the ACM, IEEE Transactions on Knowledge and Data Management*, and *IEEE Transaction on Engineering Management.* He severs on the editorial boards of seven academic journals including *Information Systems Research* and *Decision Support Systems.* In addition, he has edited (or is currently editing) 9 special issues for various MIS journals. He is a co-chair of the Second Workshop on E-Business, 2003, the 15th Workshop on Information Technology and Systems, 2005, and the IEEE International Conference on Services Computing, 2006. He is a recipient of the 2005 IBM faculty award for his work in business process management and service-oriented computing.

Huimin Zhao is an assistant professor of management information systems at the Sheldon B. Lubar School of Business, University of Wisconsin - Milwaukee (USA). He earned his PhD in management information systems from the University of Arizona. His current research interests are in the areas of data integration, data mining, and Web services. His research has been published in several journals, including *IEEE Transactions on Knowledge and Data Engineering, IEEE Transactions on Systems, Man, and Cybernetics, Information Systems, Journal of Management Information Systems, Data and Knowledge Engineering, Journal of Database Management, Journal of Information Systems and E-Business Management*, and *International Journal of Web Services Research.* He is a member of IEEE, AIS, and IRMA.

Alejandro Zunino (http://www.exa.unicen.edu.ar/~azunino) received a PhD degree in computer science from UNICEN (Tandil, Argentina) (2003). He is an assistant professor at the computer science department of UNICEN. He is also a research fellow of the National Council for Scientific and Technical Research of Argentina (CONICET). He has published over 25 papers in journals and conferences. His current research interests include: development tools for mobile agents, intelligent agents, and the Semantic Web.

Index